THE SEDUCTIVE **SHOE**

JONATHAN WALFORD

THE
SEDUCTIVE
SHOE

FOUR CENTURIES
OF FASHION FOOTWEAR

STEWART, TABORI & CHANG
New York

For Kenn

p. 1, left: ?Belgian pink and green needle-worked canvas shoe with red kid heel, c. 1710–25.
p. 1, right: Italian-made for export, red patent-leather sandals, c. 1977–80.
p. 2: American purple and black leather laced boot, c. 1915–18.

First published in the United States of America
in 2007 by Stewart, Tabori & Chang
An imprint of Harry N. Abrams, Inc.

First published in the United Kingdom
in 2007 by Thames & Hudson Ltd, London

Library of Congress Cataloging-in-Publication Data:
Walford, Jonathan.
   The seductive shoe / Jonathan Walford.
      p. cm.
   Includes bibliographical references and index.
   ISBN-13: 978-1-58479-622-0
   ISBN-10: 1-58479-622-7
   1. Shoes—History. 2. Shoes—Social aspects. I. Title.
GT2130.W35 2007
391.4'13—dc22

                              200602959

Printed and bound in Singapore by C S Graphics Pte Ltd
10 9 8 7 6 5 4 3 2 1

HNA ▮▮▮▮▮▮
harry n. abrams, inc.
a subsidiary of La Martinière Groupe
115 West 18th Street
New York, NY 10011
www.hnabooks.com

ACKNOWLEDGMENTS

The creation of this book was truly an international venture, with collectors, museums, dealers and fashion historians supplying information and images from Australia, Canada, England, Germany, Russia and the United States. I have to thank many individuals who generously gave their time and knowledge as well as access to their collections with no expectations but my sincere thanks. Clothing and fashion historians and collectors Ivan Sayers, Claus Jahnke and Melissa Leventon (curatrix.net), as well as Nazim Mustafaev of the Russian publishers Shoe Icons (shoe-icons.com, an online museum collection of historic footwear) were all especially helpful because they so readily offered their extensive collections to the cause. Lei Hidic (corsetsandcrinolines.com), Linda Ames (vintagetextile.com), Elizabeth Bramlett (fuzzylizzie.com), Jim Smiley (jimsmileyvintageclothing.com), Holly Jenkins-Evans (pastperfectvintage.com), Anne Dettmer (advintaged.com), Candy Shiveley (Contentment Farm Antiques), Susan Langley and Eduard Meier were also most generous in supplying images of shoes from their collections, as was Julia Pine for her help with fetish footwear. Bally Shoes and the North Vancouver Museum gave me free access to use images of shoes in their collections. The many members of The Honourable Cordwainers' Company (thehcc.org) clarified historic leather terms for me and Al Saguto in particular read over my glossary for accuracy. Margaret Beck helped me with techie things like downloading images from museum ftp sites, an area in which I am completely dysfunctional. Kenn Norman read and re-read the text. Ada Hopkins and Sarah Beam of the Bata Shoe Museum, along with employees of numerous other museums, patiently answered my questions about their collections, supplied images and printed off catalogue sheets from their databanks for my use. Lastly, I want to thank Beth Levine who graciously agreed to share some reminiscences of being a shoe designer in the 1950s and 1960s as a foreword for this book.

CONTENTS

FOREWORD
BY BETH LEVINE

SHOES ARE SO INTIMATE. THINK ABOUT IT. SHOES ARE SO PERSONAL, SO CARING, SO FRIENDLY, SO FLATTERING. SHOES ARE SO EXASPERATING AND HURTFUL IF YOU **LET THEM SEDUCE YOU**.

I landed in the shoe business because my shoe size was 4B, the sample size for modelling for shoe buyers in the late 1930s. I was also the 'guinea pig' who wore the shoes for fit and design. I thought it was a serious responsibility. I learned a great deal and eventually became a shoe designer. I was lucky that my first job was with Palter De Liso. Vincent De Liso was the shoemaker par excellence and a solid, creative, honest designer. They sold to Bonwit Teller, Saks Fifth Avenue, Neiman Marcus, Marshall Field and high-grade stores across the country, plus one in London, so they had to be good in quality and fashion. Their competitors were Delman, Seymour Troy, La Valle, Perugia (at Saks) and other quality makers, such as Newton Elkin, Congenni and Strassberger. All had a passion to compete in making the best product.

Making shoes used to be called 'The Gentle Craft'. Sometimes I wondered! My husband and I loved Seymour Troy – we were so pleased that he sought us out after we began our business. Seymour Troy was so creative, so interesting and interested in the theatre, a brilliant storyteller, elegant and dapper, who always wore his hat 'just so'. He was ruthlessly copied and enjoyed foiling the copiers in ingenious funny ways.

Herbert, my husband, had been a newspaperman writing for a theatrical magazine and a fashion paper. He wanted to do something that 'I could hold in my hand'. A friend convinced him to come into his shoe business for a while as sales and advertising manager. When we went into the shoe business, many were leaving it. We thought we would find a niche in high-grade feminine shoes that you did not need but wanted. It worked. We made the soles look more delicate than they were by finishing the soles of our day shoes like evening shoes, playing with colour and trimmings. The French, when they embellished the heels and parts of shoes with embroideries or tiny jewels, had a wonderful, simple expression for them: 'Venez y voir', 'Come see this'.

In 1964, Herbert Levine Company introduced the aerodynamically designed 'Kabuki' pumps to give the illusion of flight, allowing the wearer to feel as if she were walking on air. Their jet-stream defiance of space prompted Levine to observe in retrospect, 'I should have called them "airplane" pumps'.

We sought the best workers and there were many in 1948. Herbert said, 'I spent thirty years falling asleep counting pairs.' To keep a factory busy is not always easy – but we managed it because the shoes sold. We had a slogan 'get over the buyer to the consumer'. It worked. We respected our customer and the shoes told her we did.

Owning your own business helps. Having an audience helps. Herbert was inspirational in thinking that I could solve any problem. So I would go to it and create. 'Make clear see-through Lucite heels without screws,' he suggested, so I did it. I had the freedom to experiment with funny things (he could not fire me). Almost every new idea we presented – a new last, a new boot, a new construction – was resisted. Why are so many people afraid of 'the next new thing'? When our new ideas were accepted and worn by some, they sold like hot cakes and immediately were copied. My sister, Ruth Ballin, a wonderful creative artist and designer, used to ask, 'Why does everybody want to be first second?'

Actors and dancers are very careful about their shoes and feet, as they should be. When Bette Davis was to appear on stage, she and her designer came to us. As she was getting ready to leave I told her we could put something on the soles that would quiet the sound and also prevent slipping – she strode across the room at her full five-foot-one-inch height, declaiming 'I hate pussyfooting – I want to be heard!'

Janis Paige played a stern fashion editor in a Broadway production. She selected chic, meticulous, low-heeled shoes but also a pair of black crocodile pumps with a two-inch thin curved sexy heel. I felt I had to tell her that her character would never wear such a heel. She said, 'Shh, the heel is a giveaway to the sexy girl I am underneath.'

I met Jonathan Walford at the Bata Shoe Museum in Toronto, Canada. It is a fabulous shoe museum that was built by Sonja and Tom Bata and is a 'must see'. The footwear collection is WOW! Jonathan's knowledge and information is fascinating reading. Learn a lot and enjoy.

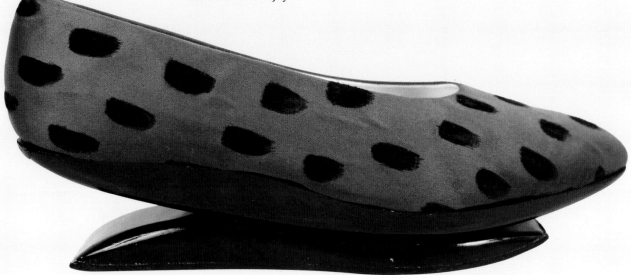

Canadian or American red leather, vinyl and plexiglass
Spring-o-lator mules, unlabelled but date stamped
'December 29, 1955'. They were modelled in a fashion
show held in Vancouver, where the newspapers reported
them as the first pair in the city.

INTRODUCTION

Footwear is primarily an invention of necessity to protect us from the elements. However, over the centuries and in almost every culture, footwear has taken vastly different forms, proving that there is far more at play than mere protection. Footwear in the Western world is under the influence of fashion, and change is the fodder of fashion.

Of all the arts, fashion is the most responsive to change because of its ephemeral nature. Styles, shapes, construction, decoration and etiquette change when the experiences and thoughts of society change. Fashion expresses the gender, age, economic strata and social echelon of its wearer. Fashion can facilitate or hinder comfort, health and ease of movement. It reflects cultural ritual, morality and sexual liberation. It responds to foreign influences, political turmoil, economic stability and artistic sensibility. It is made using the latest scientific developments and technological innovations. It is influenced by popular culture and leading personalities. Everything that shapes our world affects and inspires fashion and by looking at historical fashion within the context of when it was made we can understand how it came about.

Fashion must be vital or it can only be defined as wearable art. Like the riddle – does a tree make a sound if it falls in the forest and there is nobody around to hear – fashion must be received in order to be called fashion. Runway haute couture is only a suggestion until it is purchased and worn. The most successful fashions are those that are copied through licence, inspired interpretation or counterfeit. In fashion, imitation really is the sincerest form of flattery and the greatest sign of success.

Vivienne Westwood put a pair of blue mock-croc platform shoes on the feet of model Naomi Campbell for a 1993 fashion show without unrealistic expectations of the shoes actually selling. But when they felled Campbell on the catwalk it made international headlines, and Westwood has since sold about 300 pairs, a large portion of sales coming from museums and collectors. Is it fashion if a supermodel falls on the catwalk but only museums buy the shoes?

There have always been eccentrics who push and pull fashion ahead and behind its time, but most women bought their shoes in stores or ordered them from their shoemaker to fall in line with what was au courant. Here follows the history of women's fashion footwear since 1600.

French etching of a shoemaker's workshop by
Abraham Bosse, c. 1635.

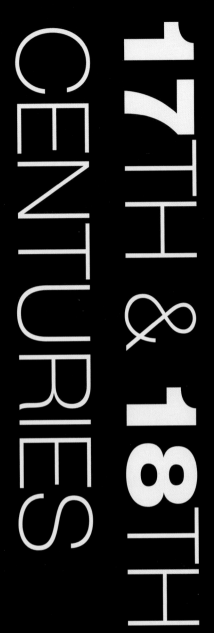

17TH & 18TH CENTURIES

Clothing was originally developed for protection, modesty and utility. In early civilizations dress came to express the status and cultural ideals of the society that created it. Particular shoes were defined by their construction, style and even colour. They were named first by the Greeks and later the Romans, who provided the root for many of our present-day footwear styles, including *soccus*, *sandalium* and *muleus* (sock, sandal and mule). During the late Roman (Byzantine) Empire, Christian morality deemed it sinful to expose the body. St Clement of Alexandria in the third century AD preached humility for women, commanding them not to bare their toes. Byzantine footwear covered the feet, and shoes replaced the sandals that both men and women had worn for centuries. As Islam expanded throughout Rome's old eastern territories in the eighth and ninth centuries, Christianity reinforced an alliance in what was once Rome's western domain. Irish footwear from this period is nearly identical in style to that created by Egyptian Christian Copts 2,500 miles to the east – evidence of the cultural bond Christianity had formed over Western Europe.

Europe emerged from the Early Middle Ages in the eleventh century as warring kingdoms united by the Christian church. These European states began crusades into the Holy Land, coming into contact with Islamic scholarship and goods. Nobility had their appetites whetted by souvenirs of exotic silks and embroidered fineries brought home by crusaders. Over the next few hundred years trade routes developed and mercantile capitalism was born.

Fashion became the privilege of the upper classes and was available on a sliding scale of diminishing advantages from the royal family down the social ladder. Any pretension to dress above one's station was limited by social hierarchy. Expensive materials and excessive styles were royalty's most visible way of staying ahead of moneyed merchants. But, when the cost of dressing well did not create enough of a gap between the nobles and the mercantile class, sumptuary laws were placed upon materials, styles and decorations, restricting their use to persons of appropriate status. Restrictions against obscene or excessive fashions were set by the church, who, together with the state, attempted to keep the classes in their place.

Footwear and clothing were similar for both sexes until the fourteenth century. Shoes were generally flat-soled with almond-shaped toes. Pointed toes appeared in the eleventh century but rarely in an exaggerated form, if for no other reason than it would have been impossible for women to walk in floor-length gowns with elongated toes. By the mid fourteenth century, however, men's clothing tightened and shortened, bringing shoes into full view and making them prime candidates for elaboration. The toes of men's shoes became so long that they protruded several inches in front of the shoe and were known as 'crakowes' in England or 'poulaines' in France, after their supposed Polish origin. They were also known as 'pykes' or 'pikes' because of their pointed shapes and were identified as a fashion folly in 1361 and 1362 in the *Eulogium Historiarum*: 'Beaked shoes, one finger long, which are called "Crakowes"; they are judged to be the claws of devils rather than the trappings of men'. Some accounts refer to toes being over a foot in length and requiring chains to attach the tip of the toe to a garter or belt to prevent the wearer from tripping, but it is difficult to ascertain medieval fact from fiction and there is no evidence that such an example ever existed. From dated documents, art and archaeological evidence it is clear that pointed toes of two to five inches were very much in fashion during the late fourteenth century throughout Europe. The style subsided in around 1400 but was revived in the mid fifteenth century becoming even more popular than before. At least one royal edict limited their length in 1463, when England's Edward IV proclaimed, 'No knight under the state of a lord, esquire, gentleman, nor other person shall use nor wear...any shoes or boots having pikes passing the length of two inches'. This fashion crackdown was extended two years later to include everyone. A papal bull followed in 1468, which called the style 'a scoffing against God and the church, a worldly vanity and a mad presumption', but neither royal edict nor papal bull dissuaded followers of the poulaine. A victim of its own success, the style only fell from favour when fashionable nobles abandoned long toes because they had become too common. By 1490 the style had all but disappeared.

By the early sixteenth century the Italian Renaissance was causing the arts and sciences to flourish. Italy was unquestionably the wealthiest place in Europe and had the best access to trade silks and leathers and some of the most sophisticated industries for producing quality textiles. Conspicuous consumption of sumptuous cloths, leathers and decorations impressed foreign visitors and inspired fashions abroad. The trend for white or light-coloured leather shoes, often slashed or punched to reveal colourful linings or hose, came from Italy's lead. However, with the dawn of Protestantism in Northwest Europe, men's footwear from England to Germany took on a different look from that of Catholic Southern Europe.

Men took to exploring a new dimension in their footwear: width. A recurring trend in fashion history is for a reactionary opposite of what is in vogue to become the new fashion. By the 1520s broad-toed shoes, variously called 'scarpines', 'bearpaws' 'cowmouths' or 'hornbills', were the new style in Northwest Europe. These square- or round-toed shoes were as wide or wider than the ball of the foot and often flared outward. The toes were padded and instep straps were often used to keep the shoes in place. Whether the style was seen as anti-Catholic is not recorded but with the ascension of England's Catholic Queen Mary, who favoured Spanish dress, a law was passed to limit toe width.

With the exception of their footwear, both men and women were victims of fashion excesses. The length of women's skirts prevented their footwear from expressing exuberant style and their outlet for excess went to the opposite end of the figure: headdresses. With the introduction of platform soles in Italy, however, this was about to change. It is perhaps only logical that after the dimensions of length and width had been explored, height would be the next venture.

Ancient Greeks first put platform soles on their actors' sandals to suggest performers were playing important persons, and the women of that time adopted cork-soled platform sandals called *Cothurnus*. In the late fifteenth century aristocratic Venetian women revived the style to reflect physically their high status. Platform or stilted mules, called 'chopines', ranged in height from a few inches to upwards of a couple of feet. Although in existence as early as 1500 the style did not spread quickly and seems to have been worn rarely outside Italy and Spain. Most period references to chopines and all surviving examples date from the late sixteenth and early seventeenth centuries. Foreigners who remarked on them in their journals regarded chopines more as a curiosity than as a serious fashion. Even if not worn widely outside Southern Europe, the style was known throughout the continent, and even William Shakespeare commented on them in *Hamlet* (Act II, Scene II) in 1600: 'Your Ladyship is nearer to heaven than when I saw you last by the altitude of a *chopine*.' One of the most famous accounts of the style appears in *Coryat's Crudities* (vol. 1, p. 400, 1905), Thomas Coryat's travel book from 1611:

> 'So common in Venice that no woman whatever goeth without it, either in her house or abroad...so uncomely a thing, in my opinion, that it is a pity this foolish custom is not clean banished...there are many of these chapineys of a great height even half a yard high....By how much the nobler a woman is, by so much the higher are her chapineys. All their gentlewomen...are assisted and supported either by men or women, when they walk abroad, to the end they might not fall.'

Called 'depraved' and 'dissolute' by the church, the style was slow to disappear despite the fact that women of the oldest profession donned them, lowering the shoe's status for women of breeding. As late as 1648 period accounts refer to Venetian women appearing as walking maypoles in their chopines.

Fashion began to change in around 1600 as the barriers in dress distinction between classes started to break down. Sumptuary laws continued, but they were more often proclaimed to secure domestic economies and industries than to keep the masses from affecting style, which had proven difficult to enforce anyway. Fashion became a commodity that was traded throughout Europe, remaining elitist through consumption, quality and extravagance. The privilege of fashion was available to anyone who could afford the cost and could maintain the life of idle pleasure that it was designed to accommodate. The working classes adapted high fashion into simpler modes using humbler materials and were only restricted by cost and practicality. To define noble from common, wealth and position were made conspicuous through refinement. Conscious gentrification of the upper classes was studied through poise, language, manners and even gait. The very steps of the upper classes became affected through the establishment of a toe-heel stride, where the ball of the foot touched the ground before the heel.

It is from around the year 1600 that examples of fashionable dress have survived in any quantity. Shoes, gloves, jackets and other articles of clothing were saved and passed down through generations, eventually finding their way into public museums and private collections. These survivors give us examples of fashion in reality, even if most of them represent only elite style. Before 1600 there are few examples of dress that are not archaeologically recovered, although some religious vestments managed to dodge destruction and were often made from fashionable garments left to the church by wealthy patrons. As early as 1439 an account of the Countess of Warwick exists, which donated her green cloth and gold gown with wide sleeves to Our Lady of Walsingham in Norfolk and other garments to Tewkesbury Abbey in Gloucestershire.

The elite of the medieval period owned few garments, but by the seventeenth century fashionable wardrobes had been expanded. Those not adhering to pious puritanical principles spent fortunes on embellishment: ruinously expensive cordovan leathers, elaborate embroideries, imported gilt lace and fine silk ribbons. The accumulation of wealth brought with it a taste for finery and the creation of surplus garments; many elaborate items were worn infrequently and thereby escaped destruction through use. These garments were too valuable to be given to the needy and instead were kept for posterity or sentiment, or with plans to be reworked.

When heels upwards of an inch were externally applied to the soles of shoes in the 1590s there was little distinction between men's and women's styles. Footwear fashion briefly enjoyed the admiration of both sexes. The addition of heels to soles was made possible a century earlier by the development of welt construction, which did not require turning the shoe right side out after being sewn, as had been the case with turn-shoe construction. Welt construction made it possible to use a thick leather sole, which kept its shape in the arch and accommodated the lift of the heel height. With the introduction of heels, shoes were made without left or right definition and could be worn on either foot. It even became the practice by some to swap the shoe between the right and left foot on a daily basis to result in more even wear. Straight soles reduced the cost of keeping an inventory of pairs of lasts for left and right in every size and heel height. Straight soles would remain in use for the next two hundred years, gradually becoming less popular during the nineteenth century.

At the end of the Renaissance a gradual change in the meaning of fashion for men and women began to take effect. Men's clothing and footwear slowly became more utilitarian while women's clothing and footwear became more elaborate. This was partially precipitated by men's clothing becoming more tailored in the fourteenth century. Men wore their wealth on their back to express their social status and, although some sumptuary laws prohibited men without the requisite wealth from wearing silk or embroideries, the cut of cloth was rarely prohibited. For example, in 1471, Scottish women whose husbands were not wealthy enough to be allowed to wear silk doublets or cloaks were themselves permitted to wear silk collars and sleeves. Women's clothes began to take on the display of high fashion while men's clothing became plainer and more sober. This trend became more evident in the seventeenth century.

In England, the shift was more abrupt. During the Civil War and Commonwealth period (1642–60) both sexes experienced a period of sobering dress when Royalist furbelows became unfashionable. The tailored dark wool suit and low-heeled shoe was born in this period and steadfastly became a standard in men's dress over the following centuries. When Charles II regained the throne in 1660, men's fashion briefly adopted the embellishment of French styles but this was not sustained.

Women's fashion recovered from plainness and once again took up the use of lace and silks and high-heeled shoes.

By the middle of the seventeenth century France had become a beacon of style for all of Europe to emulate. The excesses of baroque were indulged under Louis XIV, and the fashions and arts of France, favoured by European nobility, spread throughout fashionable society. Heels remained at about the same height for both sexes until the 1660s; by the 1690s women's heels were taking on greater elevations, towering upwards of four inches. Despite this, 'well-heeled' women's hem lines made shoes virtually invisible. Continental European heels, especially in France, Spain and Italy, were thinner and usually taller as ladies lived in cities for most of the year, whereas English heels were thicker and often lower, being more sensible choices for living on country estates. This differentiation remained the rule until hem lines inched toward the ankles in the mid eighteenth century. Suddenly there was an interest in high thin-heeled shoes, and by the 1760s English ladies had abandoned their sensible heels to take up the French curvaceous pompadour heel and later, in the 1770s, the Italian stiletto-like heel.

Buckles first came into fashion because of their practicality. Samuel Pepys refers to putting on buckles for the first time in 1660, and by the end of the seventeenth century the use of buckles overtook that of ribbon laces on men's footwear. Women's shoes were slower to feature buckles because they caught on hem lines. Rising hem lines and the use of panniers (side-hoops) that held skirts clear of the feet in the mid eighteenth century, however, provided the opportunity for ostentatious buckles, and a mania for large silver and gilt buckles set with paste and semi-precious stones ensued. Buckles on men's shoes were larger than those on women's footwear, but both sexes displayed their shoe jewelry to its best advantage when they bowed or curtseyed. With extended foot and downcast eyes the buckle became the focal point during introduction.

In the later years of the eighteenth century mercantile and industrial wealth had created an affluent, educated yet politically under-represented middle class. The American and French revolutions exploded out of this imbalance, and the resulting new democratic order placed everyone on the same level and ostentatious display fell from fashion. Heels disappeared from women's shoes in the 1790s, and in the early months of the French Revolution the French National Assembly passed a vote that all deputies give up their shoe buckles for the benefit of the treasury. Fashion was about to be expressed in a very different manner.

>> FLAT SOLES

Flat-soled shoes were made until the 1610s even though heels started to be added in the 1590s. Before the addition of heels, soles were sometimes given small wedges using a lift or two of leather. High heels were probably inspired by the tall platform chopines made fashionable in Venice in the sixteenth century.

Pinking, slashing and punching were inexpensive methods of decorating leather shoes in the late sixteenth and early seventeenth centuries and were used on all classes of footwear, although the most profusely decorated examples are found on higher end products. Until the 1640s shoes were often unisex in style, with only the width of the heel seat determining the sex of the wearer (narrower heel seats were made for women). Boots generally were made only for men, but there exist a few scarce references to riding boots for women, although women also wore shoes for the activity.

Spanish or Italian flat-soled leather shoes,
c. 1600.

>> CHOPINES AND PLATFORMS

Chopines were known across Europe by 1600 but they were rarely worn outside Italy and Spain. Surviving examples of these tall pedestal mules over six inches in height are always made of leather or suede, suggesting that they were intended for outdoor wear. Shorter versions, usually dating from the seventeenth century, are often covered in silk velvet and decorated with tack work, tassels and silver lace and were probably worn indoors.

A more practical platform shoe style found some favour with women who wanted to increase their height under the long skirts of the period. A preference for light-coloured footwear, especially tan and white, prevailed among the elite because it suggested an idle lifestyle of indoor pleasure. The working classes wore more practical black and brown leather, often waxed, but sometimes of ooze (the old name for suede).

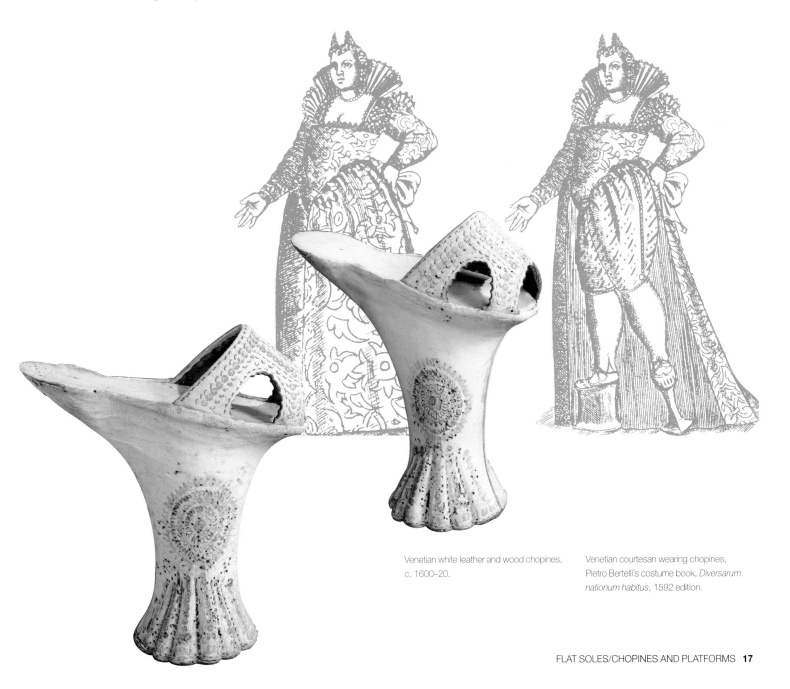

Venetian white leather and wood chopines, c. 1600–20.

Venetian courtesan wearing chopines, Pietro Bertelli's costume book, *Diversarum nationum habitus*, 1592 edition.

Ooze was fashionable in the seventeenth century because it imitated velvet but was more practical for footwear. The large oval side openings (as illustrated here), dubbed 'drawbridge' style by the French in 1617, were fashionable in the first half of the seventeenth century, shrinking in size on most shoes after the 1650s and disappearing during the 1680s.

Swiss engraving by Matthäus Merian of a husband helping his wife with her shoes, c. 1615.

Italian white leather shoe with wood platform sole and heel, c. 1610.

English portrait, *Mary Curzon, Countess of Dorset*, William Larkin, c. 1612.

Fashionable London lady in winter costume by Wenceslas Hollar, 1643.

>> ROSES AND LATCHETS

Very little footwear survives from the seventeenth century, so we must rely upon period journals and art for information. In the English portrait of Mary Curzon her shoes are clearly seen, but they are more visible than they would have been in reality, partly due to artistic licence. Skirts were held away from the body by the use of a farthingale, an early seventeenth-century undergarment used to create width in the skirt at the hips. With skirts held clear of the feet, shoes were often highly decorated with 'roses', ornaments of silk and lace, which were introduced on footwear in the late sixteenth century and became their largest in the 1610s to hide the closure of latchets. Latchets were flaps or tabs that were extended from the sides of the shoe and had holes at their ends that were tied with a string or cord through corresponding holes on the tongue or extended vamp. Roses were attached using a different pair of holes on the vamp or tongue.

The image by Hollar in 1643 of a fashionable London lady represents a period for which it is particularly difficult to find surviving English footwear: the Civil War and Commonwealth period, 1642–60. Clearly visible here, however, is a large rose made of multiple loops of silk ribbon. Roses gradually shrank in size, partly due to collapsing skirts that were no longer held away from the body and therefore interfered with the movement of the feet. Large roses disappeared from use in the 1660s.

Italian leather slap sole shoe with heel, sole and toecap covered with olive-green silk and straw appliqué to simulate marquetry, c. 1650–70.

>> SLAP SOLES AND SHAPES OF TOES

Originally appearing as removable overshoes for men's heeled outdoor footwear to keep the heels from sinking into muddy, mucky streets, slap soles quickly became a constructed element of the shoe. Some shoes had the heel attached to the back of the sole but most surviving examples do not, and the heel slapping the unattached sole on every step resulted in the style's name. No known image between 1630 and 1690, when this style was fashionable, illustrates a woman wearing a pair, but several examples of women's slap-sole shoes survive. Although primarily intended for outdoor wear, slap soles occasionally appeared on women's indoor shoes.

The round toes of the early seventeenth century tapered to an oval, then gradually to a pointed shape with square tips and, by 1650, to a definite square shape. However, there were overlapping styles and no clear progression in toe shapes from year to year.

>> RED HEELS

Although fashionable in silhouette, this shoe exhibits the influence of regional style with its red-painted stacked-leather heel, which was typical of some provincial styles of the period found from Alsace to the Netherlands. The shoe came from an old American collection and may possibly have been worn in the Dutch colonies of present-day New York State.

Red heels normally suggested aristocratic wear, but this shoe, in its construction and finishing, was definitely made for a member of the merchant class. In the late seventeenth century heels were more often than not made to contrast with the upper, and it is often quoted that in France Louis XIV decreed that red heels were to be the exclusive privilege of the French aristocracy. While this sounds typical of Louis's strategy to provide privilege but not power to his court, there is no evidence that such a decree was ever made. Red heels were already in use by the late 1610s and being worn at court by the 1630s, long before Louis ascended the throne. Louis wore red heels throughout his life, as recorded in his portraits, but they were also fashionably worn throughout Europe, their popularity attributable to the influence of the French court. While they were usually associated with grand dress outside France, their strict association with aristocratic wear within France was probably the result of custom, not edict. In the years leading up to the French Revolution this link was voiced, and in 1780 an attack on Marie Antoinette appeared in a pamphlet entitled *Portefeuille d'un talon rouge* (the wallet of a red heel), condemning the aristocracy through their connection with red heels.

Dutch or American ooze shoe with red-painted stacked-leather heel and reproduction silk rose, c. 1650–65.

English blue silk mules with forked square toes and silver gilt-thread embroidery, c. 1660–85.

>> SQUARE TOES AND SILK PANTABLES

Mules have been worn since the late Roman Byzantine period. By the seventeenth century, most mules were intended for indoor wear and were covered with silk and embroidery, although plain leather styles for outdoor use were also worn. The term mule was replaced by 'pantable' in the late 1670s when French style and words were influencing English culture. Pantable is an anglicization of the French word for mule, *pantouffle*.

The elongated square toe was first seen on women's shoes in the late 1640s and gradually fell from favour in the late 1680s and early 1690s, at the moment when the toes of men's shoes became the most extreme square shapes. Women's square toe styles varied and included tapered almost pointed toes with squared-off tips, broad shallow shapes and even extreme forked and flared styles. Today's slang term 'being a square' comes from the eighteenth-century slam 'square toes', meaning out of date or old fashioned. This was directed in particular at men, who wore square-toed shoes when they were no longer in vogue. The most famous use of this criticism is in a Thomas Rowlandson caricature of 1784 in which a son calls his father 'old square toes'.

The vamp of the olive silk mule is covered in a florid patterned silk brocade. This style of brocade patterning was produced by the Chinese for export to Europe and became known collectively as

'bizarres'. European silk production was centred in Italy and France until the emigration of the Huguenots in the last quarter of the seventeenth century. They brought their skills to countries tolerant of Protestantism and set up silk-weaving centres in Spitalfields, (England), Krefeld (Germany), Stockholm (Sweden) and Gouda (the Netherlands). In an attempt to bolster the fledgling domestic silk industry, an English edict in 1699 proclaimed that the wearing of Chinese silks was illegal. Similar edicts followed in other countries. With Chinese silk brocades illegal for outerwear, European silk weavers continued to weave silk brocades in Oriental-style 'bizarre' patterns until the 1730s when rococo floral designs came into fashion.

This mule (above) was presented by Prince William III to Sarah Hammersley. Little is known of this lady other than she was born in 1665 and was the granddaughter of Hugh Hammersley the Lord Mayor of London in 1627. The title 'Prince' dates the mule to after 1677 when William married Princess Mary, daughter of the future James II and niece of the then reigning King Charles II. Sarah would have been in her mid-to-late teens when she received this gift. Ironically, it was under William and Mary that the Anglican Church was made the official faith of England in 1690, thereby securing England as a welcome haven for Huguenot silk weavers.

?Italian white suede shoe with red kid heel
and slap sole, c. 1695–1705.

>> HIGH HEELS

Between 1685 and 1720 women wore high-heeled shoes in combination with high hairstyles and caps to create a tall slender silhouette, the perfect vision of baroque verticality. The high heel reportedly came into existence in 1661 after Monsieur Philippe, the brother of Louis XIV, was ridiculed for his lack of height by his wife, Princess Henrietta Anne of England. Monsieur Philippe immediately instructed his shoemaker to add an extra two inches to his heels, but Henrietta Anne informed the king of these plans and Philippe, on his next entrance into court, found that Louis had added two inches to his heels too. Louis liked high heels and made them a fashion at court. Women's styles started to diverge from those of men in the 1660s, and by the 1690s the difference was obvious. Women's shoes had high, slender heels, pointed toes and continued the use of ribbon laces, while men's shoes had lower heels, broad square toes and used the new fashion for buckle fastenings.

White suede, which had been so popular with the elite during most of the seventeenth century for indoor and outdoor shoes, particularly at court, was by the 1660s beginning to fall from favour, and by the 1690s was rare, especially undecorated as in this example. Its light colour suggested privilege, as the wearer obviously did not walk muddy streets or go out on wet days. Leather remained popular for daywear, while silk brocades were preferred for more formal occasions and indoor use.

French etching of a lady trying on shoes, artist unknown, c. 1690.

French fashion illustration, *L'Hyver*, c. 1690–93.

>> FRENCH BAROQUE

After 1710 women began to wear buckles more frequently, although ribbon ties were preferred until the 1730s as buckles tended to catch on hem lines. The small silver buckles used at first consisted of a single T-shaped prong that hooked through a button-like hole on the latchet closure. The straps extending from the quarters and closing on the instep were referred to as latchets, languids or straps, their exact definition being somewhat open to interpretation.

By the 1720s footwear had become more graceful due to the balanced proportions and curvaceous contours perfected by French rococo artistic sensibility. Women's shoes in the early eighteenth century were still unseen but for the toes peeping out from under floor-length hem lines. Heels became curved, echoing the domed soles and upturned needle-pointed toes. Uppers in bright rich colours, charming patterned brocades and delightful embroideries entertained the eye.

Mules were popular throughout Europe until the eighteenth century when the combination of the very high heel and the backless upper made the style less practical and they almost disappeared from English women's wardrobes. In France, the mule became the shoe of the boudoir because its tendency to not remain upon the foot made it suitable for states of undress and intimate liaisons. Rococo artists fancifully depicted their subjects wearing mules in garden settings, but in reality the style rarely ventured into the sunlight.

Lady on Her Day Bed (previously known as *Presumed Portrait of Madame Boucher*), François Boucher, 1743.

French silk pantouffles (mules) embroidered with silk and silver thread, c. 1720–30.

>> ENGLISH HEELS

Britain has a long-held reputation for being a nation of the sensibly shod, a reputation that was deserved in the early eighteenth century when English footwear had sturdy thick heels. This was because an English lady resided most of the year at her country estate, only venturing into the city or spa for social reasons or for a shopping trip to see her dressmaker and shoemaker.

The fashions worn in France were much emulated in England from the beginning of the Restoration (1660), but shoes were only influenced by the French-style domed soles and upturned pointed toes. The practicality of the English heel overrode the artistic merits of the continental style. The effects of rococo ornamentation were not as obvious on English shoes, which appeared heavier because of the heel shape. However the same elements of grace and ornament were evident in the finish of such areas as the tongues, which were decoratively cut in peaks, cupid's bows or Van-dykes (serrated).

Because elite English women set the fashions by adopting more practical heels than their French or Italian counterparts,

Three English shoes with latchets for ribbon-tie closures, c. 1700–25.

middle- and working-class English shoes were similar in style to higher-end fashions. Only the quality of the construction and materials changed according to the wealth and status of the wearer.

Wooden overshoes, worn for the purpose of protecting leather and textile shoes from the muck and wet of the streets, had been in use since the medieval period, and pattens with iron rings attached to the underside of wooden overshoes had been in use since the early seventeenth century. The English invented a style of overshoe, called clogs, that first appeared in the 1680s and consisted of a wood or cork block fitted to the arch of the shoe with a leather sole and straps often covered with the same material as the shoe. Clogs were worn in cities, primarily to protect fine shoes. The unusual combination of clog-pattens, with a fitted arch but wooden sole and iron ring, as pictured here, were probably made for country wear. Pattens were generally considered appropriate only for the lower classes or wear in the country, yet period references to their wear in spa towns suggest that they were really only deemed *déclassé* in London.

English low-heeled brocade silk shoes, probably made for an adolescent girl, c. 1730–40.

English wood clog-pattens, c. 1730–60.

Top: English shoe with buckle closure, c. 1730–45 and original clog overshoe.

English olive wool twill winter shoe, c. 1730–40.

>> WINTER WARMTH

The Irish, Scottish and Welsh used the same thick sturdy heel as the English in the early eighteenth century. Dutch and German heels were somewhere between the English and French heels, being neither as thick as the English heel nor as thin as the French.

Wool was commonly used for winter footwear in Britain, while velvet was preferred on the Continent. The finest quality wool broadcloth, of which these Irish shoes are made, was beaten, boiled, stretched and scraped in the manufacturing process to create a tight weave with waterproof qualities. The process for making wool broadcloth was developed in late medieval Italy, but by the eighteenth century England was the largest producer. The English olive wool twill shoe was likely made for a woman of the merchant class. The embroidery on the Irish pair, however, denotes a higher status for the original wearer; embellishment was a sign of wealth and was generally unaffordable to the masses. A shoemaker would not have undertaken the needlework ornamentation of uppers.

Instead an embroiderer would have been employed in the manufacture of the upper before the shoes were made, although some ladies who had trained in the domestic arts before marriage would have been capable of such needlework.

Irish wool shoes with colourful floral embroidery, c. 1735.

English cream silk shoe with metallic braid appliqué, a simple upper decoration used since the early seventeenth century. The English heel provides a slightly curvaceous silhouette with a thin waist, c. 1745–55.

>> THE ENGLISH TAKE ON THE POMPADOUR

English shoes lost their pointed toe during the 1740s and 1750s and buckles replaced laced closures. By 1760 women's open-front robes were often worn with petticoats cut shorter to reveal the shoes and buckles. The panniers or side hoops that held the skirt away from the body and the shorter skirts allowed buckles to become quite large and elaborate without catching hem lines. As shoes became more visible, the practical heavy English heel began to lose favour. Heels became slimmer, moving towards the more curvaceous French heel, now known as a pompadour heel after Louis XV's mistress, Madame de Pompadour. In 1753 the English publication *Receipt for Modern Dress* quipped, 'Mount on French Heels when you go to the Ball, 'tis the fashion to totter and show you can fall.'

Since the late seventeenth century a welt was used between the forepart of the sole and the upper and was made a decorative feature of the shoe's construction. The visible welt was called a rand and was made of a folded piece of, usually, white kid through which the stitching of the sole and upper was done. By the late 1760s the rand was reduced to a utilitarian and near invisible piece of leather

English shoes made of rose silk faille with metallic brocade tape decorating the vamps. Made for the American market and worn in Connecticut by Catherine Dexter for her wedding in 1756.

Bottom: English silk shoe with pompadour heel, c. 1765–75.

English silk brocade dress with design of trellis and floral nosegays, c. 1765.

the same colour as the sole, creating a lighter looking sole.

Until the late eighteenth century most fine shoes worn in the American colonies were imported from England. The American shoe industry was just beginning to develop in the 1750s, primarily in and around Lynn, Massachusetts, and most American-made shoes from this period were low-heeled leather shoes of crude construction. American buckles also tended to be plainer than European ones but imported fancy buckles were not uncommon and were popular as wedding and sweetheart gifts.

>> FRENCH BOURGEOIS STYLE

This is a typical, albeit rare, example of a low-heeled shoe donned by the bourgeois. By the mid eighteenth century men's footwear was low-heeled for all occasions, and this shoe resembles a man's style in many ways but for the narrower heel seat and wedge-shaped heel. Ladies' footwear was generally high-heeled for all occasions, and even the few exceptions had a heel height of at least an inch. A lady may have worn a shoe similar to this one for travelling or for walking in country gardens.

The construction of this shoe exhibits slightly cruder materials and stitching than one would expect to find in a major urban centre like Paris, suggesting that it was made by a provincial shoemaker. As such it is exactly what the women pictured in the Arles dressmaker's workshop are wearing: low-heeled shoes suitable for their working-class status. They are dressed fashionably, even though their costumes exhibit some regional influences, because their work would require apparel suitable for meeting clients. While it was not the custom for ladies to walk the streets at this time, women of the working and trade classes had no alternative and so required suitable footwear. The sole of this shoe has darkened from being wet, indicating it was worn outside.

>> BUCKLES

Buckles originally came into fashion because of their usefulness, and the first buckles used by men in the 1660s served mainly functional purposes. However, Louis XIV, The Sun King, liked a little fantasy with his function and in 1685 he ordered a pair of diamond-studded buckles for 351,258 livres – an enormous sum for the period.

A translation of a French publication from 1693 appears in *The Story of Jewelry* by Anderson Black (Morrow & Co, 1974):

> 'Certain young people have recently launched a new fashion: they have set out to close their shoes and their breeches with buckles at the expense of ribbons….They claim the buckles are more convenient. Ribbons, however, are more proper and modest than these gaudy new closures, which, moreover, make them suffer as they irritate the bones of the vain ones, which should quickly make them repent their exhibitionism and their extravagant ideas. Let us sincerely hope that all sensible persons with strong notions of honour will abstain from the usage of these vulgar ornaments. It is up to all fathers to solemnly warn their young that such ostentation is forbidden by Holy Scripture.'

The sanctimonious warnings did not work. The same source informs us that in 1733 in France theatre tickets proclaimed: 'Entry forbidden to persons with laced shoes'. Arbitrary, perhaps, but no more so than today's dress codes forbidding men to enter a restaurant in trainers.

Women followed men's lead, and between the 1760s and 1780s buckles became enormous pieces of jewelry, interchangeable between one pair of shoes and another, much like brooches.

Such ostentatious displays of wealth met with no approval from the working class in the years leading up to the French Revolution. The National Assembly of France's legislative session on 22 November 1789 opened with Le Maréchal de Maille making the patriotic gift of his gold buckles after a vote had been passed that all deputies give up their valuable shoe buckles for the benefit of the treasury. Buckle fashions came to an abrupt end, not only in France but throughout Europe. By 1791 buckle manufacturers in Birmingham sought an audience with the Prince of Wales, the future George IV, begging him to help save their industry, which had flourished over a fifty-year period. He promised to support them by example and influence and made buckles regulation court wear. However, the fashion dandy Beau Brummell, who considered dress and taste a fine art, announced to his fashion followers, including 'Prinny', the Prince of Wales: 'No more colour. No more fantasy, and certainly no more jewels. One must give up one's shoe buckles for the stricter laced shoe.' Outside of court wear, some men retained the plainest of steel buckles, considering 'shoe strings' too foppish. Most men had given up buckles by 1810 except for, ironically, working-class American men who wore them until the 1820s.

English silver buckles set with paste stones, c. 1780.

>> NEW HEELS

The heavy English heel had disappeared by the 1770s and the French heel was being displaced by the even thinner Italian heel, which had a partial wedge that acted as a shank to support the span of the arch. The Italian heel was sometimes even reinforced with a metal rod, the same construction method as used in the stiletto heel by Italian shoe designers in the mid 1950s (see p. 192). The English publication *Gentlemen's Magazine* remarked on this style in 1776:

> 'Heels to bear the precious charge,
> more diminutive than large,
> slight and brittle, apt to break,
> Of the true Italian make.'

Toes became pointed again by the late 1770s, and the latchets slowly began to slip down the vamp so that buckles could be more prominently displayed. As is often the case in fashion history, styles become their most extreme before being abandoned, and buckles were at their largest and most ornate in the 1780s, just as slip-on shoes decorated with bows and ruching became fashionable. Leather, linen and wool shoes were gaining favour for everyday use, allowing fancy shoes to be made of lighter and more delicate dressmaking silks, including taffeta, spotted silk damask and satin. Small delicate sprigs of embroidery, paillette (spangle) and silver-and gilt-thread appliqué began decorating toes as heavy brocade silks fell from use.

English silk brocade shoes with round toes, c. 1765–75. These shoes have a small floral brocade pattern that probably matched a gown. The practice of matching shoe and dress textiles was common from the late 1760s to about 1780.

English blue silk shoes with Italian heels and silver thread and sequin appliqué on the vamps, c. 1785–89.

?American spotted silk shoes with silver lace-trimmed bows, c. 1785–89.

German striped ticking linen shoes with a typical German heel with an extended wedge to support the arch, like an Italian heel, but using a right angle between the neck and wedge, c. 1775–80.

The Spruce Sportsman or *Beauty the Best Shot*, hand-coloured engraving, London, c. 1780.

English green Morocco kid slip-on shoe with upturned toe, c. 1786–87.

French fashion plate from *La Galerie Des Modes* depicting upturned toe shoes, 1786.

>> ORIENTALISM

A peculiar fad in 1786 and 1787 was for shoes with upturned toes, which were referred to as 'Kampskatcha' (sic) slippers or shoes in the 'Chinese taste'. Although closer in appearance to shoes from the Near East, the style did represent the eighteenth-century fascination with Orientalism that permeated the decorative arts. The influential movements of Naturalism, Orientalism, Neoclassicism and Gothic Revival all had their roots in the eighteenth century. Their full effect, however, would not be felt until the following century, with the exception of Neoclassicism, which was about to become very evident in the last decade of the eighteenth century.

>> NEOCLASSICISM

The new French and American republics drew inspiration from classical models of democracy, underscoring the already emerging taste for classicism in the late eighteenth century. Sandal-clad Greek and Roman sculptures inspired footwear design in the 1790s. Artists had depicted their sitters wearing sandals since the Renaissance, but their paintings were intended to portray an historical, timeless or divine quality and did not reflect any fashion for wearing sandals. The painting by Boilly from 1797 (see p. 44) shows what appears to

be a fashionable woman wearing toe-baring sandals, but the subjects of this image are the *Incroyables* and *Merveilleuses*, the anti-fashion extremists of the day, who represented atypical fashion of the late 1790s. In the winter of 1799, Madame Tallien, one of Paris's society beauties, and two of her friends appeared at a state function clad in tunics and sandals with purple straps and rings on their toes. The following day Josephine Bonaparte, on behalf of the first consul of France, made it known to the three ladies that such excess would not

English brown and yellow kid shoes,
c. 1792, worn by Emma Dobson of
Chatham Lodge, Harrogate, Yorkshire.

be tolerated, poetically adding, 'The time of the fable is over, the Reign of History is beginning'. Even in liberally minded France, open-toed sandals were too salacious for society. Illusions to and suggestions of nudity were de rigueur if executed cleverly, but bare feet visible in a sandal were taking things too far. The neoclassical solution was to use trompe l'oeil in the form of painted straps and cut-outs with underlays in closed-shoe styles to create the impression of déshabillé while retaining propriety. When worn with coloured stockings that matched the underlay colours, the illusion was complete.

The elongated pointed toe of the 1790s also fooled the eye by making the foot seem narrow. A tiny foot was considered genteel and elegant, and fashionable English women envied the Duchess of York who was famed for her very small feet. Elizabeth Simcoe, wife of the first Lieutenant Governor of the province of Upper Canada from 1792–96, sent some moccasins to her sister in England and wrote in

?English red kid and blue silk heel-less shoes with yellow stitching and sequins, c. 1798–1800.

English brown kid and embroidered pale-blue striped silk damask shoes with pink silk throat ruffles and top line binding, small heels, c. 1795.

her journal in April 1792: 'I think them very pretty for little children in the house, but I should be afraid if older ones wore them, their feet might be too large ever to wear the Duchess of York's shoe'. It was a common misconception that tiny shoes resulted in tiny feet and the width of feet could be trained in childhood by wearing constricting footwear. Both men and women wore shoes considered too tight in width by today's standards and this habit remained well into the twentieth century, especially with women.

English black japanned leather shoes with matching galoshes, c. 1792–97.

>> PEDESTRIANISM

English streets began to be paved in the 1760s and more ladies took up walking, abandoning transportation by carriage and sedan chair. By 1780 the fashion for taking a promenade along the newly paved streets of London led to walking dresses with ankle-length skirts. A fad for walking everywhere became a much-practised sport, known as pedestrianism.

Women needed suitable footwear to protect their thin-soled shoes from damp and muck. Boots were slowly added to their wardrobe in the 1780s, but did not become common until the 1790s and were as thin-soled as the shoes, really only offering protection in fair weather. Wooden overshoes and pattens continued to be worn but were relegated generally to rural situations and were awkward to wear for any length of time. The English stopped wearing clogs fitted to the arch of the shoe when thin Italian heels were taken up in the 1770s. The search for a suitable replacement resulted in the development of foothold galoshes made of waterproofed lacquered leather.

A pair of English galoshes with japanned
leather toecaps and spring heels covered
in kid leather, c. 1790.

Irish or English leather boots, c. 1795.

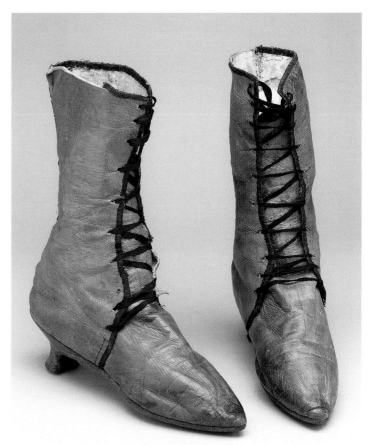

Japanning, an early form of patent leather, came into use in
around 1790 because of its waterproof qualities. The flesh side of
the leather was painted several times with black varnish and oil,
pumiced between coats to create a high-gloss finish that damp could
not penetrate. In 1785 a British patent was taken out by Alexander
Gillies for spring galoshes consisting of toecaps with forepart soles
and kid-covered spring loops to hook around the heels. In description,
they match perfectly the pair of galoshes pictured.

'At The Shoemakers', Pattison's Shoe Shop,
London, c. 1825–28.

19TH CENTURY

By 1800 the Industrial, American and French revolutions had dramatically restructured social order and the middle class became power plebeians, setting the standards of taste and decorum for all society. Conspicuous elitism was no longer in style: shoelaces, painted leather and cotton jean displaced ornate buckles, gilt embroidery and silk brocade. Footwear lost its high heels in the last decade of the eighteenth century, reflecting the democratic ideal that everyone is born on the same level. Neoclassical interpretations of Greek and Roman styles of dress were evident in empire-line gowns and sandals, representing the interest held in these ancient democracies, which were models for the new order.

The middle class replaced the aristocratic pursuit of leisure with the pursuit of material wealth. Fashionable men now worked for a living and their fashions took on the sobriety of English tailoring and shoemaking. Plain tailored dress had its roots in the English Civil War of the mid seventeenth century when the pursuit of elegance was displaced by political turmoil. Even the extravagant King Louis XIV toned down his dress in the later years of his reign. Influenced by English style, Louis appeared more serious and authoritative in the European political arena wearing dark wool suits and plain footwear with lower heels. By the time of the French Revolution at the end of the eighteenth century, Anglomania and the adoption of English style swept France.

The English industrial economy picked up speed in the second half of the eighteenth century bringing wealth to its owners and investors. Although working class by occupation, industrialists were becoming economic equals of the nobility in the nineteenth century. Industrialists' daughters married up the social ladder to gentry looking to replenish depleted family fortunes. Bettering oneself became possible through money. While men intimated their position through subdued business attire, their wives and daughters reflected the new elitism by always dressing au courant – not by over-indulging in opulence but by remaining in step with the latest style.

In the aftermath of the French Revolution, Napoleon Bonaparte led his country to war against the rest of Europe until 1815, a consequence of which was a breakdown in fashion communication resulting in an inconsistent fashion image. In shoes, the use of low heels and the shapes of toes varied. Military supplies took precedence over civilian dress and the production of soldiers' footwear was of the greatest priority, even in Canada and the United States where the War of 1812 was fought. The shortage of military footwear was made clear in many period references to the practice of removing boots from the feet of fallen soldiers for re-use.

Northampton became the centre of English shoe manufacturing during the Napoleonic Wars because of the large orders placed for men's military footwear. To meet quotas, improvements in shoemaking were necessary. Marc Isambard Brunel reintroduced a sole-riveting process in 1810, originally developed in Roman times, that allowed military footwear to be made by unskilled labourers. But the end product was unsatisfactory and, when the factory burned down in 1815, the process was abandoned. The English also developed a press for cutting out leather and perfected the pantograph, a machine that allowed mirror images of left and right lasts to be made proficiently.

Crooked soles, with left or right definition, were brought back into women's footwear as early as 1801 but they were slow to catch on, largely due to the cost of purchasing shoes made for each foot rather than straight soles that could be worn on either foot.

With peace, Northampton became the centre for men's footwear production. The French were rebounding economically after the war and began making and exporting women's silk and kid shoes using a streamlined cottage-industry production method. France was regaining its former place as the leader in women's fashions and became the largest exporter of women's shoes until the 1860s.

By the 1820s fashion was noticeably progressing through identifiable seasonal changes reported in monthly fashion periodicals. Fashion reporting dates back to late-seventeenth-century France when fashion plates first appeared, but at the time they were more prized for their art and were acquired by collectors of prints. From 1778 to 1787 the first regular fashion publication, *Galérie des Modes*, was published in France, but it was an elitist publication and had a small circulation. In England, German-born Rudolf Ackermann reinvented the fashion plate during the Napoleonic Wars by creating periodicals devoted to women's interests. *Ackermann's Repository*, published in London from 1809 to 1829, provided middle-class English women with information on style and fashion. Its coloured fashion plates with full descriptions, intended to serve as dressmakers' guides, appeared alongside information and illustrations on interior decoration as well as literary reviews and reports on commerce and travel. When hostilities ceased between England and France, the fashion periodical, of which several were being printed by the 1820s, served to create a cohesive fashionable style.

In 1830 *Godey's Lady's Book* was the first of many American fashion periodicals to be published. Even if the fashions pictured upon the pages were unobtainable from their London or Paris sources, American women were at least aware of what was in vogue. Contrary to the myth that North Americans were years behind in style, fashion was delayed only by the length of time it took a boat to cross the Atlantic, and fashionable women who craved the latest mode and feared appearing colonial or backwards were limited only by their means. There is, in fact, much evidence of many American women dressing above their situation, often inappropriately or unseasonably, to prove their social class in the officially classless republican American society of the mid nineteenth century. Many European visitors noticed and commented in their journals on women walking in tiny French silk slippers on the unpaved streets of American cities. After 1850 American fashion periodicals included reports on the latest modes from Paris and London as well as Philadelphia and New York where the journals were published. Advice was often dispensed regarding beauty, art, taste, culture, design and etiquette. Editorials advised ladies on what not to wear as much as on what to wear and it was usually through these reports that many women learned of what was fashionable for their feet.

The late 1830s and 1840s was a period of great change within many countries experiencing political unrest and revolt. Ever-growing industrialization meant the complete upheaval of long-standing social and economic structures. The anti-industrial Luddite revolts in the 1810s had no effect on industrial progress and factories continued to scar the horizon, mechanization replacing craft. Romantic ideals of the picturesque began to infiltrate the arts as an antidote to an industrial reality and design became historically inspired. By 1840 the arches of Gothic cathedrals inspired the design of steel-beam railway bridges. The Gothic arch also influenced the silhouette of women's costume. Women's dress had evolved from the interpretations of Greek tunics with ankle-length hem lines that hung freely about the body to tightly fitted bodices with corseted waists and full skirts that swept the floor. Boots and shoes abandoned colour and decoration as feet disappeared under hem lines widened by the addition of cumbersome petticoats. In public, a woman expressed her taste and decorum through her dress and deportment. Virtue, grace and propriety were a woman's domain in this era.

Progress could not be stopped and technology continued to pick up speed, despite a sentimental fondness for a romanticized past that was expressed artistically. Patents for sewing machines had been issued as early as the 1790s, primarily due to the need for sewing leather shoes. An early sewing machine designed for commercial use employed a chain stitch and was patented by Frenchman Barthelemy Thimonnier in 1830, but a revolt by workers in fear of losing their jobs to technology destroyed the machines. Chain stitching was found to be unsuitable for sewing leather uppers anyway, since one pulled thread could unravel the whole seam. American Isaac Singer's 1856 patented lock-stitch sewing machine was the first to sew leather as well as cloth, and heralded a series of changes in the American shoemaking industry. Over the following thirty years American footwear production became the most prolific and profitable in the world and remained that way for the next hundred years.

American Lyman Blake developed the first machine for attaching soles to uppers in 1858 using a sturdy chain-stitched seam directly through the sole. Chain stitching may not have been suitable for sewing uppers but it was fine for sole construction as long as the thread was waxed to give it more 'grab'. The thread was also partially imbedded in the sole leather, making it less likely to come undone. Blake sold the principal interest to fellow countryman Gordon McKay, who went on to finance the construction of the first machines. The American Union Army gave McKay his first large commission to make soldiers' boots in the early 1860s and the process was in common use by the mid 1860s.

Wooden-pegged soles had been made in the United States since the 1810s and were exported to Europe as early as 1842, but these earlier versions were hand crafted and laborious to make. A machine for attaching soles with wooden pegs was invented in 1859. Wooden pegs performed exceptionally well in wet weather because they swelled to make the sole waterproof and were used for a variety of footwear from women's utilitarian buskins to military boots for the American Civil War.

The Goodyear welting machine, in use by 1877, was developed by Charles Goodyear Jr., the son of the man who invented the process of vulcanization nearly forty years earlier. A Goodyear welt imitated the difficult stitching of a leather shoe through the upper, welt and sole. Unlike the McKay stitching machine, it did not puncture the bottom of the sole and thus made shoes more suitable for wet weather. This development put an end to the production of peg-soled shoes in the United States.

Invented in 1883 by Jan Matzeliger, the lasting machine copied the multiple motions of pulling an upper around a last and tacking it into place before attaching a sole. The machine brought this previously time-consuming and exacting job down to a minute's worth of work that a semi-skilled labourer could perform.

Numerous developments, many but not all of them American, improved the production of footwear throughout the nineteenth century. The vulcanization of rubber discovered in 1839 by Charles Goodyear revolutionized the overshoe industry. A machine to manufacturer metal eyelets was developed as early as 1823 but was used sparingly by the shoe industry until the 1860s. A process for making shoes with cemented or glued soles was patented in 1858 but would not revolutionize the manufacture of ladies' dress shoes until the 1930s. Leather rollers and splitters; machines for welting, closing, screwing and riveting soles; and the American idea of shoe boxes in the 1830s, which allowed for efficient stock management and safer exports, all contributed to the American market's ability to inexpensively mass-produce and export a variety of quality sewn footwear.

England's Great Exhibition of 1851 displayed the prowess of English hand shoemaking. Shoemakers created footwear of exceptional quality for the exhibition, pushing the limits of fashion with brightly coloured boots and shoes that reintroduced heels. These styles were more than a decade ahead of the general footwear mode and small heels began to slowly return to footwear in the late 1850s. Steel shanks were added for arch support and tall curvaceous heels, resembling the pompadour French heel of the mid eighteenth century, came back into fashion in the late 1860s, providing fodder for fashion periodicals to scold its followers. The eighteenth century inspired all areas of the arts and was evident in footwear with the reintroduction of buckles and bows on the toes of shoes and boots. Women's costumes took on similarly elaborate trimmings, with fringes and pleats, buttons and tassels. The large mid-century skirts diminished in size and by 1870 the bustle had appeared at the back of the dress. Skirt fronts fell closer to the body by the mid 1870s allowing the decorated toes of shoes and boots to be seen while walking.

At Philadelphia's 1876 Exhibition, American manufacturing expertise focused on the future of machine production rather than the development of style or the finest examples of hand craftsmanship. By this time, European exports to North America were rapidly declining as Americans were becoming the largest producers of shoes in the world.

The preponderance of plain brown and black footwear from the late 1870s until the 1910s was occasionally alleviated by the addition of beaded toes on dressier styles. American machine-beaded styles began to flood the European marketplace in the 1880s. Orders dried up for bespoke work as cheaper American ready-mades stocked

European shelves. Elite hand shoemakers survived by specializing in superbly crafted boots and shoes. Some American ladies would even cross the Atlantic to purchase the very best couture footwear by makers like François Pinet in Paris, who is recognized as the founder of footwear couture in the way that Charles Worth is given the same honour for haute couture. The age of the shoe designer was upon us!

A growing movement for health and physical exercise resulted in the emergence of sports footwear in the second half of the nineteenth century. Walking and riding had been the only strenuous activities deemed suitable for ladies in the early nineteenth century and acted as catalysts for the introduction of boots into women's wardrobes. A variety of lawn sports, including shuttlecock and battledore (badminton) and croquet, became popular during the century but they were more social than strenuous activities and were usually performed in fashion footwear. After 1860 the more aerobic recreations of ice-skating and tennis and, late in the century, bicycling and golf became popular. These activities required appropriate footwear and lead to the introduction of new styles of performance-enhancing shoes, most notably the invention of the rubber-soled sports shoe, which would become the most influential shoe style of the twentieth century.

The liberated woman, called the 'New Woman' in the 1890s, played sports, attended university and even travelled without a chaperone. She wore tailored suits and required a variety of footwear in suitably mannish styles to match her daily activities. A less strident vision of the modern woman was popularized by the American illustrator Charles Dana Gibson who drew humorous and sentimental sketches in the 1890s of beautiful young women portrayed as confident, healthy, active and intelligent. The Gibson Girl, was a well-known and emulated icon of the period, and there was even a front-laced shoe style named after her in England.

By the turn of the century, goods and fashion knowledge were exported around the world as fast as steamships and railroads could take them. Efficient public transport systems linked suburban homes to city centres where the new department stores held a wide variety of goods under one roof. This increased women's ability to purchase and stay 'in step' with the latest styles. If all else failed, customers could order goods by post or telephone from catalogues. Wealthy American women travelled to Europe for high-fashion clothes and footwear but also bought quality constructed domestically manufactured ready-mades. The shoe industry was one of the largest employers in North America at the turn of the twentieth century and manufacturers and retailers needed to compete for their share in the marketplace. Manufacturers learned quickly that trade cards, broadsides, billboards and magazine advertisements promoted brand names and encouraged repeat business from loyal clients. The new economy of mass consumption had begun.

English olive leather shoes with gold-
stamped design and yellow silk tassels,
c. 1800–10.

>> DEMOCRATIC SOLES

Durable and affordable, leather footwear was more democratic than the silk shoes of pre-revolutionary France. By 1800 most footwear was made of leather with silk used only for trims and ribbon laces. The term sandal was used at this time to refer to any closed-toe shoe with laces that crossed over the instep and tied around the ankle.

Heels had vanished from almost all footwear by 1800, in keeping with the new democratic philosophy that all people were born on the same level, although the occasional wedge or tiny heel still appeared in the early 1810s. Fashion colours were borrowed from the then recent excavations at Pompeii and were inspired by Napoleon's military campaigns in Egypt and Italy. Colours of the classical world were revived – white, tan, pastels, rich tones of Pompeii red and Nile or crocodile green – and new, quick and inexpensive techniques for applying colour and pattern to plain surfaces on leather shoes were introduced with roller-printed kids and leathers.

Costumes Parisiens fashion plate, showing the closed-toe sandal-slipper with ankle laces, 1803.

English printed leather shoes with pink silk ribbon bows at throat, c. 1805–12.

An 1801 advertisement from Philadelphia offered ready-made crooked-soled shoes (left and right shapes), but straight-soled shoes would continue to dominate all shoe production until the 1870s, not falling completely from use until the 1890s. Most early examples of crooked soles were bespoke, while ready-mades were made with straight soles.

>> WALKING BOOTS

Women only wore boots for horse riding until the late 1780s, at which point they also began to wear them for walking. First known as the demi-boot, half boot or high-low, the new style was mid-shin in height and had a single-lace front closure. Knotted at the bottom, the lace was laddered through the holes and tied at the top.

Gaiters were an alternative to boots and proved more popular in France than England. Borrowed from men's military dress, gaiters protected the stocking from spatters and dashes of mud and were known as 'spatterdashes' in England, the origin of the word 'spats'. Many of the early boots made of cotton with leather toecaps copied the look of gaiters over shoes.

Walking for sport was known as pedestrianism and was a prescribed activity for men and women for the improvement of their health. This was not a stroll, rather a brisk activity that required good posture and stamina, what we would call hiking today, and was considered a suitable social exercise for young ladies. Jane Austen

depicted many of her novels' heroines involved in pedestrianism in both town and country settings. She even suggested in her 1804 novel, *The Watsons*: 'You should wear half boots, nankin galoshed with black looks very well.' In that same year, across the Atlantic in York (present-day Toronto), an advertisement for boots from the retail establishment of St. George & Company was printed in the *Upper Canada Gazette*: 'Lately arrived from New York...a valuable and extensive assortment of half boots, morocco and leather'.

The fashion for boots gained popularity throughout the early years of the nineteenth century. The English fashion journal *Ackermann's Repository* reported on fashions in Berlin and it noted in 1815: 'The ladies wear demi-boots...of red kid or morocco, or satin'. In the 1827 English publication *Crispin Anecdotes*, the writer complains: 'It is to be regretted that many ladies should prefer the wearing of boots to the use of the shoe.'

>> INCONSISTENT FASHIONS

After Napoleon installed himself as Emperor of France in 1804, silk began to reappear on evening shoes. His coronation had spared no expense, drawing more on classical Imperialism than on democratic idealism. Classical motifs became style inspiration, with gilt-embroidered laurel wreaths, lyres and Greek key designs decorating French court robes. Josephine's own court shoes were made of white silk taffeta, gilt-embroidered with bees, the symbol of the Empire.

The Napoleonic Wars meant that there was no consistent fashion image from the late 1790s until the late 1810s as both France and England determined their own fashions, sometimes continuing to do so even into the 1820s. English fashion journals in the 1820s, like *Ladies' Monthly Museum*, reported fashions in London and Paris as having different styles. Women's footwear exemplified this confusion in fashion authority with different toe shapes running concurrently: pointed toes (1790s–1810), almond-shaped toes (1800–25), rounded toes (1805–35), and squared-toe tips (1810–30). Eventually the squared-toe tip broadened and became the dominant style from 1830 until 1880.

High heels became unpopular after the French Revolution and were completely abandoned on European women's shoes by

the early 1810s. However, in around 1815, men started to wear trousers instead of breeches and a strap was attached to the hem of each leg to keep them taut and straight. These straps hooked under the shoe and were anchored by the heel, which also kept the strap from wearing through by being walked on.

Heels, which had hardly disappeared from American women's shoes, began to make a comeback. The height of the heel was never great, usually consisting of a few layers of leather, but by the early 1830s the heel again vanished from American women's shoes, not destined to be reintroduced for twenty years.

American wool shoe with stacked leather heel, c. 1820.

English illustration from *Ladies' Monthly Museum*, June 1823.

>> THE SANDAL-SLIPPER

Originating in France in the 1790s, the sandal-slipper only became the predominant style of shoe in the 1810s. Shoes in the early nineteenth century had no support or counter in the back of the upper, so the back part could be collapsed to slip the foot into the vamp and then pulled up around the heel once the foot was in place. A drawstring around the top line secured the shoe to the foot, although not always successfully as period literature often refers to the problem of losing slippers. To compensate, silk laces were attached at the sides, which crossed over the instep and tied about the ankle to keep the slipper in place. The laces resembled the straps of classical sandals and the shoe became known as the sandal-slipper. Ribbons tended to slip or become untied, but the problem was remedied after the development of elastic in 1839, when elastic loops started to replace silk ribbon laces.

Coloured footwear began to gain popularity, especially as the shoe was seen under ankle-high hem lines. It was often the custom from the 1790s to the 1810s to match shoe colour with the colour of the gloves or silk ribbon belt. After 1810 shoe colour was also often matched to the colour of the purse or dress trimmings. During the 1820s classical colours began to be replaced by darker

sombre hues, such as aubergine, plum, purple, navy blue, forest and bottle green and grey, all of which became favourites in the 1830s.

Prunella, a durable worsted satin-weave wool, was commonly used for footwear in the 1810s and 1820s. *La Belle Assemblée*, an English fashion periodical, noted in 1833: 'Prunella shoes are become so common that no lady wears them'. Despite this fashion snobbery, prunella remained in fashion for daytime footwear until well into the 1860s.

English satin silk sandal-slippers with silk ribbon laces, c. 1815–30.

American silk wedding sandal-slippers with
silk ribbon laces, 1818.

>> FRENCH INDUSTRY

By 1820 France was the leading producer and exporter of ladies' ready-made straight-soled silk and kid sandal-slippers, maintaining that position until the early 1850s and remaining a strong exporter until the onset of the Franco-Prussian war in 1870. The French predominance in the ladies' shoe market was of concern to other leading shoe-producing nations, particularly England, who placed a duty on imports of foreign footwear in 1827.

French supremacy was a result of hiring out piecework. Women sewed the kid and silk uppers together and then sent the completed uppers to professional shoemakers, who made lasts and soled the shoes. The shoes were returned to the seamstresses for finishing with ribbon bindings and laces. By the 1840s this form of cottage industry was common in Europe and North America, and many small factories only employed shoemakers who specialized in making lasts and soling shoes. The era of one shoemaker making a shoe from start to finish was becoming archaic by 1850.

Parisian shoes were notorious for their narrow widths and in most cases the foot was wider than the sole. This resulted in the upper being pulled under the foot and many surviving shoes show wear on this area of the uppers.

French coloured etching of Paris shoe seller by Lanté and Gatine, c. 1817–22.

French lithograph of woman sewing boots and shoes by Charles Philipon, published by Charles Tilt, London, c. 1828–30.

La laborieuse Cordonnière.
(Paris.)

Straight soles were easier and cheaper to make than soles defined for left and right feet. An advantage of these straight-soled French shoes was that they could be bought in multiple pairs, mixing and matching the shoes until they were all worn out. Silk shoes were often marked inside with a 'D' (*droit* or right) and a 'G' (*gauche* or left) by the manufacturer to show which foot they were intended for. This eliminated any confusion about putting the shoes on the opposite foot, which might reveal damage from previous wear.

French shoes were identified easily by their lack of an upper back seam. Nonetheless, shoes were being made and sold as 'French' in London and New York where they copied the seamless back – something that today would result in a lawsuit for infringement. *The Boot and Shoe Manufacturer's Assistant and Guide* reported in 1858: 'Most of the so-called French manufacture is the product of American artisans. This amiable deception is practiced in order to gratify the whims of those who lack confidence in the skill and taste of American manufacturers.'

>> SQUARED TO FLARED

The square toe of the late 1820s to the early 1880s had a definite chronology in style. It began as a tapered toe with a squared-off tip that had become quite broad by 1830. The square toe continued to broaden until the ball was the same width as the toe, and by 1845 the toe was sometimes even flared beyond the width of the ball. During the 1850s the sharp corners slowly softened into a square toe with rounded edges. In this final incarnation, the square toe remained the fashion until the early 1880s, when it became rounder and then pointed.

Square-toed sandal-slippers of the 1830s resemble today's ballet slippers for a good reason. Dance historians dispute when dancing upon the toes was first attempted, however, it is generally accepted that Italian Marie Taglioni was the first prima ballerina to become known for her demonstrations of en pointe dancing in around 1830. This type of dancing was made possible by the addition of wooden blocks and lambswool cushioning to the square toes of sandal-slippers, and the style has remained in use by ballerinas ever since.

Soles of three French sandal-slippers, left to right: c. 1830, c. 1845, c. 1855.

French black silk sandal-slippers with flared toes, c. 1845.

>> FOUL WEATHER WEAR

Iron-ringed pattens, commonly used since the early seventeenth century, continued to be worn into the 1830s, although a hinged wooden clog without an iron ring also became popular from the 1810s to the 1830s. Women had worn clogs and pattens primarily to protect their health by preventing their feet from getting cold and damp, indoors and out. Elizabeth Simcoe, wife of the Lieutenant Governor of Upper Canada, reports having worn clogs on board ship in 1791 because the floor of her cabin was never dry. However, despite their intention to preserve health, clogs and pattens proved useless in deep muddy streets and occasionally were even dangerous. French writer Aurore Dupin,

better known as the male-attired and -named George Sand, wrote in 1831:

> 'On [a] Paris pavement I was like a boat on ice…my pattens sent me spilling, and I always forgot to lift my dress. I was muddy, tired and runny-nosed, and I watched my shoes and clothes go to rack and ruin with alarming rapidity – So I had a box coat cut for me out of heavy drab stuff, with matching trousers and waistcoat…I can't convey how much my boots delighted me, I'd have gladly slept in them.'

For North American women, an alternative to pattens were moccasins. In a letter to a friend in 1797, Elizabeth Russell of York

(present-day Toronto) writes of acquiring a pair of moccasins to send to her English friend as a gift, and that Mrs. Simcoe (the same lady who wore clogs in her boat cabin) wore them over her shoes. Anne Langton reported in *A Gentlewoman in Upper Canada* (Toronto, Clarke, Irwin and Company, 1950) in c. 1840: 'Footwear…was generally moccasins…and over these another pair of moccasins for out of doors'. Apparently, the use of moccasins was already known in England, as the English publication *La Belle Assemblée* reported in 1828 that moccasins were useful as overshoes. Whether these were imported Native moccasins from North America or a European copy is not known. *Godey's Lady's Book* illustrates a moccasin in January

1861, calling it a carriage shoe. However, it closely resembles a type of Native moccasin that is attributed to the Iroquois in many ethnological museum collections, even though the style often had an additional leather sole suggesting an intended fashion use.

Europeans travelling to South America in the late sixteenth century recorded that the natives of Brazil made shoes, bottles and balls from the cured latex sap of a tree called *cachuc*, meaning 'weeping wood'. The English scientist Joseph Priestly discovered that this substance rubbed out pencil marks and thus the name 'rubber' was born. The elastic and waterproof qualities of rubber interested late eighteenth century scientists, but they were hampered by the fact that although the rubber flowed out of the tree in liquid form, it soon solidified and then decomposed.

Rubber galoshes were made in Brazil by pouring latex over clay forms and curing them in a plume of smoke from a fire of uricuri palm nuts that contained high amounts of acetic acid and phenols. The smoke stopped the rubber from decomposing but turned the galoshes a dark-brown colour. When the galoshes were sufficiently thick after several applications, they were left to cure for a few days and then the clay was washed out.

Although Brazil was a Portuguese territory, the English had been given access to its ports in exchange for helping Portugal against Napoleon's army. The first large shipment of galoshes from Para in Brazil to England was made in 1823, but the hefty cost of shipping made them expensive. The first shipment to America in 1825, a considerably shorter journey, still required them to retail in Boston at US $5 per pair (about US $95 in today's money). The 'India Rubbers', as they were known at the time, were also problematic as they became soft and sticky in the summer and brittle in the winter. Regardless of their problems and expense, sales grew to half a million pairs per year by 1842.

Charles Macintosh, working as a chemist at his father's textile dyestuff factory in Glasgow, was looking for a use for naphtha, the waste product from cooking coal to create gas for Glasgow's new gas works that opened in 1818. He discovered that naphtha dissolved

Brazilian moulded rubber galoshes, c. 1830.

rubber and that a thin sheet of rubber slurry could be sandwiched between two layers of textile to create a waterproof fabric. The cloth was patented in 1823, and in 1830 he entered a partnership with Thomas Hancock to produce raincoats and cloaks, known as 'Macintoshes'. This process, however, still resulted in the rubber hardening in cold weather and the original products were said to be extremely smelly.

In 1839 Charles Goodyear discovered that when rubber was heated with sulphur it created a refined rubber that was stable and elastic, returning to its shape after being stretched and unsusceptible to external temperatures. This critical discovery produced little profit for Charles Goodyear, who had borrowed huge amounts of money for his research and ended up signing over the American patent to his assistant and financial backer Nathaniel Hayward. He also lost the English patent to Thomas Hancock who, probably inspired by the hellish sulphuric smell during the heating process, called the method 'vulcanization' after the Roman god of fire and volcanoes. In later years Hancock admitted that he stole the research after being able to smell the sulphur and beat Goodyear in the patenting process. The first vulcanized rubber galoshes were marketed in 1844 and quickly turned into a profitable industry. Goodyear died in 1860, US $200,000 in debt.

American rubber galoshes, impressed on sole 'Goodyear Shoe Co. Naugatuck, Conn. Patent 1844'. Presumably made of vulcanized rubber with a lining but it is difficult to ascertain as the rubber has hardened over time, which even vulcanized rubber will do eventually.

American red and beige woven cotton
shoes with black glacé kid toes, c. 1845.

American resist-dyed plum velvet shoes with
glacé kid vamps, c. 1840–45.

>> STYLE AND SENSIBILITY

Compared to Europe, most North American cities had poorer roads and non-existent transport systems. North American women tended to walk out of necessity rather than for recreation. In 1832 Englishwoman Mrs Frances Trollope toured the United States and reported that American women 'never wear boots, and appear extremely shocked at the sight of comfortable walking shoes and cotton stockings….They walk in the middle of winter with their poor little toes pinched into a miniature slipper, incapable of excluding as much moisture as might bedew a primrose.' Mrs Trollope was partly correct as boots had fewer followers on that side of the Atlantic than in England. Some American women were wearing India rubber galoshes in the 1820s and 1830s for outdoor walking in the wet or cold, but these galoshes were expensive and in short supply. By the 1840s leather shoes, including those in the typically American light-tan colour often referred to as café au lait, textile shoes and ankle boots with toecaps of patent or glacé kid and double soles were being made for general street wear. While these walking styles were only slightly better at resisting the damp than a silk or light kid sandal-slipper, they were at least fashionable options that were better suited for inclement weather. The American fashion journal *Leslie's Magazine* reported in 1843: 'The insane practice that formally prevailed of ladies walking the streets in winter with their feet in light kid slippers has most fortunately subsided and has been replaced by India Rubbers, double soles and gaiter boots.'

American café-au-lait-coloured kid shoes, c. 1840.

American fashion plate, *Godey's Lady's Book*, December 1838.

The English publication *Ladies' Repository* noted in 1843: 'Amidst the frosts of winter and the damp of spring the devotee of fashion may be seen walking the street with no more substantial covering for her feet than the silken hose and Parisian sole – affording scarce greater protection than the stocking itself and this not withstanding the many instances in which such exposure annually results in early death or a broken constitution.' This alarmist statement suggests that the fashion for style over sensibility was also an English problem.

Ill-fitting Parisian sandal-slippers with narrow soles did little to restrict the natural foot shape, but sturdier leather shoes with laced closures were less forgiving. The English publication *Handbook to the Toilette* in 1841 stated: 'There scarcely exists an Englishwoman whose toes are not folded one over the other, each of these crooked, and their nails almost destroyed.' The New York publication *Sergeant's New Monthly Magazine* contained a similarly sensationalist statement in April 1843: 'Comfort…is unhesitatingly sacrificed on the altar to vanity. Do not two thirds of the sex willingly suffer a cramping and curtailing of the feet and its attendant evils, to which the iron torture-shoe anciently used by the inquisitors bears no slight resemblance?' Nineteenth-century fashion journalists were prone to exaggeration but their concerns were not pure invention.

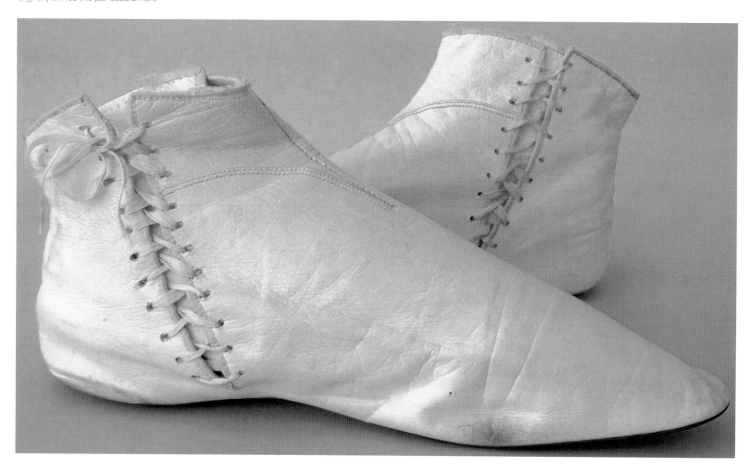

>> BLACK AND WHITE

The fashion for coloured footwear rapidly declined when hem lines hit the floor in the late 1830s and shoes became invisible. The broad and bright palette that had been available shrunk to a few sombre hues of brown, dark blue, forest and bottle green and some deep purples, with taupe, putty and café-au-lait coloured leather shoes in the United States. Black and white footwear increased in use until by the mid 1850s fashion writers were specifying only black and white footwear. *Ladies' Repository*, an English publication, commented in 1850: 'White or black satin slippers with silk stockings must be worn for the evening'. Another English publication, *The Toilette*, went further in 1854, pointing out: 'Coloured shoes are exceedingly vulgar;

delicate pinks and faint blue silks have been advocated but white satin, black satin or kid or bronzed kid are neater and more elegant.' The American publication *Peterson's Magazine* confirmed in January 1855 that 'nothing can be more elegant than a pure white or black satin shoe'.

However, the introduction of the wire-frame petticoat in the mid 1850s influenced ladies' footwear because of its tendency to tip when dancing or walking, exposing the foot and ankle. Interest was renewed in coloured and decorated footwear. Colours exploded back into fashion with the German perfection of aniline (synthetic) dyes in the late 1850s. A whole new range of purple shades and other,

often gaudy, new colours like apple green (previously only attainable by using arsenic) and electric blue were now possible. The taste for plain black and white footwear did not disappear but was augmented by these new colours in the early 1860s. *The Englishwoman's Domestic Magazine* reported in 1862: 'A great revolution has taken place in the *chaussure* for the black shoe or boot…coloured ones are substituted to accord nicely with dresses, blue, violet, scarlet and green morocco.'

French black silk sandal-slippers, c. 1850.

American white kid shoes with silk bows, labelled 'S. Driver, Salem, Massachusetts', c. 1850–60. These belonged to the sister of Enoch Lincoln, Governor of Maine in the late 1820s, who named Augusta as the capital of the state.

>> ADELAIDES

In around 1830 side-laced boot styles, called Adelaides after the Queen consort of King William IV, were introduced. All known surviving examples date from after the ascension of Queen Victoria, suggesting that they found little popularity at first.

Feminine modesty was embraced when skirt hems dropped to the floor just before Victoria became queen in 1837. Adelaides became popular as daytime wear, hidden beneath the full skirts, which only increased in fullness over the next twenty-five years. With the introduction of wire-frame hoop skirts, or crinolines, in the mid 1850s women were relieved of the burden of multiple petticoats. Hoops, however, tended to tip and expose the ankle. In the 1856 publication *Every Lady Her Own Shoemaker*, the author acclaims boots:

'If the wind blows one's skirts away from the feet, one's ankles are not so much exposed.' Boots therefore became necessary for maintaining daytime respectability in public and were also worn often in the evening.

Adelaides were also known as gaiter boots in the United States, referring to a boot with a cloth upper trimmed with leather toecaps and counters. The side lacing was turned toward the inside of the ankle to make for a dressy appearance, but with every step the ankle joint rotation loosened the closure. The Adelaide began to fall from favour as front-laced boots made a comeback and button boots emerged in the late 1850s (see p. 78). The side-laced closure style was used only occasionally after the 1860s.

American black prunella wool side-laced boots, c. 1850.

American pale-green silk taffeta side-laced boot, c. 1860.

>> ELASTIC-SIDED BOOTS

Adapting the idea originally developed in 1785 for spring-loaded loops to attach foothold galoshes, Englishman Joseph Sparkes Hall sewed spring coils inside channels on the side gussets of pull-on ankle boots in 1837. A prototype of his idea was presented to Queen Victoria but the style did not go into general production. Sparkes Hall also experimented with using triangular pieces of rubber, but results were not satisfactory. Improvements in the elasticity of rubber after the discovery of vulcanization in 1839 led to the development of elastic thread, which when woven into webbing could be used as gussets on ankle boots. Sparkes Hall's elastic-sided boots were hugely popular and became known as 'gore' boots and 'Congress' boots in the United States. They were later referred to as 'Garibaldi' boots in Europe, after the Italian statesman.

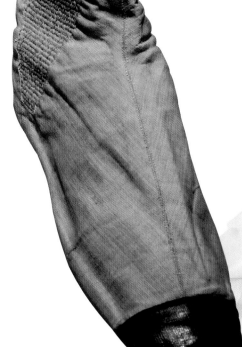

English prototype boots of cotton with black-patent toecaps and metal springs set in channels on either side of the ankle. Made by Joseph Sparkes Hall in 1837 and presented to Queen Victoria.

American manufacturers had a problem keeping up with initial demand for the boots because of the restrictive English patent. The American journal *Godey's Lady's Book* reported in August 1848:

'About one year since the Congress boot has been introduced into the United States, the demand has been so great that few have been able to obtain them. This is not the fault of the shoemakers. This boot is a patented article, and they are compelled to pay six cents for the privilege of making every pair....As a dress boot it is the perfection of neatness. The Congress boot has received the marked and continued patronage of Queen Victoria. It is also very generally worn by the first ladies in England and our own country. They combine all the good qualities of a beautiful gaiter with none of the trouble and inconveniences. The elastic gore is an admirable and invaluable support to the ankle, making the boot fit snugly, and giving it a light, graceful and captivating appearance....The manufacture of the Congress boot is steadily progressing. The exact elasticity required having been obtained, the boot is now believed to be most perfect worn.'

The style was used for informal house shoes in the late nineteenth and early twentieth centuries when it was known by a variety of names, most commonly the Chelsea boot. In its last incarnation in the 1960s it was called the Beatle boot.

American silk Congress boot, c. 1865.

?Hungarian gilt-embroidered button boots, c. 1860–68.

>> BUTTONS AND BALMORALS

The 1860s was the decade of the boot. Numerous publications voiced their preference for boots over shoes for all occasions, most probably because the huge crinoline undergarments did little to stop drafts and boots were considered more healthful and modest. Shoes were certainly still worn, especially at the end of the decade, but those that survive were usually made for house wear or eveningwear. Boots made entirely of leather, rather than of cloth with a leather trim, were more common by 1860.

Button closures and front lacings displaced side-laced closures and relegated elastic-sided boots to more utilitarian wear in the 1860s. Button closures required the use of a buttonhook to do them

up and could not be adjusted during the day when the foot and ankle swelled, but their tailored ankle-flattering style made them firm favourites. Front-laced boots were known as balmorals, after Queen Victoria's Scottish castle retreat. The Queen herself popularized the style as English publication *The Habits of Good Society* suggested in 1859: 'Victoria has assumed the Balmoral boot. With these...the high-born lady may enjoy the privileges which her inferiors possess – she may take a good walk with pleasure and safety.'

Canadian white leather button boot, worn
for a wedding, 1869. Scalloped edging was
especially fashionable after 1867.

American illustration of lady wearing balmoral boots with her walking dress with elevator skirt, *Peterson's Magazine*, March 1861.

Canadian white cotton balmoral boots, worn for a wedding, 1867.

>> BARRETTES

With the demise of sandal-slippers in the late 1840s and early 1850s, the term sandal disappeared for a few years from the shoe lexicon. American fashion journal *Peterson's Magazine* reported in January 1855 of a novelty seen in Paris for shoes with bands on the instep that any lady could re-create by remodelling an existing pair of shoes. By the late 1860s the style was commonly available, especially in boots, and was called the barrette or sandal-boot. It was perfect for wearing with coloured stockings that matched or complemented the dress as they showed through the bands on the leg and instep. Sandal-boots sometimes featured ornate cut-outs instead of plain bands and were made until the early 1920s.

Canadian or American black leather sandal-boot, c. 1868–80.

French black silk barrette shoes, c. 1865–70.

>> ENGLISH PROWESS

Industrial capability, an expanding empire and timely social reforms made England the most powerful nation for most of the nineteenth century. The Great Exhibition of 1851 was a milestone in English national pride that highlighted all that was good about industrialization. The potential for human progress through technology and prosperity seemed limitless. Queen Victoria, who opened the exhibition, even expressed these ideals as religious responsibility: 'The progress of the human race resulting from the labour of all men ought to be the final object of the exertion of each individual. In promoting this end we are carrying out the will of the Great and Blessed God.'

Fashion footwear in 1851 was generally black or white, undecorated and without a heel. Footwear made for the Great Exhibition was more typical of footwear from 1861 than 1851, as it was designed to showcase workmanship, pushing the limits of fashionable style in the process.

Queen Victoria reigned during this period of English prowess and the age has become known as the Victorian era, even in countries not historically associated with the British Empire. The legacy of Victoria's reign has been passed on in the appellation of places and objects associated with the Queen, her family and even her residences, such as Balmoral, her Scottish home after which

English shoes made for London's Great Exhibition of 1851.

front-laced boots were named (see p. 78). Victoria can be credited with the resurgent interest in Scottish tartan since her Scottish heritage was her strongest link to British ancestry. Victoria's husband, Albert, the Prince Consort, had numerous items named after him, including the male version of the side-laced Adelaide boot and the rounded-cut tongue of a shoe upper popularly used on house slippers (see p. 88). Queen Victoria permanently adopted mourning dress after the death of Albert, popularizing the strict observance of mourning procedure and creating a fashion for sombre colours in the late nineteenth century.

English silk tartan ankle boot, c. 1860–65.

French white silk slippers with hand-
embroidered grapevine design,
c. 1855.

>> CHAMELEONS

A renewed interest in the decoration of shoes for home and evening wear developed with the introduction of cage-frame hoops in the mid 1850s as skirts tended to tip and sway, exposing the foot and ankle. Machine chain stitching, not suitable for sewing shoe uppers, was useful for producing decorative embroidery.

Shoes with coloured silks underneath decorative cut-outs and with machine-stitched designs were first shown at London's Great Exhibition of 1851, but they were not in general production until the mid 1850s. The style was available in different coloured silks, most commonly rose and blue but also green and yellow. *The Englishwoman's Domestic Magazine* reported in 1867: 'Chameleons are made in bronze and the toes ornamented with open lace appliqué satin inserted in a kind of pocket...[which comes in] various colours...ready to fit in, so with your blue dress your shoes are blue, and so on.' No known example with interchangeable coloured silks exists, but in all likelihood the reporter misunderstood the term 'chameleon' and gave his or her own interpretation based on the chameleon lizard that could change its colour.

Dyeing dark-brown kid leather with red dye, obtained from the cochineal insect, created the deep purplish lustre that became known as bronzed kid. This leather finish first appeared in 1846 and became very fashionable from the 1850s to the 1880s, remaining in use until the 1920s.

French bronzed-kid chameleon shoes with decorative cut-outs and blue silk underlay, with machine-stitched embroidery on the vamps, c. 1858–65.

Fashion illustration from *Godey's Lady's Book*, depicting morning toilette: the dress, bonnet and shoes (chameleons) suitable for morning wear at home, July 1859.

French bronzed-kid chameleons with decorative cut-outs and rose silk underlay, with machine-stitched embroidery on the vamps, c. 1858–65.

>> BERLIN WOOLWORK

Canvas embroidery or Berlin woolwork, known today as needlepoint, was a popular domestic pastime for women in the mid-nineteenth century, especially from the 1850s to the 1870s. The name reflects its German roots and the city where the brightly coloured loose-twisted wool was manufactured and where the charted patterns were first produced. Patterns were exported particularly to England and the United States where the fashion for Berlin woolwork was most prevalent, and they were commonly reprinted in ladies' fashion journals. The patterns were especially popular in the publications *Godey's Lady's Book* and *Peterson's Magazine*. During the American Civil War there were shortages in European imports as well as limited leather production for civilian and military footwear. Necessity created a pastime at home for making slippers and other kinds of footwear with textile uppers. Not only Berlin woolwork was used but also other kinds of needlework, such as braid appliquéd wool and embroidered velvet. Berlin woolwork slippers were, however, a favourite.

The needlework was carried out at home and the completed uppers were then taken to a shoemaker to be made up. Berlin slippers were not only worn by women but were also frequent gifts to men – surviving examples are more often than not barely worn masculine slippers, suggesting that they were perhaps not always appreciated. A poem by M. T. Morrall expressing the distaste for Berlin woolwork appeared in 1852, entitled *The Husband's Complaint*:

'I hate the name of German wool, in all its colours bright;
Of chairs and stools in fancy work, I hate the very sight;
The shawls and slippers that I've seen, the ottomans and bags
Sooner than wear a stitch on me, I'd walk the streets in rags.'

American floral-embroidered Berlin woolwork slipper uppers, c. 1855.

Opposite: American Berlin woolwork graphed patterns for slippers from *Godey's Lady's Book* and *Peterson's Magazine*, 1857–72.

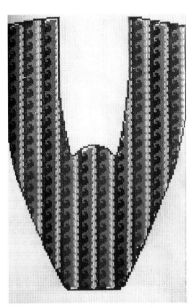

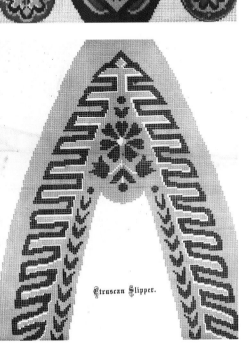

Etruscan Slipper.

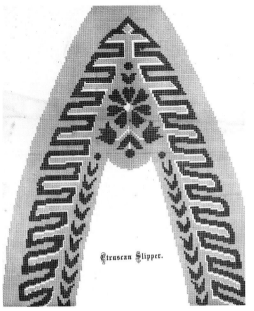

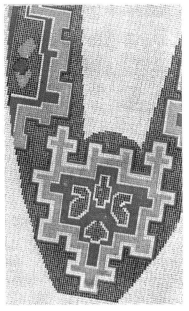

>> ROCOCO REVIVAL

During the 1850s the throat was cut higher and counters were used in the back parts of uppers. These developments displaced any need for laces or elastic loops to help keep on shoes and the sandal-slipper disappeared. Decorative treatments were applied to the throat, including such fancy cutting as zigzag 'Vandyking' and rounded-cut 'Albert' tongues. Small bows trimmed with lace and small decorative buckles also began to appear. *Godey's Lady's Book* reported in March 1860: 'The slippers made by all French houses are decorated with rosettes, ribbon, and lace, sometimes mixed with silk....Other slippers, of black patent leather, have, not at the edge, but in the middle on the top of the foot, a large gold, steel or silver buckle placed on a black ribbon.'

By the 1860s these ornaments and trims became features of the shoe and were inspired by seventeenth- and eighteenth-century modes. The American publication *Peterson's Magazine* stated in November 1864: 'Steel and gilt buckles on bows of velvet or ribbon

are indispensable.' In 1863 large multiple-loop 'Fenelon' bows appeared, so-called after the seventeenth-century French writer of the same name. In the United States shoes decorated in this way were sometimes referred to as 'Marie Antoinette slippers'. Buckles, although rarely functional, had grown in size by the late 1860s and the shoes that sported them became known as 'Molières' in France, 'Cromwells' in England and 'Colonials' in the United States.

Heels were shown at the Great Exhibition in 1851 but did not begin to reappear on most shoes until the very end of the 1850s. Low at first, they were beginning to reach heights not seen since the 1780s by the end of the 1860s. Along with rococo heels, buckles and bows, mules also came back in vogue. Some publications referred to them as 'Du Barry' slippers, paying homage to the Ancien Régime of French aristocrats who had favoured the style over a century before. Mules found less use in England and North America than in Continental Europe, as had been the case when Madame Du Barry herself was alive.

American white kid shoes with white silk Fenelon bows and brass buckles, c. 1863–70.

Canadian white kid shoes with white kid Fenelon bows, c. 1863–70.

American black kid walking shoes with
grosgrain ribbon ties, c. 1865–75.

American illustration of dress and shoe, *Godey's Lady's Book*, November 1869.

French or Italian gilt-thread embroidered plum velvet mules with silk lining, c. 1865–75.

French shoes made from Turkish kilim
uppers, c. 1860–65.

>> EXOTICISM

Western empires gained faster access to the world marketplace with the development of rail transportation and steamships by the mid nineteenth century. Portugal and England had well-established trading ports and access to India, China and South America. The Netherlands had the only regular access to Japan until the Americans opened up the country to trade in the 1850s. France, Italy and Germany had access to African and Middle Eastern goods. Western nations traded for exotic textiles from foreign lands, satisfying the taste for novelty that the West had first acquired with the return of soldiers from the Crusades, nearly a thousand years earlier.

A kilim is a reversible tapestry weave of hard-twisted wool or silk. Produced primarily in Turkey, kilim shoes (above) were popular from the mid 1850s until the 1880s and originally came into fashion during the Crimean War (1854–56). The Russian and Ottoman empires were in conflict over control of the Crimean Peninsula and Western Europe supported the Ottoman Turks, which revived an interest in the Turkish and Persian arts throughout the West.

Turkish gilt-thread embroideries, Persian kilim weavings, British Indian beetle-wing appliqué, Chinese 'forbidden' stitched silks and numerous other delicately worked textiles from foreign lands appealed to romantic-minded Victorians. They had fashionable shoes made up from the imported goods, which were sometimes already formed into shoe uppers specifically designed for the Western market.

Fashionable but impractical straw shoes (opposite) were novelty items in the 1860s and 1870s and were popular tourist souvenirs from the island of Madeira. Fashion journals described the style as ideal toilet slippers or bathing slippers at the seaside.

Exoticism was not restricted to goods from halfway around the world however. Regional European workmanship and styles, such as the Scottish ghillie and Hungarian boot, found appeal in other Western countries.

Madeiran straw shoes lined with rose-coloured
silk, made for export, c. 1860.

American black leather riding boots with Hessian-style scalloped top line, trimmed with a black silk cord bow. Pink kid lining in the tops and white kid lining in the feet but unlined in the shaft, c. 1866–74.

>> EQUESTRIAN FOOTWEAR

Boots were essential riding gear as they were necessary for protection and for commanding the horse. Various styles of boot were worn by women in the seventeenth and early eighteenth century until the Hessian pull-on type came into fashion in the late eighteenth century. It remained the dominant style of boot for avid riders, and it is from this model that the modern riding boot eventually evolved in the late nineteenth and early twentieth centuries. However, from the sixteenth century until well into the nineteenth century it was not uncommon for women to wear shoes for riding. Even in the late nineteenth century, catalogues advertised styles similar to ankle-high street boots as suitable for riding.

Kid lining, as in this example, offered more sensitivity to the rider when giving signals to the horse through foot and leg commands. The field-boot closure, laced like a corset in the middle of the shaft, provided the snuggest fit at the ankle and was the easiest to put on and take off. A lady rode sidesaddle at this time, but this pair has spur rests at the back of each boot, which would have allowed her also to ride astride. It was normal for young ladies to train on both the nearside and offside of the horse in a reversible sidesaddle so as not to overdevelop one side of the body. These boots have straight soles, with no left or right foot definition, so the spur rests may also be in place on both boots

LADY'S RIDING BOOTS.

to permit the rider to swap boots, evening the wear over a longer period of time (as was the custom with leather footwear with straight soles).

American illustration of riding boots in the Hessian style.

American illustration of riding dress, *Godey's Lady's Book*, June 1854.

English cartoon from the publication *Punch*, 2 October 1869.

>> THE RETURN OF HIGH HEELS

By the early 1870s the high Louis heel had returned to fashion due, in part, to the eighteenth-century rococo revival that had been gaining favour in the decorative arts since the end of the 1850s. The addition of high heels was made technically possible by the introduction of shanks, metal supports inserted between the sole and insole that supported the arch of the foot. The curvaceous high heel was set as far forward as possible on the sole to visually foreshorten the foot. High heels also helped fashionable women perfect the Grecian bend, the early 1870s fashion for a slightly forward tilt to the upper body. The posture was more easily

"THE GRECIAN BEND."

French black silk button boots with black kid toecaps, white-stitched embroidery and black silk Louis heels, made by Perchellet, 1875. This is one of eight nearly identical pairs of boots purchased in Paris in September 1875 and shipped to Santiago, Chile. This style of boot with its scalloped top line and tassel was sometimes referred to as a 'Hungarian' or 'Polish' boot and was fashionable from the mid 1860s to the mid 1870s.

achieved through the adoption of the correct corset, bustle and high heels.

Pious fashion journals scolded women who adopted high heels. The American publication *Ladies' Treasury* warned as early as 1868: 'High heeled boots are universal, notwithstanding that medical men have been writing very severely against them. They say the fashion causes corns, cramps, lameness at an early age, lessens the size of the calf and thus makes the leg lose its symmetry.' A similar American damning of the high heel appeared in *The Complete Home* in 1879:

'They are amongst the most dangerous things in the world....The human figure was meant to stand erect, well planted upon its feet: whatever throws the body out of this ordained equipose disturbs nearly all of its functions....To these high and ill-placed heels, which destroy the balance of the body, may be attributed much of the prevalent spinal disease, a very large proportion of the diseases and weaknesses of the eye, and not a few cases of insanity.' These statements present editorial opinion and hearsay as fact, which is typical of sensationalist late-nineteenth-century publications. Although based on truth, articles were exaggerated for dramatic impact. In fact, the heel had a less detrimental impact on the foot than an ill-fitting shoe.

French blue kid shoes, labelled 'Chausseurs pour Dames – J. A. Petit – Paris – rue St. Honoré 334 – Maison à Trouville', c. 1868–75.

>> SEA BATHING

Many physicians considered sea bathing merely therapeutic until the mid nineteenth century. By the 1860s, however, bathing had become a popular pastime. Women mostly donned sandal-boots that consisted of cotton shoes with cork or espadrille soles and wool-twill laces, but sandal and mule styles were also worn. They were not intended to be waterproof, rather they offered protection to the soles of the feet from hot sand and sharp stones. They also ensured modesty, especially when worn with stockings as was common until the 1910s. The sexes were segregated on bathing beaches until around the turn of the twentieth century when a few beaches began to allow mixed-sex bathing. Women, especially in England, changed into their bathing dress in wooden carts, called bathing machines, which they entered from the beach on one side in their street wear and exited on the other side in their bathing costume, ready to go in the water.

French fawn cotton bathing sandal-boots with purple wool trim and embroidery and braided straw espadrille soles, unlabelled, c. 1870–74. They were probably purchased for wear at one of the seaside resorts, such as Dieppe or Trouville. The embroidered image on the vamps shows a woman wearing Breton peasant dress.

American illustration of bathing dress with various footwear styles including a sandal, *Peterson's Magazine*, August 1870.

>> READY-MADES AND COUTURE

Bright gaudy colours were abandoned by the mid 1870s when earthy rich colours – garnet, maroon, russet, emerald and brown – were considered more tasteful. By the late 1870s the skirts of women's dresses fitted closely to the front of the body and were often ankle length for outdoor walking, bringing shoes back into full view. While taste and decorum specified plain styles of dark-coloured footwear for the street, decoration and colour flourished in the salon or ballroom.

The French established the ready-made shoe market when they exported the sandal-slipper early in the century, but by the late 1860s it was American ready-mades that were beginning to flood the market. *The Leather Trades Circular and Review* stated in England in 1868: 'Bespoke is generally giving way to the buying of articles ready made.' It was particularly the American exports of machine-beaded shoes that displaced the tradition of European bespoke footwear. Beaded toes were very fashionable in the 1880s, especially after 1885, and *The Young Ladies' Journal* reported from Canada in January 1888 that 'shoes are embroidered with beads over the toe...others are ornamented with a butterfly of jet beads'.

Austrian bronze-beaded kid shoes by
Robert Schlesinger, c. 1885–92.

A few shoemakers survived the onslaught of inexpensive American ready-mades by specializing in workmanship that machinery could not reproduce. These shoemakers transformed themselves into designers, turning their hands to making shoes of the finest materials in the most artfully executed designs with exquisite finishing. The leader in this new field of shoe couture was Paris shoemaker François Pinet, who attracted an elite clientele, including wealthy American women from across the Atlantic.

By 1890 makers' labels regularly appeared on footwear. Paper labels had been on some shoes since the late eighteenth century, but were now replaced by shoemaker, manufacturer or retailer labels stamped in ink on linings, incised into soles or woven into sewn labels. Some manufacturers introduced logos and brand names for product lines. The power of the label was being recognized by consumers and it often listed accolades including exhibition prizes and royal warrants. Beginning in the 1880s, some American manufacturers even stamped the retail price on the sole, reassuring the consumer that merchants were not marking up goods beyond a reasonable profit margin.

American steel-beaded black kid shoes, unlabelled, c. 1882–88.

American printed velvet shoes, unlabelled, c. 1882–90. Typical of the cheapest American styles made for export, these shoes were attached to each other by the cotton twill tape top line binding at

the back seam of each shoe. This tape was also used to hang the shoes on display in a shop from a hook or rod and was cut off by the owner after purchase.

French embroidered boots by François Pinet,
c. 1882–88.

>> BETTER FITS

In 1872 the English publication *Dress and Care of the Feet* reported: 'Formerly, the great majority of women's shoes were made upon lasts that were straight, and the same is true even yet.' Although shoes for right and left feet had been available since the beginning of the century, their general adoption over straight soles was a slow process, especially in women's shoes. It was not until the 1880s that left and right sole shapes were in place in most footwear.

Shoes and boots had become more constructed by the 1880s, with interlinings, shanks and stiffeners in the toes and the back parts of uppers. Sturdier leathers were also being used for utilitarian boots. These developments supported the shape of the shoe or boot but constricted the foot. American manufacturers introduced standardized widths in shoe sizes in the mid 1880s. With the universal use of left and right sole shapes, shoes and boots now fitted much better than they had throughout most of the century. Vamps were generally shorter in the early 1880s, gradually lengthening toward the end of the decade as toes became more pointed.

American illustration of fashion footwear, *Godey's Lady's Book*, December 1889.

American illustration of fashion footwear, *Godey's Lady's Book*, July 1889.

There was no distinguishable preference for boots or shoes in this period as both were made for every occasion. There was, however, a tendency for increasingly masculine styles, including laced oxfords for daytime and some evening styles. Aestheticism, an earthy Japanese-influenced palette and Queen Victoria's permanent mourning status influenced the colour and ornamentation of footwear. The majority of shoes were black, brown or white, with some pastel and rich colours for eveningwear.

American red silk and gold kid evening oxfords, c. 1880–88.

American bronze kid beaded oxfords, labelled 'Cammeyer', c. 1878–82.

English black silk shoes with embroidered toes depicting the motto 'God Save the Queen', honouring the diamond jubilee of Queen Victoria. Labelled 'Stagg, Mantle & Co., Leicester Square', 1887.

American copper satin evening pump,
c. 1889–95.

>> PLAIN AND ELEGANT

Button and front-laced boots were available concurrently in the 1880s and 1890s, but laced closures were preferred for more utilitarian wear because they could be adjusted throughout the day and were easier to put on and take off. Button boots were considered neater and more tailored, as the American fashion magazine *Demorest's* wrote in 1879: 'There is little likelihood of any style superseding the buttoned boot, which is…the most elegant for…promenading, visiting and house wear.' *Demorest's* confirmed this view in 1883: 'buttoned boots are the undisputed rulers of the shoe kingdom'. *Godey's Lady's Book* noted in February 1885: 'No fancy work, embroidery, stitching, beading, or even irrelevant fancy buttons are visible. The boot is ornamental only in its quality, which is of kid, the finest and softest. The toe portion is roomy yet shapely. The heel, with not a suggestion of the "French bend" about it, is yet graceful, and the sole of the foot is broad enough to allow promenading without having to stop every few moments to give a rest to the pinched and rebellious foot.'

English bronze-kid button boots, c. 1885–92.

Most walking boots made between the 1860s and the 1910s were black or dark brown as it was understood that darker colours made feet look smaller. The demise of the square toe in the 1880s was controversial, as many felt the square shape was healthier for accommodating the toes. With a wider sole, however, the toe shape became less important as long as the proper fit in length and width was obtained.

With the introduction of pointed and spade toes (see p. 112) in the 1890s the debate about foot health was stirred up again. For the first time in shoe history alternative toe styles were available for consumers who preferred not to follow the mainstream fashion for elongated or pointed toes. Manufacturers offered square toes and round toes as alternatives and, although they never sold as well as the pointed styles, they pleased many customers.

Canadian leather boots with patent-leather toecaps, labelled 'J. McPherson & Co., Hamilton', c. 1890–95.

Ladies' Waukenphast Button

SIZES, 2 to 7. WIDTHS, A, B, C, D, E.

No.
4612. Ladies' French Kid, Patent Leather Tip, Waukenphast, Button.................$5 00
4613. Ladies' French Kid, Patent Leather Pointed Tip, Waukenphast, Button............... 5 00
4614. Ladies' French Calf Foxed, Kangaroo Kid Top, Waukenphast, Button, Hand Sewed.. 5 00
4615. Ladies' Straight Goat Foxed, Kangaroo Kid Top, Waukenphast Button, Hand Sewed.. 5 00
4616. Ladies' Calf Foxed, Kangaroo Kid Top, Waukenphast, Button, Hand Sewed...... 4 00
4617. Ladies' Calf Foxed, Kangaroo Kid Top, Waukenphast, Button, Hand Sewed Welt. 3 00
4618. Ladies' Straight Goat Foxed, Kangaroo Kid Top, Waukenphast, Button, Hand Sewed Welt............................ 3 00

LADIES' CALF BUTTON BOOT.

SIZES, 2 to 7. WIDTHS, A, B, C, D, E.

4619. Ladies' French Calf, Kangaroo Kid Top, Button. Hand Sewed, Caledonian Tip........$5 00

LADIES' CALF BUTTON AND LACE BOOT.

SIZES, 2 to 7. WIDTHS, AA, A, B, C, D, E.

4620. Ladies' French Calf, Button, Hand Sewed, Kangaroo Kid Top, Pointed Toe.........$5 00
4621. Ladies' Calf Lace, Kangaroo Kid Top, Hand Sewed Welt................................ 4 00
4622. Ladies' Calf Lace, Kangaroo Kid Top, Hand Sewed Welt................................ 3 00

LADIES' BLACK CLOTH TOP, BUTTON, PATENT LEATHER POINTED TIP.

SIZES, 2 to 7. WIDTHS, A, B, C, D, E.

No.
4623. Ladies' Black Cloth Top, French Kid Foxed, Patent Leather Pointed Tip, Button, Hand Sewed.........................$5 00
4624. Ladies' Black Cloth Top, Soolma Kid Foxed, Patent Leather Pointed Tip, Button, Hand Sewed Welt....................... 4 00
4625. Ladies' Black Cloth Top, Soolma Kid, Straight Foxed, Patent Leather Pointed Tip, Button, Hand Sewed Welt............... 4 00
4626. Ladies' Black Cloth Top. Soolma Kid Foxed, Patent Leather Pointed Tip, Button, Hand Sewed Welt....................... 3 00
4627. Ladies' Black Cloth Top, Soolma Kid Foxed, Patent Leather Pointed Tip, Button, A.J.C. 2 50

LADIES' BLACK CLOTH TOP, BUTTON, PATENT LEATHER TIP.

SIZES, 2 to 7. WIDTHS, A, B, C, D, E.

4628. Ladies' Black Cloth Top, French Kid Foxed, Patent Leather Pointed Tip, Button, Hand Sewed..........................$6 00
4629. Ladies' Black Cloth Top, French Kid Foxed, Imitation Tip, Piccadilly Toe, Button, Hand Sewed......................... 5 00
4630. Ladies' Black Cloth Top, French Kid Foxed, Patent Leather Straight Tip, Button, Hand Sewed......................... 5 00
4631. Ladies' Black Cloth Top, French Kid Foxed, Patent Leather Tip, Medium Toe, Button, Hand Sewed,......................... 5 00
4632. Ladies' Black Cloth Top, Soolma Kid Foxed, Patent Leather Straight Tip, Button, Hand Sewed Welt....................... 4 00
4633. Ladies' Black Cloth Top, Soolma Kid Foxed, Patent Leather Pointed Tip, Button, Scalloped Back, Hand Sewed Welt........... 4 00
4634. Ladies' Black Cloth Top, Soolma Kid Foxed, Patent Leather Pointed Tip, Piccadilly Toe, Button, Hand Sewed Welt.............. 4 00
4635. Ladies' Black Cloth Top, Soolma Kid Foxed, Patent Leather Pointed Tip, Button, Hand Sewed Welt....................... 3 00
4636. Ladies' Black Cloth Top, Soolma Kid Foxed, Patent Leather Straight Tip, Medium Toe, Button, Hand Sewed Welt............... 3 00

American illustration of boots from A. J. Cammeyer catalogue, New York, spring 1894.

Canadian glacé kid spade-toed boots, labelled 'John McPherson Company Ltd., Hamilton', c. 1895–1902. This company is listed in the 1890 Canadian shoe and leather directory as manufacturers of a thousand pairs of boots per day.

English rubber-soled sports shoe by Joseph Box, 1886.

Illustration of tennis players, *Peterson's Magazine*, May 1889.

>> THE DAWN OF THE TRAINER

Toward the end of the nineteenth century women began to participate in activities that were far more aerobic than the social lawn games considered appropriate for young ladies earlier in the century. In the 1860s skating and gymnastics were taken up, but it was lawn tennis that opened the door to more strenuous exercise in the late 1870s. Rubber-soled 'croquet sandals' had been made for genteel lawn activities in the 1860s, but for lawn tennis a well-fitting shoe with a rubber sole was required. *Demorest's* magazine recommended in 1883:

> 'French heeled shoes are incompatible with good tennis playing. The real lawn-tennis shoe for ladies is of black French kid, laced on the instep with any coloured ribbon to suit the

costume, and with India rubber soles....it most effectually preserves the feet from dampness, cannot possibly injure the lawn-tennis court...and the danger of slipping when the grass is damp is entirely avoided.'

In 1876 the Liverpool Rubber Company began producing a shoe with a rubber sole that was marketed in 1885 as a plimsoll. The shoe had a red rubber sole that resembled the Plimsoll line on ship hulls. By the 1890s various rubber-soled shoes were being produced, mostly in the United States and Canada where they were known generically as tennis shoes, although the term 'sneakers' appeared as early as 1894.

TENNIS—COSTUMES.

>> THE HUNT FOR LEATHER

The leather on this pair of pumps, or court shoes, has been stamped or boarded to resemble alligator skin, a technique used to compensate for the dwindling supplies and increased cost of real alligator skins. Alligator was first used in the southern United States in the early nineteenth century for footwear and saddles, but it was not very durable and fell from favour in the late 1820s. No examples of shoes made of alligator from this period are known, but the American painter John J. Audubon commented on the alligator hunt for this purpose in 1820. There was a brief revival of alligator footwear during the American Civil War when supplies of footwear and leather had been cut off to the south due to blockades. In *A Confederate Girl's Diary*, Sarah Morgan Dawson of Baton Rouge, Louisiana, wrote on 21 May 1862: 'Behold my tender feet encased in crocodile (sic) skin…from my pretty English glove-kid, to sabots made of some animal closely connected with the hippopotamus!'

Following the Civil War, the French and Russians took to using alligator for everything from upholstery and luggage to saddles and bookbindings. They employed an improved tanning method developed by the French that made the skins waterproof and more hardy. By the 1890s footwear manufacturers were using alligator once again, although the skin was preferred for uses other than footwear. Hunting depleted alligator numbers in the wild and prices rose, necessitating the stamping of leather to imitate alligator for all purposes. Other reptile leathers, including lizard and snake, were experimented with but did not come into general use in footwear until the 1920s.

American black leather pumps stamped to imitate alligator, with red heels and high-flared tongue with buckle. Labelled 'Colonial – R.H. Macy & Co., New York', c. 1885–92.

>> POINTED AND SPADE TOES

The predominant feature of 1890s high-fashion footwear was the pointed toe, which visually lengthened and narrowed the foot. The style came from France in the late 1880s, when concerns over the narrowness of the toes lead to the elongation of the vamp, creating what became known as the spade toe. The spade-style toe alleviated any pressure on the toes and was fashionable from the mid 1890s

English barrette boot with pointed toe by Joseph Box, c. 1890–96.

into the early years of the twentieth century. The curved neck of the Louis heel was exaggerated in the 1890s to place the base of the heel as far forward under the foot as possible, visually shortening the overall length of the shoe. The high instep was also considered attractive, and the higher the heel the more pronounced the top of the instep became.

Russian Empire (Congress or Poland) laced boot with scalloped top line and spade toe, labelled in Cyrillic 'Vindman', from Lodz, present-day Poland, c. 1898–1904.

French black kid pump with silver sequin
decoration, c. 1896–1904.

American red kid slipper, labelled 'Laird
Schober & Co., Philadelphia', c.1898–1904.

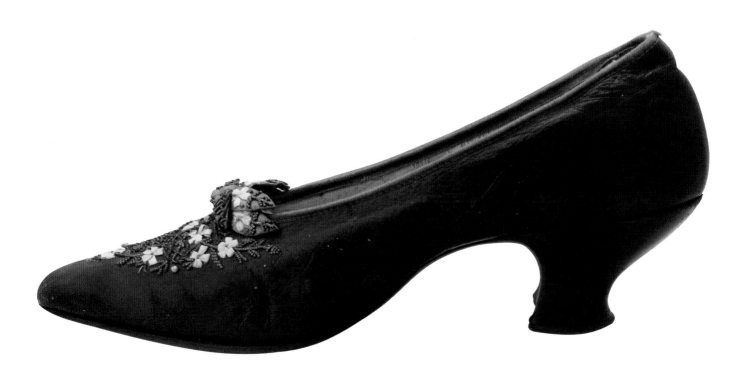

American bronze kid shoes with embroidered
vamps and spade toes, c. 1896–1904.

>> UPTURNED TOES

After disappearing from use in the mid eighteenth century, suede returned to fashion in the 1890s. The velvety surfaced leather would go on to find a permanent place in the production of footwear in the twentieth century, at times – in the early 1950s and early 1990s – being more popular than leather.

Upturned toes in the Turkish or Oriental style (depending on which period manufacturers were trying to equate the origins of the upturned toes with) were revived several times, although no incarnation met with any great success. Upturned toes were well reported in 1786 and 1787, and reappeared sporadically from the early 1870s to the mid 1890s, usually on slippers or mules. They would reappear again in the late 1930s and then on and off until the early 1960s, usually on slippers.

Green suede oxfords with upturned 'Turkish' toes, labelled 'A.J. Cammeyer, 6th Ave Cor 20th St. New York', c. 1894–97.

American illustration for carriage boot from *The Shoe Retailer*, 21 September 1904.

American velveteen and fur-trimmed carriage boot intended for wear over a pair of shoes, c. 1900–05.

WE ORIGINATE THE STYLES

This is one of our late styles in carriage boots.

These jobbers carry
GUPTILL SLIPPERS
in stock:

Clark-Hutchinson Co.,
·Boston and New York.

Vinsonhaler Shoe Co.,
St. Louis,
Southwestern Agents.

Williams-Marvin Co.,
San Francisco,
Pacific Coast Agents.

Designed and Made by
HERVEY E. GUPTILL,
Haverhill, Mass.

>> CARRIAGE BOOTS AND ARCTICS

Carriage boots of velvet, lined with fur or quilted silk for warmth, had been available since the 1860s and enabled ladies to travel in comfort during the winter. They found most favour in North America where winter weather was more extreme, but they were not intended for walking on slushy pavements. By the 1890s carriage boots were made with rubber soles and galoshes, and were available either as boots, worn in place of shoes, or with a hollow heel, to be worn over a pair of shoes. By the turn of the century in the United States, rubber-soled versions intended as overshoes or boots were known as 'Arctics'. Carriage boots without rubber soles fell from use by 1910, and the popularity of Arctics increased in the early 1920s as fashion boots lost favour. In the 1940s salt began to be used to melt icy pavements and Arctics and galoshes became essential as one puddle of the resulting slurry could ruin leather footwear.

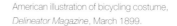

>> BICYCLING BOOTS

When bicycling became fashionable for women in the 1890s their costume was adapted – shortened skirts or bloomers – for riding astride. Usually tall boots were worn to protect the stockings from mud and damp. Lace hooks were used on the upper half of the front-laced closure to allow the laces to slide more easily, adjusting to the movement of the calf muscle. Many bicycling boots also had a metal ring at the top of the closure to secure the tags or aglets of the laces and so prevent the laces from becoming entangled in the bicycle chain. As an alternative to boots, gaiters were sometimes worn with shoes, and by the early twentieth century shoes alone were preferred, worn with strong cotton-knit stockings, often in tartan or striped patterns, like golf stockings.

American russet leather boots, c. 1896–1900. Russet-coloured leather was very much in vogue in the late 1890s and early twentieth century for sports and summer footwear.

>> THE BAR SHOE

Generally, leather was preferred for most footwear in the late 1890s and early 1900s, although silk was still worn for wedding and evening attire but on a much smaller scale than before. The bar or strap shoe was introduced in the 1880s and became increasingly popular until it was the predominant style of women's shoes in the 1920s. Shallow vamps that almost appeared not to allow for the thickness of the toes were typical of shoes from the mid 1890s until the first few years of the twentieth century, disappearing by 1904.

Knock-on heels, identifiable by their straight breast and curved neck, were cheaper to attach to shoes than Louis heels, recognizable by their curved breast with the sole running continuously down the neck to the top lift. Knock-on heels were usually shorter than Louis heels because they were attached to the shoe by a single screw and a few nails after the shoe was completed, making them less sturdy and likely to snap off while being worn.

In 1892 *The American Shoe and Leather Gazette* reported that white shoes were appearing for summer wear, most frequently at the seaside. White leather shoes made before 1910 had a tendency to yellow due to the tanning method used for doeskin. By the 1910s, white cotton, kid or cow leather, which did not yellow, was used instead, therefore making white shoes more appealing for summer wear.

49A. Common Sense, with best dongola kid, low heel and wide
toe, flexible
soles, sizes 2½
to 8, E width
only.

$1.50.

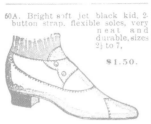

50A. Bright soft jet black kid, 2-
button strap, flexible soles, very
neat and
durable, sizes
2½ to 7,

$1.50.

51A. Dongola kid, with extension
soles, English
walking style,
sizes 2½ to 7,

$1.50.

52A. Tan goat kid, with turn flexible
soles, a neat
up-to-date
shoe, sizes
2½ to 7,

$1.50.

53A. Choice bright kid, with turn
soles, well-made, neat and stylish,
sizes 2½ to 7,

$1.25.

54A. Dongola kid, old ladies' comfort shoe, full fitting, turn flexible
soles, sizes 2½ to 8.

$1.25.

55A. Genuine goat kid, with turn
soles, kid toe-cap, kid-lined, beat
it if you can,
sizes 2½ to 7,

$1.00.

56A. Tan pebble, with rather heavy
soles, great
value, sizes
3 to 7, no half
sizes,

85c.

57A. The milk maid's friend, heavy
leather, hard to wear out soles,
sizes 3 to 8,
no half sizes.

75c.

Ladies' Slippers.

58A. A New York style, very swell,
fancy black-beaded vamp and
strap, hand-turn soles, the best
American
make, B, C
and D widths,
sizes 2½ to 7,

$3.00

59A. Genuine patent calfskin, with
bright kid back, hand-turn soles,
sizes 2½ to
7, C and D
widths,

$2.50

60A. Black beaded strap sandal,
very pretty, with turn soles and
medium high heels, sizes 2½ to 7,
C, D and E
widths,

$2.50.

61A. Fine selected American kid,
plain, with thin turn soles, very
neat and perfect fitting, with wood
heels or leather, state which you
prefer, C, D and E widths, sizes 2½
to 7,

$2.00.

62A. The popular full fitting kid
turn flexible soles, one strap sandal,
sizes 2½ to 7, D and E widths,

$1.75

63A. Our leader, choice glazed kid,
one strap, with flexible soles,
neat, durable and comfortable,
sizes 2½ to 7, D and E widths,

$1.50.

64A. Bright glazed kid, turn flexible
soles, with low heel and plain wide
toe, common-sense shape, E width,
sizes 2½ to 7,

$1.25.

65A. Genuine kid, with flexible
soles, kid lined, medium toe and
leather heel, great value, sizes 2½
to 7,

$1.25.

66A. Solid comfort dongola buskin
with elastic over the instep, turn
flexible soles, sizes 2½ to 8,

$1.20.

67A. "Snowball," American white
kid sandal, with turn soles, kid
lined, sizes
2½ to 7,

$1.20.

68A. One strap, goat kid, with flexible soles, easy fitting, kid lined,
beat it if you
can, sizes 2½ to 7,

$1.00.

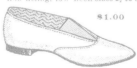

69A. Prunella buskin, flexible soles,
fine fitting, low heel, sizes 2½ to 8.

$1.00

70A. Snowflake white kid sandal,
high heel, cotton lined, sizes 2½
to 7,

95c

71A. The housemaid's friend, one-
strap sandal, with soles rather
thick, can be worn on the street,
sizes 2½ to 7,
splendid
value,

85c

72A. Best imported fancy repp carpet slippers, with leather sole, a
great wearer, sizes 3 to 7, no half
sizes......................85c

73A. Fancy carpet, McKay sewn
soles and low heels, sizes 3 to 7, no
half sizes,
50c.

74A. Prunella buskin, elastic over the
instep, sizes 3 to 7, no half sizes,

40c.

75A. Heavy leather kitchen or outdoor slippers, sizes 3 to 7, no half
sizes,

35c.

Misses' and Children's
Boots.

76A. Genuine kangaroo buttoned,
spring heel, little heavier than kid,
and will wear better. (For full description of this excellent leather,
see page 83.)

Sizes 11 to 2 ..$1.50
Sizes 8 to 10½.. 1.20
Sizes 5 to 7½ .. 1.00

77A. Kangaroo laced, with spring
heel,
Sizes 11 to 2........$1.50
Sizes 8 to 10½....... 1.20
Sizes 5 to 7½........ 1.00

78A. Best quality dice calfskin, laced,
medium heavy, neat
and durable, spring
heel,
Sizes 11 to 2 ..$1.50
Sizes 8 to 10½.. 1.25
Sizes 5 to 7½.... 1.00

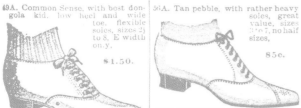

At the turn of the twentieth century the United States held the controlling interest in the production of ready-made shoes. Manufacturers of ready-mades in other countries, primarily England and Germany, were expanding their factories but to compete they needed the same machinery already available to Americans. Furthermore, American patents held most shoe production technology, so manufacturers had to purchase or rent the machines and technology from the patent holders. Once the machines had been acquired, a commission had to be paid for every pair of shoes produced.

Patented in 1884 and perfected by 1900, the American innovation of chrome tanning produced leather more cheaply and faster than traditional tanning methods. It would take several years for the European shoe industry to catch up with America and in 1914, just when it seemed possible, World War I began. Shoe production in Europe shifted from civilian fashion footwear to military boots. Chrome tanning became the most common process for making leather for military footwear and eventually displaced traditional tanning methods for the production of most leather.

During the 1890s ladies' monthly fashion journals had transformed into fashion magazines, a subtle but profound difference. Fashion journals relied almost entirely on reader subscriptions and reported on fashions from a heavily editorialized perspective. The fashion magazine, on the other hand, reported fashions with little editorial comment, but relied heavily on advertisers of middle-class products that were well established and more restrained than the cutting-edge Parisian style pictured in the articles. Advertising was still in its infancy at the turn of the century but American shoe manufacturers quickly learned its benefits. Shoe companies used many of the now well-known tricks of the trade to develop brand recognition, and Florsheim was one of the first businesses to take out advertisements in national magazines. Its investment paid off when it provided free eye-catching store-window displays to stores that carried its product. This meant that wherever the store was located there was already a customer base familiar with Florsheim thanks to its advertisements.

The use of a trademark to sell shoes was pioneered by The Brown Shoe Company when they introduced cartoonist Richard F. Outcault's Buster Brown comic-strip character in 1904 at the St. Louis World's Fair. The company had failed to purchase the exclusive rights, however, and Buster Brown became the trademark for scores of products, including cigars and whiskey, but he remained most associated with selling children's shoes. Mary Jane, Buster's girlfriend, was introduced to market girls' instep strap shoes in about 1909. The campaign was so successful that all shoes of this type became known generically as 'Mary-Janes'. In 1916 the United States Rubber Company recognized that by advertising their Keds brand tennis shoes as 'sneakers', they appealed to the target market of teenage boys who used the term. And, Converse became aware of the power of celebrity endorsement when they hired basketball player Chuck Taylor in 1921 to travel the United States promoting the game and the Converse brand basketball shoe. It was thoroughly understood by the 1920s that label recognition and product loyalty meant money in the bank for

In the 1910s most footwear, still unseen under the hem, was black, brown or white. If ornamented, the shoe or boot was usually the same colour as the decoration so as not to warrant undue attention. There were dressy shoes for smart occasions, but the vast majority of ready-mades were durable and serviceable leather shoes and boots. Many women wore suits or skirts with tailored blouses for daytime functions, appropriately pairing their wardrobe with brogues, bluchers, oxfords or balmorals. *McCall's Magazine* lamented in 1904: 'What an excellent thing it would be if there should be a revival of 1830 manners…for in those days rudeness such as one so often finds now, was quite unknown. It seemed to come in together with heavy boots, but in the day when women wore only thin slippers, their steps and their voices were lighter, less hurried, less boisterous. And yet there were merry times among young people we are told, and far more marriages.' It was clearly the opinion of this fashion editor that heavy boots were the cause of the ruination of society.

By 1911 petticoats were reduced in fullness and skirts designed for walking inched toward the ankle. With the advent of World War I in 1914, hem lines began to rise. As skirts grew shorter walking boots became taller to keep up with the shrinking hem line. By the armistice in 1918 the hem was so short that boots could grow no taller, creating an unsightly gap between the top of the boot and the hem of the skirt, and shoes became preferred footwear for all occasions.

The 'between the wars' era of the 1920s and 1930s was the heyday of the burgeoning fashion-shoe industry. Shoes were as important a part of an outfit as the hat and as noticeably out of place if not au courant. The Depression made money short for many, but American shoe sales dropped only marginally. Overall, the American shoe industry saw growth during the 1930s, despite the economy, with many manufacturers actually expanding. New England, the original home of the American footwear industry, was now the centre for well-established shoe brands, rubber footwear and the production of shoe machinery and grindery (the trade name for tacks, staples, rivets and other materials used in shoemaking). In the heart of the American Midwest, St. Louis, the largest shoe-making centre in terms of pairs produced, manufactured footwear mostly for domestic sale. The shoes stocked the shelves of chain stores, an emerging form of retail. National shoe chain stores came to prominence in this between-war era. Kinney (founded 1894), Edison Brothers and Thom McAnn (both founded 1922) and Jarman (founded 1930) were the largest chain stores and were instrumental in changing how most Americans shopped for much of the twentieth century. Kinney had set the trend early by creating customer loyalty through low prices. It was attention to price that gave birth to the shoe-chain phenomenon and the larger a chain became the greater volume of stock and cost leverage it had. Half of all American retail footwear sales in the 1930s were from chain stores, despite a backlash from small merchants and wholesalers who campaigned against chain-store pricing.

New York was the centre of American high-fashion footwear production and was the only shoe-manufacturing region in America to feel the profit pinch during the Depression. Ladies' dress shoes in the 1930s were made using cement construction, a new method that resulted in a level playing field for European shoe manufacturers who could now compete with American ready-made dress shoes. Companies like Bally in Switzerland and Ferragamo in Italy began exporting their shoes to the US in the late 1930s, cutting into New York fashion footwear sales.

However, just when competition was becoming stiff everything changed when, once again, war broke out and European manufacturers switched to military production during World War II (1939–45). When the United States entered the war in late 1941, many American shoe factory workers went into service or found better paid jobs in wartime industries. Salaries rose to meet the competition for employees, and continued to rise after the war to attract workers from the steel and building industries. The California construction method for making women's and children's platform sandal casuals was developed during the war, more from a shortage of skilled labour than materials. Leather was in especially short supply during the war and civilian footwear was rationed. Inventive replacements were needed, especially in Continental Europe where there was little leather to spare outside military use.

When wartime restrictions were lifted at the end of the war, American manufacturers quickly resumed full-time production. The American footwear industry thought in terms of thousands of pairs per style and could not profitably supply small runs of high-fashion footwear, especially with high labour costs. After the war, Germany and England, previously Europe's largest producers of footwear, were not in the economic position to prioritize the redevelopment of their shoe industries. Italy, however, began to experience its 'economic miracle' – the term Italians used to describe their postwar recovery – which was partly spurred on by a carefully planned government-sponsored exhibition showcasing modern Italian design that toured the United States in 1951. This brought attention to Italy as a country with a tradition of design excellence and quality craftsmanship. The typically smaller Italian industries allowed for more limited and more affordable runs of high-fashion footwear.

Unable to find a manufacturer who would take a chance on a style that was not a guaranteed top seller or was expensive to produce, some American designers found Italy the perfect location for manufacturing their fashion shoes. American shoe importers Marx and Newman created the brand 'Amalfi' in 1946, which comprised shoes made by various small Italian shoe manufacturers. Many American importers and retailers turned to Italy for quality ready-made footwear, making Italy one of the major export countries in postwar Europe.

In the late 1940s there were four hundred influential high-fashion footwear companies in New York, such as Palter De Liso, Delman and I. Miller, and important designers like David Evins, Seymour Troy and Beth Levine. By 1960 the Italian market had cut into the American fashion footwear business so significantly that there were only 100 companies still operating in New York.

Postwar America was becoming suburban and the suburban woman was not concerned with cutting-edge fashion; she shopped at chain stores. With the dawn of modern consumerism, chain retailers located in suburban roadside plazas and in the newly introduced indoor shopping mall. They could also afford to promote their low-priced nationally available products through print, radio and the new medium of television. The 'Payless' shoe chain started with one store in Topeka, Kansas in 1956. By using a grocery-store self-service concept and by selling inexpensive imports, the company quickly grew to nearly 500 stores by 1972. Chain retailers could keep products at a low price by importing their stock from countries where manufacturing costs were less. Southeast Asia, especially the Philippines, became a major producer of rubber and plastic footwear in the early 1960s, and in the 1970s Spain and Brazil became major leather-shoe exporting countries, providing Italy with greater competition in the fashion footwear marketplace.

The peak production year for footwear in the United States was 1968, with over 640-million pairs made. Twenty years later a quarter of that number would be produced. Manufacturers, wholesalers, retailers and importers had been merging with or acquiring each other since the 1950s when Italy started exporting shoes. The growing number of exporting countries pushed existing companies to merge into ever-larger mega-shoe corporations, upgrading production and streamlining management and distribution to remain profitable.

A catalyst for the increased amalgamation of the American shoe industry came in the form of the branded athletic footwear revolution of the 1970s. Sales of unrecognized brands began to decline and athletic shoes took top sales over fashion footwear. Shoe chains that sold only their own labels were unable to supply Adidas three-striped runners or Nike swoosh-marked trainers, but old-fashioned store loyalty was dead and consumers now shopped by brand alone. In 1973 Bruce Katz, working for his father's import business in Boston, saw that among the shoes in plain white boxes was a line made from a leather called 'Rockport'. He printed the name 'Rockport' on the boxes and this simple piece of branding turned their business into a multi-million-dollar industry that was bought out by Reebok in 1986.

Retailing diversified at the end of the twentieth century to include catalogue sales, factory outlets, televized home shopping and e-commerce. The shoe chain was disappearing, or at least the pioneers of shoe-chain retailing were disappearing. Nine West, then the newest of the big shoe chains, transformed the old family-oriented bargain-basement feel of their retail outlets by modernizing with an up-market look.

Today, American footwear manufacturing is all but gone. Most Americans wear shoes made in Italy, Brazil, the Philippines and, since the 1990s, China. Those shoes still produced within the United States come from a division of one of the mega-corporations. This is not just an American trend. Many shoe companies around the world are conglomerates of smaller firms that have been bought out or taken over, especially since the early 1990s. The recessions of the early 1980s, early 1990s and early 2000s have been difficult for the shoe industry, and many established companies have not survived the economic downturns. The last two recessions in particular were devastating to shoe companies who were operating on marginal profits. This was not due to lack of sales but because of corporate over-extension: some retailers could be found on one street more repetitively than fast-food restaurants or banks.

With the increase in middle-class wealth, shopping habits changed during the twentieth century. While American women often own over twenty pairs of shoes today, in 1940 women owned on average between six and eight pairs. During the early 1990s recession, the overspending that had been typical in the late 1980s stopped. Women started wearing the shoes they already owned and simply did not buy any more for a year or two. Companies scrambled to regroup since their futures were based on unrealistic forecasts made during the economic boom of the late 1980s.

The fashion image has become so multiplicitous that there is no longer one predominant silhouette. Fashion is now a series of trends that comes and goes from season to season. Platform pumps, stiletto-heeled sandals, or pastel ballerina flats: they come, they go, they come back again. In the 1990s fashion journalists tried to impress that the platform was dead and the stiletto heel was on its way out, but those forecasts only worked when there was a unified fashion image. For centuries, women have been keeping their clothes and shoes for reasons other than sentiment, updating and altering them if they had not been worn to ruin whilst new. Today, women buy vintage, keep old favourites and add trendy items for a season's wear to update a look that incorporates basics from several years back. The moulded plastic sandal, marketed as jellies, was a cheap and cheerful summer shoe in the early 1980s, returning as a fashion trend in the summer of 1995 and again in the summer of 2004. In the summer of 2005 vintage butterfly appliquéd cowboy boots became the rage after pop stars Britney Spears and Jessica Simpson were photographed wearing them. Sales on eBay, the online marketplace, were brisk for any version of the 1970s Capezio original and went for upward of US $600. By the time manufacturers picked up on the trend, consumers had moved on and knock-offs were available for as little as US $40.

Fashion footwear is truly a worldwide enterprise now. The Swiss firm Bally is owned by an American parent company; the Czech-founded Bata firm moved to England, then Canada and is now based in Switzerland. Canadian-born designer Patrick Cox trained in and works from England but most of his shoes are made in Italy. English-born Peter Fox works from Canada and his shoes, made in Italy or Spain, are sold through his New York store. Andrea Pfister is variously referred to as a French or Italian designer, while Manolo Blahník's background and addresses are so varied that his nationality is rarely referred to. No one country holds sway over style; no one designer holds court for the fashionable elite.

The era of fashion delineation is changing. Never has there been so much interest in fashion, as made evident by media coverage, with seemingly so little high fashion worn on the streets. If we apply the rules of fashion as defined in the nineteenth and early twentieth centuries to mean popularity of design, then the biggest-selling shoe style of the past forty years is the rubber-soled trainer.

>> DECORATIVE EVENING STYLES

Evening shoes were the only styles to offer any colour in the first decade of the twentieth century. Satin pumps were available in pastel pinks, blues and greens to match evening dresses, although skirts were trained so that only the vamps of shoes were ever visible, which is where decoration, if any, would appear.

Shoes with criss-cross ribbon lacings, as on sandal-slippers of the early nineteenth century (see p. 60), were revived under the new name of Grecian sandals in the late 1880s. They found limited appeal until 1911, when they became known as tango shoes, after the fashionable dance of the era. The tango was considered scandalous when it was introduced in Paris from Argentina at the turn of the century, but American professional dancers Irene and Vernon Castle demonstrated a modified tango, sanitized of much of its overt sensuality, at respectable afternoon tea dances. Irene was photographed wearing tango shoes at many of her performances, popularizing the style by 1911. Although gradually losing favour after 1914 the shoes made a brief comeback in the early 1920s. Shoes of this kind were considered a novelty, while basics, such as black walking shoes or boots, were the bread and butter of the American shoe industry. This made American manufacturers reluctant to

American white kid pumps with beaded vamps and sandal tie ribbons, labelled 'Rosenthal's Inc., San Francisco and Oakland', c. 1911–14.

American or Canadian pink silk evening pumps with bead-trimmed rosettes at throat, unlabelled, c. 1910.

become involved in high-fashion shoes sporting too much design because they were unlikely to sell well. However, novelty shoe hits exploded a company's sales forecast, and more American manufacturers began testing the market with new styles, colours and decoration.

American lamé brocade evening pumps with metallic laces, unlabelled, c. 1913–15.

Swiss brocade pump with white silk ribbon lace by Bally, 1914.

>> MASCULINIZATION AND HEALTH

A debate had been raging since the 1870s about high heels and the injury inflicted by wearing them. By 1890 the debate had expanded to include pointed toes, and many women continued to wear low-heeled wide-toed shoes and boots. Fashionable women still wore Louis-heeled dress shoes, although heel height rarely exceeded two inches unless made to order. The pointed toe was not easily discarded, but a significant number of consumers were more concerned with foot health and comfort over style. *The Ladies' World* magazine reported in December 1899: 'Shoes made on a man's last, laced in front, with broad, projecting sole, and round, boxed toes, with low, flat heels, are worn exclusively for the street, both in tan and black.' The masculinization of women's footwear was underway.

Manufacturers were making low-heeled, broad-toed shoes and boots for daytime wear, but most toes remained narrow and sometimes pointed, only becoming more almond-shaped after 1904. It seemed that those members of the public concerned by the health of their feet had influenced mainstream styles – at least temporarily.

American black leather boots with original box, labelled 'Queen Quality' made by Thomas G. Plant Co., c. 1904–10.

High Heels and Low Heels
The Difference Shown in X-Ray Photographs
By Alexander C. Magruder, M.D.

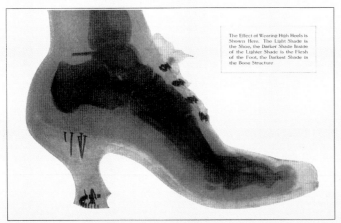

The Effect of Wearing High Heels is Shown Here. The Light Shade is the Shoe, the Darker Shade Inside of the Lighter Shade is the Flesh of the Foot, the Darkest Shade is the Bone Structure

What a Woman Gains by Wearing High Heels

ALL women like pretty feet. To enhance the attractiveness of this important point they wear high heels for three reasons. The first is that the coveted highly-arched instep is secured; the second is that the height is increased, and the third is that the foot is actually shortened in new, unnatural position by at least half an inch, measured from toe to heel. This shortening is augmented by placing the shoe heel far forward under the shoe, thus decreasing the apparent length of the foot by from one to two inches.

The two X-ray photographs which are reproduced on this page were made of the same foot under the same conditions; the only difference is that of shoes. The actual measurements of the foot show the following facts: The high heel shortened this foot half an inch; it increased the height of the instep three-quarters of an inch; and it raised the heel of the foot an inch and a half from the ground, thus increasing the height of the person practically to that extent. These figures may be verified by any one who cares to take the trouble to measure the X-ray photographs here reproduced.

What a woman gains, therefore, by wearing high heels is that the length of the foot is apparently shortened; the total height of the body is somewhat increased; the instep is made higher; and the general appearance of the foot is improved from an æsthetic point of view.

What a Woman Loses by Wearing High Heels

THE first and immediate result of wearing high heels is a general bodily discomfort. One tires more easily, is more irritable, and symptoms of nervous breakdown arise. The bones of the foot are forced into an unnatural relation to each other, as a glance at the accompanying photographs will show. But this abnormal position of the bones is a matter of comparatively minor importance.

The serious effect is that, the heels being raised and the toes remaining so near the ground, the upper part of the body is thrown forward so that the equilibrium may be maintained. In this position it is impossible to keep the shoulders thrown back. They fall forward and the chest sinks in. Full or normal breathing is impossible, and there are, as a result, areas in the apex of each lung unused—that is, the air in the apexes does not change with each respiration; they remain quiet and unused, because the muscles which expand them are not in a position to exert their full power.

The apex of each lung, especially the right, has long been recognized as the more frequent starting-point of pulmonary tuberculosis, because the tubercle bacillus grows best where fresh air does not come in contact with it.

But with lessened lung-capacity (lessened oxygenation) every organ of the body suffers. The heart appropriates the first and best blood for its own food. If this blood is not of the best quality and quantity the heart becomes weak, just as the body will grow weak when given poor and insufficient food. All other organs of the body suffer correspondingly. Of course, these organic changes are not so rapid as to be noticed at once; but they gradually appear, with cumulative effect, and sooner or later transform the girl of spirit into a listless person; the rosy cheeks to pale ones; the erect figure to stooped shoulders; the healthy, hearty, robust person to a semi-invalid or a total one.

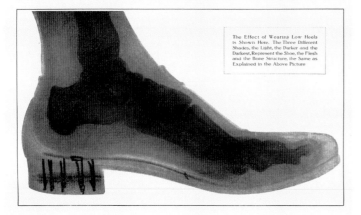

The Effect of Wearing Low Heels is Shown Here. The Three Different Shades, the Light, the Darker and the Darkest, Represent the Shoe, the Flesh and the Bone Structure, the Same as Explained in the Above Picture

American article from *Ladies' Home Journal* about the aesthetic and medical benefits and pitfalls of the high- versus the low-heeled shoe, January 1908.

Canadian photograph of a young lady wearing bulbous-toed shoes, c. 1911–13.

Canadian black leather derbies with bulbous toe, labelled 'The Empress Shoe', made by Walker Parker Co., Hamilton, Ontario, c. 1908–14.

Canadian black suede bulldog-toed button boot, labelled 'G.M.W. Co. The Duchess Shoe, London – Goodyear Welted', c. 1910–16.

A bulbous toe, called a 'nob' or 'bulldog' toe, began to appear in 1908 and allowed more room for the toes, improving circulation in the feet and legs. The bulldog toe was more popular in North America than in Europe before World War I and was a bigger hit west of the Mississippi than in the east of the United States. Often used in caricatures to ridicule its enthusiasts, the toe appeared on the feet of country bumpkins and plaid-suited travelling salesmen. Picked up in England, the style was referred to as an American toe. English, German and Swedish examples of boots and shoes with bulbous-shaped toes that were made well into the 1920s exist, long after American shoe manufacturers abandoned the style in around 1917.

Shoes did not show under the long skirts of the 1900s and the vast majority of footwear was black, brown or white and heavy soled. However, by 1911 many walking dresses and suits sported ankle-length hems, and by 1915 all hem lengths hovered around the ankle. Footwear was visible again. Styles began to resume a path toward colour, decoration and higher heels. In North America, pointed toes were popular by 1916 even though European styles shied away from extreme points. American footwear was shaped not by designers but by consumers: aside from those who demanded healthful styles, most women sought out narrower toes and shoe manufacturers followed this lead by creating pointed toes from 1916 until the early 1920s.

>> THE POPULAR STYLE

Three major elements of shoe style survived for nearly forty years with little change. The first were beaded vamps, which had been dressing up plain pumps since the 1880s. They were usually designed tone on tone, so black beads appeared on black shoes, white beads on white, steel beads on grey and bronze beads on bronze kid shoes. The second style was buttoned bar or strap shoes, which were first seen in the late 1880s and remained popular until the early 1930s. Thirdly, the Louis heel that re-emerged in the 1870s was the most common dress-shoe heel until the mid 1920s. So, a beaded-vamp bar shoe with a Louis heel looked very much the same in 1925 as it had done in 1890.

New heel styles appeared in the early years of the twentieth century, and the Cuban heel became a standard heel for walking shoes and boots by 1910. It consisted of stacked layers of leather with a tapered profile and broad top lift for a good footing, although it was also imitated in wood with a textile or leather covering for dressier styles.

American bronze-beaded kid strap pumps, unlabelled, c. 1905–15.

American pale-blue kid pumps with vamp extended into a tongue decorated with steel beadwork, Drexel Shoe Company, Omaha, Nebraska, c. 1913–17.

Canadian black-glass-beaded black leather barrette shoes with Cuban heels, unlabelled, c. 1910–16.

>> THE END OF THE FASHION BOOT

Apart from the bulldog toe, most toes on American fashion boots followed the trend for narrower pointed styles throughout the 1910s. European footwear, which at first shunned the bulldog toe, was also slower to take up the pointed style in the 1910s and continued to be made with more rounded toes.

Demand for boots declined in the 1910s as skirt hems rose and the shafts of boots were forced to grow taller. To alleviate the demand on leather, required for military use in England, boot height was restricted to eight inches in 1917. An unsightly gap of stocking appeared between the tops of boots and the hems of skirts as hems of six inches off the ground continued to rise. Many winter boots were made with wool shafts, not restricted by wartime shortages, and gaiters of wool or linen were worn over shoes to achieve the boot look without the cost of a leather boot and while remaining patriotic. By 1918 when skirt hems were eight to ten inches off the ground, boot shafts could grow no taller. Shoes had been gaining popularity over boots since about 1910 and were now worn for all occasions but winter walking. Despite this trend there seemed to be a resurgence of interest in boots just at the end of their reign when they were briefly popular for summer wear in North America in around 1918 to 1920. Many of these styles were white canvas and sported rubber soles.

German suede and black patent-leather
boots, unlabelled, c. 1916–17.

Canadian light-tan laced leather boots,
unlabelled, c. 1918–22.

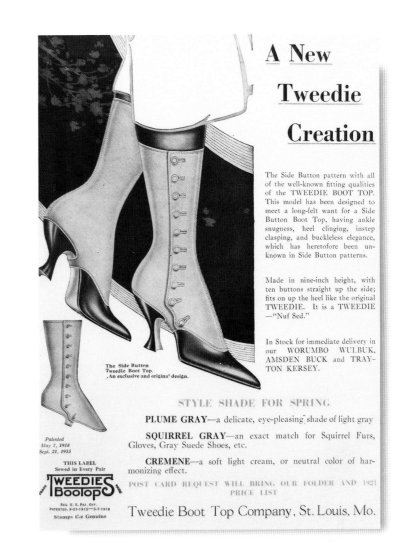

A New

Tweedie

Creation

The Side Button pattern with all of the well-known fitting qualities of the TWEEDIE BOOT TOP. This model has been designed to meet a long-felt want for a Side Button Boot Top, having ankle snugness, heel clinging, instep clasping, and buckleless elegance, which has heretofore been unknown in Side Button patterns.

Made in nine-inch height, with ten buttons straight up the side; fits on up the heel like the original TWEEDIE. It is a TWEEDIE —"Nuf Sed."

In Stock for immediate delivery in our WORUMBO WULBUK, AMSDEN BUCK and TRAYTON KERSEY.

The Side Button Tweedie Boot Top. An exclusive and original design.

Patented May 7, 1918 Sept. 21, 1915

THIS LABEL Sewed in Every Pair

TWEEDIES BootopS
REG. U. S. PAT. OFF.
PATENTED, 9-21-1915—5-7-1918
Stamps the Genuine

STYLE SHADE FOR SPRING

PLUME GRAY—a delicate, eye-pleasing shade of light gray

SQUIRREL GRAY—an exact match for Squirrel Furs, Gloves, Gray Suede Shoes, etc.

CREMENE—a soft light cream, or neutral color of harmonizing effect.

POST CARD REQUEST WILL BRING OUR FOLDER AND 1921 PRICE LIST

Tweedie Boot Top Company, St. Louis, Mo.

Canadian khaki and brown laced leather boots, labelled 'Medcalf', c. 1917–20.

American advertisement for Tweedie gaiters, 1922.

American brown kid Russian boots,
c. 1922–24.

>> RUSSIAN BOOTS AND FLAPPERS

American manufacturers misunderstood female consumers during the winter of 1921–22, which saw a shortage of rubber footwear while leather fashion boots remained unsold on store shelves. Women now wanted nothing but shoes except in foul weather. It was customary for younger women to don rubber galosh boots and not fasten the buckles, leaving them flapping. This action has been credited as the origin of the word 'flapper', although so many possible origins exist for this word that it is difficult to determine which is correct. Fringed fold-over tongues, or kilties, were also called 'flapper' tongues in the early 1920s.

By the late 1920s a new rain-boot style, fitted close over a shoe, was displacing buckled galosh boots for all bad weather except deep snow or cold conditions. Rain boots came in different colours, had wool or rayon jersey uppers, often printed in gingham or houndstooth, and were closed with dome (press studs) or slide (zips) fasteners.

The one style of fashion boot that managed to avoid an early grave was the Russian boot, a calf-to-knee-high straight-topped pull-on style that was introduced in 1921. Sales were sporadic at first but *The Boot and Shoe Recorder* reported on 6 May 1922:

'The Russian boot stands for utility, not for beauty. It can hardly be said to be a fitting and beautiful part of the costume of the modern American girl, whose skirts are short and whose feet in Russian boots are far from being petite.

Drawing of a woman in a bathing suit, wearing a coat and unfastened galoshes, summer 1922.

American advertisement for 'Raynboots', 1930.

No merchant expects the Russian boot to become a landslide proposition, but if the Russian boot could be made the compliment of the winter season and could be worn instead of flapping galoshes, there might be something in the Russian boot as an item of utility.'

By the late 1920s Russian boots were knee-high and fitted very close to the leg as either a pull-on style or fastened with a slide fastener. However, they found little popularity and were abandoned, destined not to re-emerge until the late 1960s.

>> SPORTSWEAR

Women participated in almost all the sports men played by the early 1920s and were major consumers of sports shoes. Women's rubber-soled tennis shoes had been available since the late 1870s but until World War I most sports-shoe sales had been to teenage boys. By 1920 women were buying rubber-soled shoes for general summer use, especially at the seaside, and as house wear.

Canadian or American white suede low-heeled sports shoes with leather sole, labelled 'Genuine Trot-moc Sole', c. 1910–15.

American Hood catalogue of sports shoes, 1920.

Canadian khaki cotton sports boots with brown rubber soles, c. 1916–20.

?American-made for export to Germany,
brown leather loafer with laced vamp closure
and stacked leather heel, c. 1920.

>> ORIGINS OF THE LOAFER

The loafer is a descendant of the Native American moccasin. A classic moccasin is constructed from two pieces of hide: the bottom unit and a vamp insert, which are sewn together on the top of the foot, probably to avoid dampness entering through sole-line stitches. Early fur traders and explorers in seventeenth-century New France (Quebec) adapted the traditional moccasin, making it from oiled cowhide. Additional outer soles were sometimes added to the moccasin for extra protection. By the late nineteenth century these styles were sold under the name 'camp moccasins' and felt examples appeared as house slippers.

The style was exported to Europe, but a similar shoe already existed in rural Norway: a leather shoe using a similar construction method and adapted from the footwear of the Sami (Lapp) people of the north. In 1936 the American shoe company Bass, who had been making camp moccasins since 1876, brought out a Norwegian variation of the shoe, which they marketed as 'Weejuns' (short for Norwegian) and the style caught on. Variations in the camp moccasin style appeared under different names, including 'Weejuns', 'Top-Siders' and 'Penny mocs' (so-called because a penny could be slipped under the vamp strap). The term 'loafer' was applied to the style at some point in the 1940s and proved popular with teenagers in the 1950s and early 1960s. Loafers were marketed as men's semi-casual wear in the late 1950s. Gucci's version of the loafer became a staple in men's and women's wardrobes in the 1970s and 1980s.

Camp moccasins advertisement, 1922.   Camp moccasins advertisement, 1923.

Canadian alligator-print velvet slippers or 'nullifiers' with faux-fur trim, c. 1900–10.

French quilted cream silk boudoir slippers with ermine fur and heads trimming the top line, labelled 'France – Galerie Lafayette', c. 1920.

>> SLIPPERS

Until the late nineteenth century the term 'slipper' described any indoor shoe that slipped onto the foot, including dressy afternoon and evening shoes. Slippers intended for home use only were referred to as toilet, dressing or boudoir slippers. Gradually the term slippers came to mean shoes for wear only at home. Practical leather, velveteen or felt styles were commonly made for comfort and warmth, but boudoir slippers made of lingerie silk or satin, usually heeled and artfully trimmed with luxurious materials, were also produced. Boudoir slippers were intended for more intimate wear within the bed-, bath- and dressing rooms but also appeared at the breakfast table. The trend toward a more casual home lifestyle, the changing role of women, central heating and the emergence of the en-suite bathroom have all led to declining slipper sales since the 1950s.

French or American pale-pink silk mule
with black bead embroidery, unlabelled,
c. 1905–15.

>> THE VISIBLE SHOE

The pointed toe and the Louis heel had featured since the 1890s, but by 1920 the heel had become thinner and taller and would remain predominantly that way until 1925, when a straighter heel came into fashion. Shoes were now in full view under shorter hem lines, so ornamentation was often extended beyond the vamps and footwear became available in a greater range of colours and materials to match or complement the clothes and stockings. Snake and lizard skins were fragile and did not come into general use until the mid 1920s. When used for uppers, the skins were usually lined with another leather for strength and often overlaid with leather toecaps and counters where the most wear would occur.

A problem arose for shoe manufacturers in the 1920s when shoe-chain retailers and department stores, their largest clients, ordered more novelty styles in smaller runs, including a wider range

Chinese pale-aqua silk shoes with couched silver and pastel threads. Shoes with typical Chinese workmanship were made for sale to foreign nationals, for Chinese women with Western tastes or for export, unlabelled, c. 1919–23.

of colourful and decorative shoes that changed every season. Most women, however, only bought three or four pairs of shoes each year and while retailers were trying to increase sales by offering more choice, manufacturers found it more difficult to make smaller runs of shoes profitable. As a response, manufacturers reduced workers' wages while raising prices to compensate for the smaller orders and between 1910 and 1930 the average price of shoes had doubled.

Working-class Americans could not afford these inflated costs and continued to buy plain black strap pumps for most wear. Highly colourful and decorative shoes were very occasion specific and usually bought to match a particular dress. The economy was becoming based on consumerism, but a disparity was created between those who consumed and those who were unable to afford what was produced.

American red kid shoes with crossover straps, labelled 'Tuttle', c. 1923–25.

Japanese snakeskin pumps with buttoned strap closures, labelled 'Mori Brothers – Yokohama', c. 1925–27. These shoes are lined in the quarters with leather but lined in the vamp with only cotton twill, necessitating a zigzag stitch on the vamp seams to keep them from tearing apart. The English-language label in this pair suggests they were made for foreign nationals living in the port city of Yokohama, which had been an open port for trade to the West since 1854.

American black silk V-strap embroidered evening shoes with ribbon ties, labelled 'Saks Fifth Avenue', c. 1926–30.

French blue silk T-strap embroidered evening shoes, labelled 'F. Pinet – Paris', c. 1924–26.

>> DRESSY PUMPS

Shoes that could be worn on all occasions during the 1920s were most often pumps (or court shoes), usually with single- or T-straps. The strapless pump made the leg look longer by not using a strap that cut across the instep and gradually gained popularity, displacing the strapped pump by the late 1930s.

American manufacturers in the 1920s were excellent at producing ready-made shoes but there were few American designers. The manufacturers needed designs after which to model their ready-mades and French shoemakers' work filled this void. In this way,

the French regained some of their dominance as style makers in the women's footwear industry. For those who could afford the real thing, French shoe designers produced exquisite originals for export at upwards of US $165 per pair. American tourists flooded Paris in the 1920s and regularly patronized the high-end couturiers and *bottiers*. With the onset of the Great Depression, however, Americans and their money disappeared from the city. In September 1930 François Pinet opened a shop on Fifth Avenue in New York, hoping to regain the American clients who had ceased to cross the Atlantic.

French hand-painted beige silk and blue kid shoes, labelled 'Hellstern & Son Ltd. Brevetes, Paris', c. 1927–29.

Chinese yellow silk embroidered strap evening shoes, unlabelled, c. 1926–30.

French gilded leather appliqué and green velvet T-strap evening shoes, labelled 'Perugia – 21 Ave., N. Dame – Nice – 11 Faubg St. Honoré Paris' c. 1925–28.

American machine-embroidered brown textile T-strap evening pumps, labelled 'Holly Vogue – made in Los Angeles', c. 1927–30.

French blue silk embroidered evening pumps, labelled 'Greco 4 rue des Capucines Paris, Angle de la rue de la Paix', c. 1925–27.

American purple silk brocade evening pumps with cut steel buckles, labelled 'Lord and Taylor', c. 1927–31.

American rubber and netted-cotton beach sandals, labelled 'Cuban Chic Water Wear, patent July 27, 1926, United States Rubber Products, Inc.'.

Canadian photograph of model in swimsuit, rubber bathing cap and beach sandals, c. 1934–37.

>> BEACH SANDALS

Holidaying was more accessible to the middle classes by the 1920s, when people used their 'weekends', a newly coined phrase, to travel by train or automobile to seaside resorts. Good health had been firmly linked to exercise by this time and swimming was a fashionable sport. Swimming pools began to appear at some resort hotels in the Riviera and California, and sea lagoons were built at beaches to protect an area of the seaside from surf and sea life for effective swimming exercise. Sunbathing became fashionable as a tan was a status symbol of the idle rich. Old-fashioned bathing shoes were a hindrance to swimming and ruined an even tan line. The beach sandal took the place of bathing shoes in the late 1920s, still protecting the sole of the foot but with the least amount of coverage on the top of the foot.

>> THE SPECTATOR

The American publication *Boot and Shoe Recorder* noted in its 26 December 1925 issue: 'Tell the ladies something about the folly of wearing thin soles on the street, and by that same token, tell them the incongruity of wearing heavy welts with an afternoon gown or party dress.' American women were not known for their understated taste in travelling or walking shoes. A European writer for *Ladies' Home Journal* in 1925 reported that American women had gorgeous footwear for formal occasions, but the writer could not fail to notice while waiting for a train that American women wore shoes that were too small, with their insteps bulging over the throat and the uppers made of inappropriate materials like satin and brocade.

These Austrian welt-soled shoes, typical of European-tailored footwear, would have been suitable for walking about town,

travelling or being a spectator on grassy sidelines or in the stands at sporting events. Two-tone 'spectator' shoes were first made fashionable in the United States in 1914. The style was most often produced in white canvas or leather with brown leather toecaps and counters; the brown leather protected the white from dirt and scuffs on areas where wear normally occurred. Such shoes were often called *trotteurs* (trotters) in France, suggesting their purpose. Known as brogues in England, they were named after the decoratively punched leather that had been popular since the early years of the century. In Germany the style was called a *Budapesteschuhe* after Budapest, renowned for its quality men's and women's tailored walking shoes made by hand by the city's shoemakers in the 1920s and 1930s.

Austrian canvas and leather brogue walking shoes with original shoe trees, labelled 'Coyle & Earley – Wien', c. 1928–35.

>> WARDROBE BASICS

Ladies' Home Journal recommended in 1926 a simple shoe wardrobe for those women who could not afford expensive imported French shoes or even their American knock-offs, which might be too specific in colour or decoration. If she could afford four pairs per year, a woman was advised to purchase a plain strap pump in tan or black for general service, a white sports oxford with rubber sole, a dressy afternoon pair in patent leather, satin or kid and an evening pair in gold or silver kid, brocade or coloured satin to match a dress.

American patent-leather shoes with cut-outs underlaid with white grosgrain ribbon, labelled 'Style Step', c. 1928–30.

German black suede afternoon shoes with white kid trim and interwoven instep straps, labelled 'Leiser Luxus', c.1928–32. Leiser was a chain of twenty-two stores in Berlin. The Jewish owners closed or sold the stores and left Berlin in 1936, going to the Netherlands, where they briefly operated a shoe store, and then to Argentina in 1938.

A pair of plain strap shoes or oxfords for general service in dull leather or tan and a pair of black patent or suede for dressier occasions would suffice if only two pairs could be purchased. Shoes of good enough quality at this end of the market could be bought for between US $3 and $5 per pair, but of course expensive versions of the simplest pumps were also available through high-end retailers.

English black leather shoes with brown leather straps and trim and an extended back with receptacles for lipstick, c. 1928–34. Shoemaker-made, probably for an exhibition or a special order.

>> ANKLE BOOTS

Most boots from the 1930s to the 1950s were made of rubber and worn in wet and cold weather. Fashion boots were created by designers but were never regarded as anything other than a novelty. In May 1939 Carmel Snow, editor of *Harper's Bazaar*, spoke to the Shoe Fashion Guild in New York:

'I feel sure that the question of the bootie is in your minds. We will show the boot, of course, we couldn't possibly omit it.

But whether it will be generally accepted...I think is extremely doubtful. For over a year, Mr. Perugia in Paris has been showing me his bottines. He tells me that his smartest clients order them but I have never seen any smart woman in Paris wearing them. If the French woman does not take to them easily I don't see why the American will. The best thing we have are our ankles and these boots cut the line of the ankle.'

English teal and grey kid front-laced boots with decorative stitching, unlabelled, c. 1935–38.

English black leather and suede ankle boots, unlabelled, c. 1935–38.

>> FOOTWEAR FAVOURITES

Oxfords, pumps and sandals were the most popular footwear in the 1930s. The high-heeled oxford had been in fashion since the late 1910s and was at its height in the 1930s and early 1940s. However, the newest style of the three was the sandal. The Paris couturier Madeleine Vionnet put sandals on the feet of her models in 1907, years before the style would make a serious attempt at becoming a true fashion. Toe-baring sandals were introduced at the beach in the late 1920s. Through their creative open cutwork, open sides and woven leather, closed-toe sandals were popular evening and summer wear by the mid 1930s but continued to be worn with stockings.

In the late 1920s the open-sided D'Orsay pump, named after the early-nineteenth-century dandy Count D'Orsay, was reinterpreted for women's evening shoes, often with an instep strap to keep it on. The style remained a popular dressy evening option into the 1950s. By the early 1930s a wide array of coloured silk evening shoes was available to consumers to coordinate with evening dresses, although most evening shoes sold between the late 1920s and 1970s were in gold or silver metallic leather or black silk.

More architecturally detailed construction features, such as intricate pattern cuts and decorative linear stitching, replaced the surface decoration, such as embroidery, that was so popular in the late 1920s.

Ascott

18, RUE ROYALE, PARIS

Présente ses nouveaux modèles,
ligne américaine, prêts à porter.

French advertisement for Ascott shoes,
spring 1938.

English silver lamé evening sandal, labelled 'Dolci's De Lux', c. 1932–37.

American brown suede pump with decorative stitching, c. 1935–38.

French gold kid evening pump with petit point on the vamp, showing an eighteenth-century scene with a woman carrying a staff, labelled 'Padova modele, André Perugia, 4 rue de la Paix, Paris', c. 1933–36.

English red and grey sandal-pumps,
unlabelled, c. 1932–36.

English red and grey derbies with decorative
top stitching, c. 1931–35.

American blue silk and gold kid evening shoes, labelled 'I. Miller Inc. NY', c. 1931–35.

American green silk and gold kid evening shoes, labelled 'Oppenheim Collins', c. 1932–36.

?Czech-made for export, grey and beige woven leather T-strap shoes, labelled 'Made expressly for Ingledew's Ltd. – imported', c. 1928–32.

>> WOVEN AND PLAITED

Woven leather shoes from the then Czechoslovakia were first exported in the mid 1920s and were soon copied by American manufacturers for summer wear. Dressy afternoon and evening styles were usually made of folded kid, gilded for evening wear and coloured for daywear.

By the mid 1930s Mexico was exporting huarache styles. Los Angeles shoe store Desmond's reported in the *Boot and Shoe Recorder* on 4 June 1938 that even men were buying huaraches so quickly that 'it makes it almost impossible to keep sizes on the shelves of our stores'. The Italian shoemaker Ferragamo was making his name internationally in the late 1930s for platforms and for his use of non-traditional materials. With the start of World War I, Italian and Czech imports were no longer available in North America and the dressier women's styles of woven kid were no longer in production. Low-heeled huaraches continued in popularity for casual summer wear in North America during and after the war.

Czech gold and silver woven kid sling-back
evening oxfords, labelled 'Made in Bohemia',
c. 1938–39.

Italian silver kid and crocheted cellophane
sling-back pumps, labelled 'Ferragamo –
Saks Fifth Avenue', c. 1938.

>> THE DEBUT OF THE PLATFORM

According to a fashion bulletin that appeared in the *Boot and Shoe Recorder*, Contessa Castelbarco, the eldest daughter of the conductor Arturo Toscanini, arrived in New York in early October 1937 wearing a pair of high cork-soled sandals she had purchased that summer on the Italian Riviera. The designer was not credited in the report, but the sandals were most assuredly by Ferragamo.

Platform shoes were first made for beachwear in the United States in the summer of 1938, but many designers and manufacturers included small platforms (of ⅛ or ¼ of an inch) for daytime wear and taller platforms for evening wear in their Fall 1938 collections. Other than as novelty beachwear, the style found limited success at first.

No. 1434

A novel idea in wooden soles. Curlicue heel. Upper of natural rabana straw combined with brown kid. Available also in natural and blue; natural and red.

Yʘou are cordially invited to attend Beachcraft's showing of glamorous. new play shoes for Spring and Summer selling.

During the Guild Show

HOTEL NEW YORKER

Rooms 627 and 628   May 8, 9, & 10

Beachcraft
Sandal Company, Inc.

Show Rooms: Marbridge Bldg., 47 W. 34th.
New York City
"Tony" Sarubbi, in charge of sales.
Tel. LOngacre 5-2476
Factory: 10-12 Jones St., New York City.
Tel. CHelsea 2-7798

'They'll make you tower over your husband, Mrs. Green!'

Advertisement for Beachcraft Sandal Company, 29 April 1939.

American cartoon appearing in the publication *Boot and Shoe Recorder*, 22 April 1939.

>> PEEP TOES AND SLING BACKS

Both the open toe and sling back were introduced in 1938. Open toes and backs created a problem, however, since most stockings had reinforced toes and heels and were unsightly in sandals. Appearing without stockings in town during the day was not an acceptable option at this time, as bare legs were considered inappropriate away from the seaside or home. Edna Woolman Chase, editor-in-chief of American *Vogue* had much to say about this problem to the Shoe Fashion Guild at a luncheon held in New York in May 1939:

'I want to plead with you to stop this promotion of the open-toed, open-backed shoe for street wear. From the very beginning of this fashion I have felt that it was a distinctly bad style – and I had hoped it would have an early death. You have gotten women almost barefooted now – and I won't be a bit surprised if, some day, they just walk right out on you and shellac their soles and put bells on their toes and say "To Hell with shoes!" You may say, "Well if women didn't

French plum leather sandal with pale-blue platform and heel, labelled 'André Perugia – Padova – 2 rue de la Paix, Paris', c. 1938–39.

Swiss blue leather peep-toe pumps, made by Bally for export, labelled 'Ingledew's Ltd. Vancouver', c. 1938–40.

wear them, we wouldn't make them," and I can retort, "If you didn't make them we couldn't wear them."'

Many women liked the new styles, but Chase spoke for a large number of consumers who preferred closed shoes. Variations on the theme solved most of the problems, for example, small peep toes disguised the reinforced toe of the stocking by making it barely visible and a back strip covered the reinforced heel of the stocking. Sling backs continued to be made but more often as evening shoes, when long skirts hid unsightly reinforced stocking heels, or as casual summer wear, when bare legs were permissible. Stocking manufacturers addressed the problem eventually by creating stockings without reinforced toes and heels in the 1940s.

>> WEDGIES

Introduced by Ferragamo in 1936, wedge soles were not generally shown in footwear collections until 1938. They found limited appeal until World War II started in September 1939. Wedge heels then became more common because they created the fashionable heel height but with a stable footing, something that was necessary in the wartime years when walking and public transportation replaced the use of private automobiles. Also, wedge heels could be made from wood and painted, using less leather in their production. They remained popular until after the war, sometimes worn in conjunction with a platform sole, but often not. After

1947 the wedge heel began to be used more for casual footwear, and heeled platforms or baby-doll pumps became the preferred option for dressier styles.

Suede, which had been in common use since about 1910, became very popular during the war. Suede was the sanded or buffed surface of leather and was a useful finish for poorer quality hides as the preparation process disguised imperfections. Suede was regarded as semi-dressy, suitable for daytime and evening wear, depending upon the style of shoe for which it was used. Exotic leathers – snake, lizard and crocodile or alligator – also grew in use

on fashion styles during the war as these skins were not appropriate for military footwear. Alligators, Cayman lizards and boa snakes were indigenous to the Americas and could be traded easily within the Western hemisphere. In Europe, crocodile and python were more easily obtainable and German women's shoes especially were made from these exotic skins in the early years of the war.

?German green suede and python platform
wedge pumps, unlabelled, c. 1939–41.

English black suede shoes with painted
wooden wedge heels, unlabelled,
c. 1941–44.

American black suede peep-toe pump with wedge heel, labelled 'Bullock's Wilshire', c. 1947–48.

French advertisement for A. Gresy wedge platform shoes, autumn 1945.

Canadian snake-printed leather pumps with open toes and vented vamps, labelled 'Personality Shoes' with the stamp 'W.P.T.B.', c. 1942–45.

English navy-blue oxford brogues, labelled 'Barratt's – Northampton', with a 'CC41' stamp in the quarters, c. 1942–47.

>> WARTIME MEASURES

After World War II began, shoemaking materials were in short supply, especially leather and rubber, which were required for military use. This shortage was felt most acutely in Continental Europe. When Italy went to war in Abyssinia in 1935, the League of Nations cut off the country's imports of leather. Italian designer Ferragamo worked around this by popularizing wood and cork soles. Wooden soles, both solid and articulated, were briefly used at the end of World War I in Germany and were in common use in World War II across Continental Europe. In 1942 André Perugia took out a French patent for his version of an articulated wooden sole.

Clothes rationing was introduced in Germany in November 1939. Before a permit to purchase a pair of leather shoes was issued,

a declaration had to be made to a ration officer that the applicant had only two pairs of leather shoes and that one of those pairs was beyond repair. Random checks were sometimes carried out by ration officers to ensure that claimants were telling the truth. If more than two pairs were found, the 'extras' were confiscated and the owner fined. Many women chose wooden-soled shoes that did not wear out and could be obtained without a *Bezugschein* (ration card) until the summer of 1941, at which point they too were only sold with a permit.

Shortages were less dire in the United States, and shoes of alternative materials could be purchased without ration coupons. Leather shoes were limited to a maximum of three pairs per person

German sandals with articulated wooden soles and uppers made of cotton canvas and oilcloth. Sent home as a gift by an American soldier, who wrote on the bottom: 'From Germany, 11 January, 1945'.

French pump with solid-wood platform sole and plaited-straw upper, purchased to send home as a gift by an American lieutenant who was stationed in Paris after its liberation, c. 1944–45.

per year in the United States, but this quota did not include leather-soled textile shoes, such as bedroom slippers, or any type of rope-, wood- or cork-soled shoes.

Leather shoes were actually more easily available to British civilians but rationing worked differently in Britain. In 1941, when rationing was introduced in Britain, a woman was given 66 coupons with which she could purchase whatever she liked. A pair of shoes could be had for five coupons but a coat required fourteen. An entire year's supply of coupons could be used on the purchase of a coat, two dresses, two pairs of shoes, a slip, a pair of pyjamas and three pairs of stockings. To make matters worse, by the war's end the number of coupons per year had been reduced to 36. If she liked, a woman could buy seven pairs of shoes with her coupons in 1945 but would not be able to buy any other clothing.

From 1942 British manufacturers were required to produce fifty per cent of all shoes to the Utility Standard Guidelines for Wartime Production. A 'CC41' stamp was put in shoes that met these standards, and consumers were encouraged to buy them as they avoided paying purchase tax. Although less strict, the Wartime Prices and Trade Board in Canada oversaw rationing from December 1941 and used a 'WPTB' stamp on footwear from 1942 to indicate which shoes met with wartime production standards. In Canada the rationing of clothing and footwear was lifted in 1945, but in Britain the CC41 regulations for clothing were in effect until 1949.

>> WALLED VAMPS

The high-heeled oxford had been in fashion since the late 1910s and was particularly popular in the 1930s and early 1940s. In 1938 a high-cut vamp extending almost to the top of the foot was introduced, and in 1939 a snub or walled toe also appeared. The walled toe was not in common production until after 1941 and more so after 1944. The very round toe became the origins of the baby-doll pump of the late 1940s and early 1950s, although the wall shape was dropped by 1952. By the 1940s the oxford, when paired with a Cuban or medium-height stacked-leather heel, had become a utilitarian style worn by working women, especially in the nursing field. Older women took to wearing the style for orthopedic reasons, especially during the 1950s and early 1960s when thinner, higher heels were back in vogue.

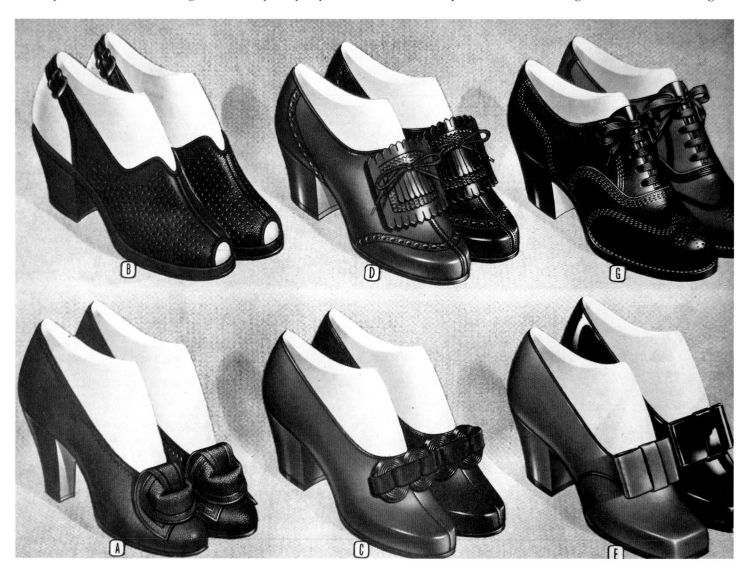

Canadian advertisement showing walled-toe styles, Eaton's Catalogue, autumn 1945.

German black suede oxfords, labelled 'Elka' c. 1948–51. Elka was a line of shoes from the manufacturer Ludwig Kopp who was located in Pirmasens, Germany, the seat of the German shoe industry.

American white suede and brown leather spectator oxfords, labelled 'The Air Step Shoe', c. 1946–50. The correspondent or spectator shoe was introduced just before World War I and was favoured from the late 1930s to the early 1950s. It was ideal for summer wear, protecting white suede and leather from scuffs and stains with its dark leather toecaps.

American leather and snakeskin platform sandals, labelled 'Creations by Henri – New York City – Paradise Bootery 1586 B'way NYC', c. 1947–51. Paradise Bootery was a small shoemaker shop in Times Square that specialized in bespoke work, creating shoes for Broadway productions, burlesque queens and brave upper east side socialites. Paradise Bootery was at its height from the postwar 1940s to the early 1970s and finally closed in the mid 1980s.

>> THE RISE AND FALL OF THE PLATFORM

Although platform shoes were introduced in 1937 they were not exactly fashion hits. Platform shoe sales began to climb in the United States in the summer of 1943 after the performer Carmen Miranda, known for her trademark platform shoes, became a star. Platforms however were generally small on most shoes. On the liberation of Paris in August 1944, Parisian women were wearing tall wooden platform shoes, taller than any commercially made in the United States at the time, and the fashion for taller platforms took off. Platform shoes were at their most popular in the United States from 1945 until 1948 and only caught on in England in 1947. They became an expression of style over necessity in the postwar 1940s, but the French, who had been wearing platforms more avidly in the late 1930s and out of necessity during the early 1940s, were eager to drop the style. In 1947 high-heeled shoes without platforms were being shown to complement the luxurious 'New Look' fashions. Platform shoes remained fashionable in Britain and the United States until well into the early 1950s despite the French lead.

American fuchsia suede sling-back platform pumps with ankle straps, labelled 'Palter De Liso New York – Bonwit Teller', c. 1947–50.

German black suede mules with polka-dot cut-outs on vamp, labelled 'Mareno Luxus', c. 1948–51.

>> CALIFORNIA CASUALS

Both of these casual summer-sandal styles were made using the Californian construction method, which was used only for sandals and was developed during World War II. The sandal was completely sewn together before a platform was inserted and a sole attached. The process did not require skilled labourers, who in the United States were in shorter supply than leather during the war.

Thousands of pairs of women's and children's platform sandals were made following this method from about 1943 until the mid 1950s, when platform soles fell from fashionable use.

Top: American rubber-soled summer casual sandal, labelled 'Kedette's' by United States Rubber Company, c. 1943–48.

Above: American rubber-soled summer casual sandals, labelled 'Summerettes – Ball Band', and an advertisement for the shoes, May 1949 (opposite).

Hawaiian wood platform sandals with straw straps, labelled 'M. McInerny Ltd. – Honolulu', purchased in 1954. The soles were most likely imported from the Philippines and the embroidered straw straps added in Hawaii. M. McInerny was one of Honolulu's oldest retail outlets, founded in 1857 as a general goods store and growing into a large department store with branches throughout the islands. The firm closed in 2003.

>> THE END OF THE PLATFORM

The platform began and ended its life as a beach sandal. By 1954 platform soles had finally disappeared from day and evening shoes and were about to be replaced on the beach by the rubber flip-flop. It may seem odd to wear platforms on the beach, but the popular theory behind this use, from the late 1930s to the mid 1950s, was that the platform would sink into the sand, keeping the feet dry and sand-free.

American articulated-wood-soled clog-sandals with red vinyl straps, labelled 'Flexiclogs pat. 2590648', c. 1952–54, and schematic drawings of the shoe from US Patent Office, March 1952.

>> BABY DOLLS

The heeled pump and sandal dominated fashion-shoe production from the late 1940s until the late 1960s. Footwear was available in a complete range of fashion colours, but black was reinvented as a glamorous colour particularly suitable for 'after five' cocktail wear, which covered any event that was semi-formal, including dining out and attending the theatre, as well as cocktail parties. Daytime-length dresses but in more luxurious materials were considered appropriate cocktail wear and were paired with suitably smart shoes. The French

French high-heeled black silk velvet pumps with gold kid trim and heels, unlabelled, possibly by Perugia, c. 1948–54. These ultimate high heels allude to a fetishism while also exhibiting the qualities of finely made shoes. As fetish subcultures evolved, particularly in the 1890s, 1920s, 1950s and 1990s, mainstream manufacturers often catered for those interested in the erotic appeal of women's shoes.

were done with the platform shoe and promoted the high-heeled pump as the ultimate in feminine style. Small platforms continued to appear on shoes until 1954, although in fewer styles with each passing year after 1947.

The immediate postwar years for most Europeans were as difficult as the war years. Rebuilding took precedence over glamour and it would be years before many women could even think about buying stylish clothes and shoes again. The rebirth of postwar fashion began in February 1947 when Christian Dior's 'New Look', as an American fashion journalist called it, was unveiled. Many fashion designers interpreted this unapologetically luxurious and feminine style, but Dior was perhaps an even better businessman than he was designer as his collection was intentionally designed to win back American women to Parisian style. The United States was wealthy and powerful, unscathed by wartime destruction, and able to afford the luxury of French fashions. However, Americans now

American black suede pumps with flocked vinyl vamps, labelled 'Coty by Lambert', c. 1952–55. The thick high heel and round toe of this style is typical of the classic baby-doll pump of the late 1940s and 1950s.

American black suede sling-back pump with ankle strap fastened by brass sword, labelled 'Stylecraft', c. 1947–50. The ankle cuff fastens with a sabre-shaped pin and chain, exhibiting fetishistic qualities.

had their own fashion and footwear designers and no longer relied on European style leads. Many American women preferred home-grown casual chic, especially postwar suburban women who were keener on raising children and dressing with comfort than appearing in the latest fashions. France did manage to regain its lead in high fashion but casual wear continued to be dominated by American design and manufacture.

English black silk crepe platform D'Orsay pumps with jewelled decorations, labelled 'Piccadilly, London', c. 1950–53.

Canadian black suede sandals with brass-wire-cage heels, after a design by Perugia, labelled 'Simpson's St. Regis', c. 1952–56.

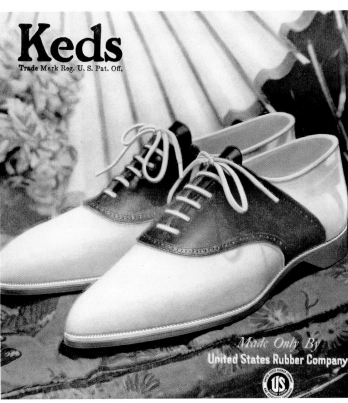

>> THE SADDLE SHOE

Originally developed as a golfing shoe in the 1910s, the saddle shoe became an icon of North American teenagers in the 1950s. The saddle look copied the effect of a short gaiter or spat being worn over a light-coloured sports shoe. They were popular with North American collegiate girls in the 1920s and 1930s, and by 1938 they were known as saddle oxfords and black-and-white or solid-coloured versions were also worn by boys. The *Boot and Shoe Recorder* reported on 4 June 1938 that their crepe soles were popular for dancing:

> 'How did this craze start? Campus fashion paved the way… turning a good classic pattern into a fast-selling volume type. On the cover of the June 7 issue of Life [1937]…appeared the photograph of a pair of dangling feet clad in socks and saddle oxfords. This picture became…famous almost overnight…. Its immediate effect on the shoe business was seen in one upstate New York department store where there was such a run on saddle oxfords that the demand could not be met.'

The article goes on to state that some factories turned to making just saddle oxfords to meet the demand, thereby reducing their production costs and passing the savings onto the consumer. In 1937 the price for a pair of saddle oxfords was between US $7 and $10, but by 1938 pairs were available for as little as US $1.98. Saddle shoes began to lose favour in the late 1950s with the introduction of suede hush puppies and penny loafers and began to disappear from catalogues after 1962.

Canadian or American red leather, vinyl and plexiglas Spring-o-lator mules, unlabelled, date-stamped 29 December 1955. These were modelled in a fashion show held in Vancouver, where they were reported in the newspaper as the first ever pair in the city.

>> THE SPRING-O-LATOR

The Spring-o-lator was a huge fashion hit in the late 1950s. Between the ball and heel of the insole was a bridge of elastic tape that stretched to secure the sole of the shoe to the foot by the tension of the elastic. American designer Beth Levine was shown the original drawings by the patent holder who had put the elastic tape in a low-heeled shoe, intending it for use as an orthopedic insole. Not seeing the potential in the original design, Beth asked to work with the idea, thinking it may be useful for a high-heeled mule. Calling their version the magnet sock, Herbert Levine shipped 36 pairs to each of three stores in Boston, Chicago and Los Angeles as a marketing test. Within days they had sold out. The Los Angeles store immediately re-ordered but cancelled the following day because other manufacturers were already producing knock-offs. The patent holder had ignored a verbal agreement with Herbert Levine for a six-month production exclusive in exchange for making the invention marketable. The patent holder registered the name Spring-o-lator and made the patent available for production by anyone willing to pay a royalty. By the fall of 1955 the style was available from numerous manufacturers.

American chequerboard brocade
Spring-o-lator mules, labelled 'Ferncraft
Exclusives – Made in Hollywood for
Iver Bros.', c. 1957–58.

American pink satin sling-back pumps with uppers extended under the sole. Trimmed with rhinestones, labelled 'Herbert Levine', c. 1954–56.

>> THE NARROWING HEEL

The round-toed high-heeled baby-doll pump was the dominant style of the early 1950s. The high heel visually lengthened the leg, accentuated narrow ankles and made calves shapelier, but designers were looking for ways to narrow the heel as much as possible. Credit has been given to Ferragamo and Roger Vivier for introducing the stiletto heel, but it was a French designer by the name of Charles Jordan (not to be confused with today's well-known Charles Jourdan) who first handcrafted thin heels of laminated wood as early as 1952. Their construction was too expensive to put into general production, but by 1954 heels were beginning to be made of plastic instead of wood and had a metal rod running the length of them for added strength. The plastic heels were then covered to match the upper. The steel reinforcing rod resembled the short-bladed stiletto weapon, which is how the heel came by its name.

This technological development meant that by 1955 heel widths were being pared down. The tallest stiletto heels, however, were generally about an inch shorter than the thicker high heels of the early 1950s; the thinner the heel, the more an illusion of height was created. By 1957 the stiletto was the most prolific heel style, even though manufacturers still made thicker heels until about 1961. Narrow heels created hundreds of pounds of pressure per square inch, pock-marking linoleum and wooden floors with every step. In 1959 stiletto-heeled visitors to the Louvre in Paris were required to use plastic heel caps to protect the antique floors.

English rhinestone-covered pumps, labelled 'Rayne', c. 1959–63.

American or French beige and brown pumps with faux-laced gypsy seam vamp, labelled 'Delman – Christian Dior – Paris', c. 1956–58.

French gold lamé brocade pump with curled tendril ornament by Roger Vivier, appeared in American *Vogue*, 1 March 1960.

Mexican tooled-leather sling-back pumps, labelled 'Entin's Shoes – hecho en Mexico', c. 1960–65.

>> WINKLE-PICKER TOES AND STILETTO HEELS

The heyday of the winkle-picker toe and stiletto-heeled shoe was from 1957 until 1963. The shape of the stiletto developed during its reign from a thick tapered style to a thinner and, after 1961, usually shorter heel. The heel was sometimes flared at the top lift, with the waist of the heel being no thicker than the steel reinforcing rod itself.

Some designers were showing pointed toes as early as 1953, but they were not put into general production. However, oval- and almond-shaped toes began appearing by 1955. In 1957 the stiletto heel was paired up with a sharp-pointed 'needle' toe, dubbed a winkle-picker in Britain after the tool used to extract snails from their shells. Small squared-toe tips also appeared in 1957 but did not gain popularity until 1962 and more so after 1964.

Aesthetically, the combination of the sharp-pointed toe and stiletto heel provided the perfect complement to the foot, ankle and calf, but from a medical viewpoint it was a terrible mix. Many women twisted their ankles on the metal spike heels, and the height of the heel and the short vamp with its pointed toe constricted the toes, causing bunions and hammer toes. These ailments would not have been so severe had women worn the style for only short periods of time, but many women wore winkle-pickers for all occasions, sometimes even while doing housework. In the early 1960s the stiletto heel was reduced in height and the forepart of the shoe was extended beyond the tip of the wearer's toes, alleviating many of the problems.

American red shantung-silk pumps with rhinestone-covered heels, labelled 'Delman – New York, London, Paris', c. 1957–58.

American blue shantung-silk pumps with black-rhinestone-decorated top line and back, labelled 'Delman – New York, Paris', c. 1959–62.

American pumps with uppers covered in guineafowl feathers, labelled 'Qualicraft', c. 1962–65.

Top: Italian-made for export winkle-picker pumps with stiletto heels, labelled 'Dolci's Princess – Made in Italy', c. 1961–64. Dolci's was a fashion shoe retailer founded in 1863 that had grown to over 200 outlets across Britain by 1963.

Italian black silk pumps with black-and-blue-beaded vamps, labelled 'Raphael Roma', c. 1960–63.

French silk pullovers designed by Roger Vivier for Christian Dior, dated 1961 and 1962. A pullover is the production term for a mock-up of a shoe upper.

Syrian square-toed pumps, labelled 'Baliorian – Alep', c.1962–64.

>> SHOE JEWELRY

Detachable buckles were a decorative and functional feature of eighteenth-century footwear. Non-functional buckles that could be clipped or sewn to shoes were popular in the early 1920s and were useful for decorating plain pumps. In the 1950s elaborately jewelled versions were revived.

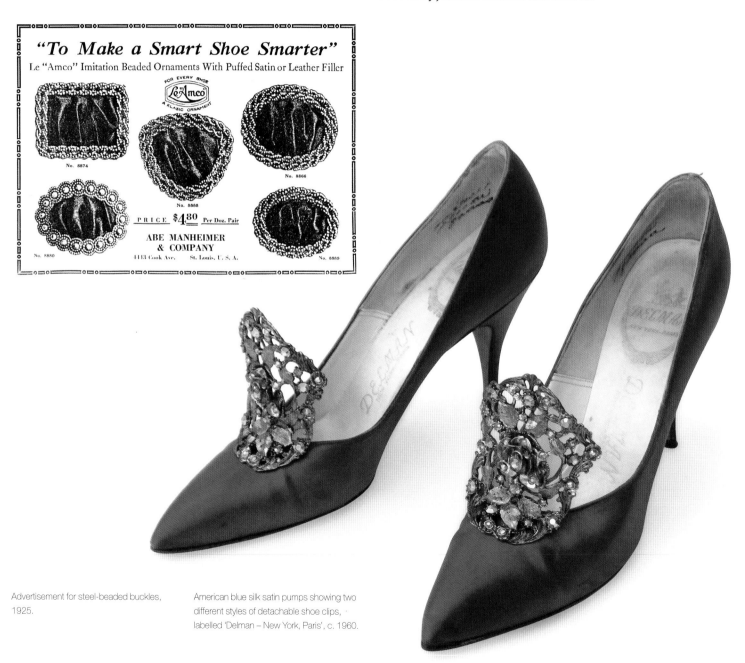

Advertisement for steel-beaded buckles, 1925.

American blue silk satin pumps showing two different styles of detachable shoe clips, labelled 'Delman – New York, Paris', c. 1960.

American or Italian black kid pumps with sole
extended and cantilevered supports without
heels, unlabelled, c. 1958–60.

>> FLOATING HEELS

The continuing search for novelty resulted in the creation of heel-
less high shoes in the late 1950s. Versions of cut-away wedge heels
date from as early as the 1940s, but it was only after an American
patent for metal cantilevered soles was granted in 1956 to Martin
Friedmann that the floating heel appeared. The cantilevered sole and
elevated mid-sole were cast from one piece of metal that was secure
enough to negate the need for a heel to support the wearer's weight.
A short-lived fad, the style lasted until about 1961.

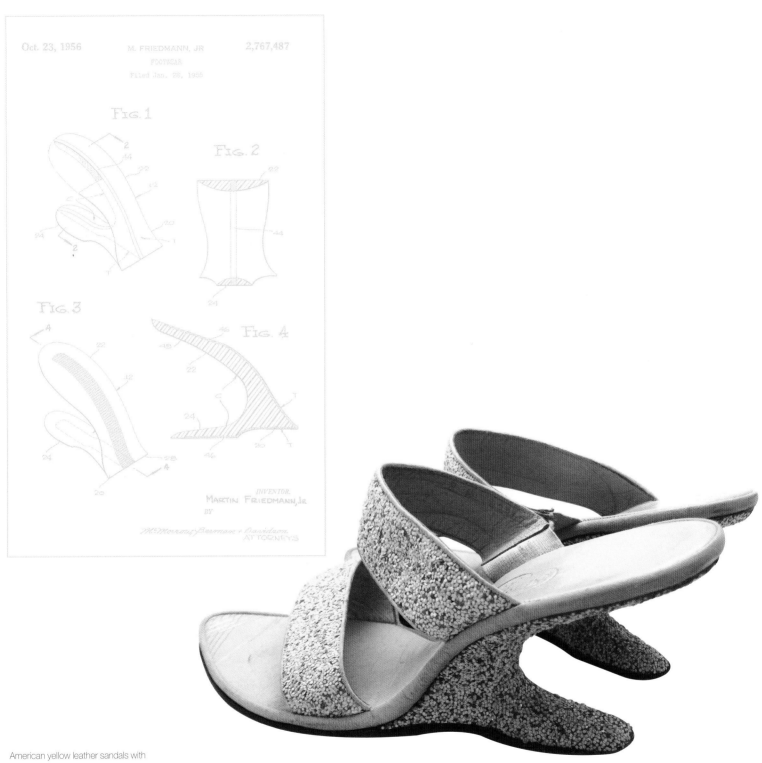

American yellow leather sandals with crushed beads applied to the straps and cantilevered wedge heels, labelled 'Mel Preston – Tip Toz – Simpson Gordon's of Charlotte', c. 1957–59. The schematic for patented heel support, 23 October 1956.

Oct. 23, 1956   M. FRIEDMANN, JR   2,767,487

FOOTWEAR

Filed Jan. 28, 1955

FIG. 1

FIG. 2

FIG. 3

FIG. 4

INVENTOR.

MARTIN FRIEDMANN, Jr

BY

McMorrow Berman + Davidson.

ATTORNEYS

?American green and black brocade pump with Louis heel, c. 1961–65.

Canadian advertisement for Louis-heeled pumps, Simpson Sears catalogue, autumn 1960.

>> CHANGING HEEL SHAPES

Alternatives to the stiletto heel included a revival of the Louis heel and low-stacked leather heels. Low-heeled shoes, usually made for casual wear, had been in constant production since the early 1940s, such as the ballet flats famously made by Capezio.

Although stiletto-heeled shoes were still being offered in department-store catalogues until 1967, the fashion for tall thin stiletto heels began to decline after 1963. The last variation on the stiletto heel was much shorter and straighter than it had been when introduced a decade earlier. The pointed toe also lost its sharp tip in the mid 1960s, with most toes becoming round or almond shaped.

Canadian advertisement from Simpson Sears catalogue, autumn 1961.

American purple leather and cream corduroy laced pumps with half-inch stacked-leather heel, labelled 'Pump Room Originals by Syd Shafron Ltd.', c. 1961–62.

Canadian black leather sling backs with black-and-white-printed pleated textile vamps, labelled 'La Boheme – by RaeSon', c. 1965–66. The printed textile on the vamps has been pleated to enhance the shoe's Op Art inspiration. RaeSon was a high-end shoe store in Vancouver that was established in 1897 and closed in the early 1990s. Shoes were manufactured for their store under their own label, so the manufacturer of this pair is unknown.

Indian-made for export black shantung-silk shoes with embroidered vamps, gold plastic soles and brass heels, labelled 'Taj of India – Berger's', c. 1962–66. Berger's was a high-end department store in Buffalo, New York.

Italian-made for export black suede sling-back pumps with short stiletto heels and rhinestone trim on the vamp, labelled 'Axels – Made in Italy', c. 1965–67.

American black lurex jersey cocktail boots
by David Evins, labelled 'Evins – made in
USA', c. 1960–64.

American winter boot advertisement,
autumn 1963.

>> THE RETURN OF THE BOOT

Manufacturers of practical rubber footwear experienced problems when stiletto heels were introduced in the late 1950s as the thin metal spikes poked through the heels of rubber and plastic galoshes and overshoes. To compensate, they made winter fashion boots with stiletto heels. Around this time several designers were playing with fashion boot designs, anticipating their imminent return. Pierre Cardin launched a low-heeled square-toed boot in his autumn 1961 collection, but the style did not meet with immediate success.

The boot came back into fashion with a vengeance in the late 1960s when it was paired with the miniskirt, which gave fashion a youthful elan. Several designers, most notably Pierre Cardin and Beth Levine, had championed the return of the boot, but Parisian couturier André Courrèges should take credit for making it work with the space-age Mod fashions of the day. Boots came back on the fashion scene at the same time as the various go-go dances became popular and were soon known as go-go boots.

Beth Levine should be recognized for taking the boot to new limits in 1967 with her stocking and stretch boot styles for which she received a Coty Award that same year.

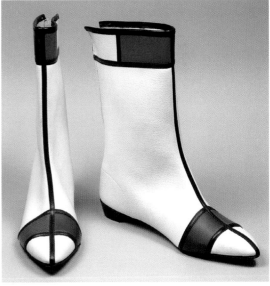

French advertisement from Pierre Cardin showing low-heeled square-toed boots, autumn 1961.

American red, white and blue vinyl boots, probably inspired by Yves Saint Laurent's autumn 1965 Mondrian-influenced dress, c. 1965–66.

American nylon stocking boots with plexiglas heels by Herbert Levine, 1967.

American stretch-vinyl animal-print boots, labelled 'Sbicca Californians', c. 1967–69.

French fashion illustration from Pierre Cardin showing thigh-high boots, autumn 1968.

Italian-made for export, brown crocodile pumps with decorative buckled straps at throat, labelled 'Made in Italy expressly for Davids, Toronto, Ontario, Canada', c. 1965–68.

American brown patent-leather pumps with large decorative buttons on the vamps and brass-studded heels, labelled 'Herbert Levine', c. 1966–69.

>> MODERN YOUTHFULNESS

As is often the case with fashion, new styles are created from a reaction to the previous mode. The winkle-picker stiletto-heeled pump of the early 1960s was conspicuously out of style amid the square-toed, low-heeled or chunky-heeled shoes of the late 1960s and early 1970s. This new fashion was designed for the first wave of the baby-boom generation and complemented long, youthful legs in above-the-knee miniskirts. Many older women were uncomfortable baring their knees and no longer followed the cutting edge of fashion. Parisian couturier Balenciaga retired in 1967, declaring that fashion was over, probably recognizing that his clientele were not keen on the new mode. The era of mature womanly glamour had been replaced by girlish youthfulness. Low-heeled pumps, although comfortable for a wide age range of women, had been the fashion of little girls in previous decades but were now a mainstream style.

The age of plastics was peaking in the late 1960s. Polyester and nylon were used in the footwear industry, but wet-look vinyl and Corfam were the new wonder materials. Corfam was developed by DuPont in 1963 and was supposed to have all the qualities of leather but without the price tag. However, the novelty of synthetic materials was wearing thin on a growing number of consumers who craved a pre-space-age world of natural materials and back-to-nature aesthetics. Corfam did not prove profitable for DuPont, who in 1969 sold the rights to a Japanese company that refined the material into a new product that appeared in the 1970s, known as ultrasuede.

Italian-made for export, brown suede
open-sided shoes with V-shaped straps,
labelled 'Creazioni Molaschi – Calzaturificio
di Varese – Made in Italy', c. 1968–71.

Forget-you-nots by Katja of Sweden at Saks Fifth Ave.

Flower power is here, gigantic in prints, romantic in hair, startling in cosmetics . . . but the absolute wildest look afoot. A totally unexpected shoe view from Katja of Sweden. And wilt these flowers won't. The colors will stay bright for you; the shoes won't sag or stiffen. This is shining CORFAM*, the shoe upper material from Du Pont that stays as supple as the day you first slip it on. Unaffected by temperature, CORFAM resists cracking. And breathes to aid comfort.

Feel free . . . you're in Corfam*

American advertisement for shoes made
from Corfam, 1968.

French fashion illustration from Courrèges, showing flat-soled shoes with large bells decorating the vamps, spring 1969.

?Italian pink and gold kid leather pumps, labelled 'Philippe le Bottier', c. 1969–71.

Canadian handmade leather sandals with instep strap decorated with brass rings, purchased from a street vendor in Vancouver in about 1971.

American or Canadian cork-soled leather sandals with square rings over instep, unlabelled, c. 1970–72.

>> HIPPY CHIC

Political, cultural and social upheaval in the mid 1960s resulted in a huge mass of American youth creating a movement that spurned established ideals and traditional fashions. They collectively became known as 'hippies' and were largely identifiable by their adoption of jeans, T-shirts and sandals. The more creative hippies sought style inspiration from ethnic cultures and historic eras. Vintage clothing and footwear were integrated with exotic textiles and humble peasant sandals for an eclectic bohemian look. Handmade clothing was preferred over ready-mades and modern materials were cast aside in favour of natural fibres and leathers. The fashion world was in as much turmoil as the real world.

At first, the American hippy movement spread ideologically and then culturally to Europe. By the early 1970s its influence was affecting mainstream fashions. Manufacturers borrowed elements from ethnic and vintage styles and incorporated them into commercially produced clothing and footwear. Leading shoe and fashion designers abandoned space-age Mod styles in favour of bohemian and historically influenced modes, and miniskirts and go-go boots were replaced by peasant dresses and granny boots.

Greek-made for export, purple suede boots with embroidered shafts, labelled 'Neil's – Made in Greece – From the Greek workshops of Jerry Edouard', c. 1970–72.

>> FOOT HEALTH

The hippies of the late 1960s promoted comfort and naturalism, reinvigorating the foot-health movement that had begun in the late nineteenth century. Negative-heeled shoes, in which the heel sat lower than the ball of the foot, were first sold in New York on 1 April 1970. This happened to coincide with the first annual Earth Day, inspiring the shoe's name. Danish yoga enthusiast Anne Kalso based her negative-heel design on a yoga pose and first started selling her Earth shoes in Copenhagen in 1968. By 1973 the Canadian company Roots was selling their version of the negative heel. Kalso ran into distribution problems and was unable to complete orders quickly enough, resulting in legal suits. Ultimately it was Roots that became the more successful of the two manufacturers. Ironically, the negative heel proved to be the cause of many foot and leg problems and the style lost favour in the 1980s.

Birkenstock sandals, with their contoured foot beds, were first imported into the United States in 1967, a few years after they debuted in Germany. A spin-off of the contoured foot bed was the 'exercise' clog in which the toes had to grip the clog, supposedly improving muscle tone and circulation. Although Birkenstocks are recognized by most consumers as being plain ugly, they show no sign of falling from favour. Sales for the original contoured foot bed sandals were higher in the 1990s than in the 1970s, inspiring trainer and sport-sandal manufacturers to use contoured foot beds.

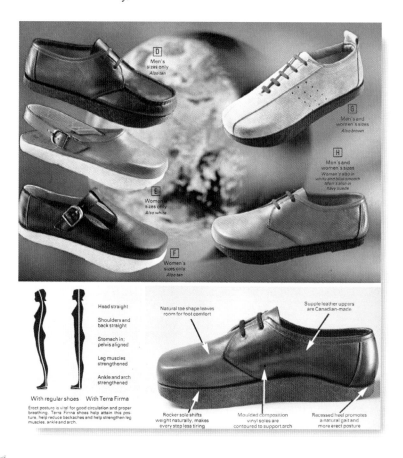

Canadian advertisement for negative-heeled shoes, Eaton's catalogue, spring 1975.

>> PLATFORM EMPOWERMENT

Some designers were showing a few tall platform styles as early as the mid 1960s, but consumers did not respond and the styles were not put into production. In 1969 small platforms began to appear on some shoes and were well received, opening the door to increasingly higher platform shoes in the early 1970s that drew inspiration from their 1940s ancestors. High heels, although still chunky, were reintroduced on shoes without platform soles by 1970 and were preferred by more mature women who would not wear platform shoes again.

The fashion market was fractured in the early 1970s and different fashions were aimed at different age groups. The majority of designers and manufacturers, however, targeted the baby-boom demographic of women under the age of thirty. In 1974 platforms were at their peak and were available at heights of five and even six inches. The ultimate novelty was a shoe with a detachable acrylic platform sole that was made famous when John Fuqua, an American football running back, wore a pair with live goldfish in the heel. These were available under the El Padrino label and were imported by the same company that made 'crayons', with their colourful acrylic soles, popular in the early 1980s. Platform shoes added height to women, making their legs appear longer and psychologically empowering them as they were raised up to men's eye level.

Italian or American multicoloured leather and vinyl platform oxford, c. 1972–74.

English or American illustration of a woman
with platform shoes, c. 1972.

Italian red and black PVC-coated leather platform sandals, labelled 'Creazioni Bologna – Made in Italy', c. 1972–75.

Italian red snakeskin and wood clog platform shoes, c. 1973–76.

German snakeskin open-toed shoes,
labelled 'Leiner, Junge Mode, Echt Leder',
c. 1972–76.

American vinyl and snakeskin open-toed
sling back, labelled 'Herbert Levine',
c. 1971–73.

>> CLOGS AND MULES

After 1975 the platform began shrinking in height as thinner, taller heels returned to fashion. A small platform had the benefit of creating a seemingly high-heeled shoe or boot that was in reality not that tall once the height of the platform was subtracted. Wedge heels, too, were popular in the late 1970s, giving the same illusion of height but in a style that offered a sturdy footing.

Mules and clogs also returned to fashion in the mid 1970s, usually in natural wood and earthy leather colours. Clogs had been a working-class shoe until the early twentieth century, never intruding in the realm of fashion. When Italian clogs were sold under the brand name of 'Candies' in the United States in 1978, they became one of the hottest-selling styles of the century and were much copied. Mules were saved from the brink of obscurity when high-heeled versions, often with clog bottom units, were revived in the mid 1970s.

A novelty that came late in the platform shoe era was the clog-skate. Pop Wheels were the most popular brand and were intended

?Italian wood clog sandals with leather straps, unlabelled, c. 1976–79.

to cash in on the roller-skating trend of the late 1970s. First marketed in 1978, Pop Wheels were at the height of their popularity in the spring of 1979 when they were being sold at Macy's in New York for US $38 a pair. The fad did not last long and by the end of 1979 they were no longer selling. This was due to a waning interest in platform soles and roller skating and also because of problems with the wheels, which tended to collapse suddenly while in use. The platform died out with disco and the decade, and by 1980 platforms were unavailable in any store or catalogue.

Italian-made for export, brown leather mules with stacked-leather heels, labelled 'Nickels – Made in Italy', c. 1978–80.

Canadian advertisement for macramé-strap wedge sandals, Eaton's catalogue, spring 1978.

American wood and leather clog-skates, labelled 'Pop Wheels', c. 1978–79.

French or Italian snakeskin sandals, labelled 'Andrea Pfister Paris – Made in Italy', c. 1975–78.

>> THE SEXED-UP STILETTO

The sandal moved beyond its hippy reinvention in the late 1960s and by 1975 was being made in sexy high-heeled styles using metallic leathers and exotic skins. Snake was the 'in' leather of the 1970s and was featured in every shoe designer's collection and at every price point. As the baby boomers hit thirty, their tastes turned toward more mature, provocative styles and the platform was cast aside.

Returning to fashion in the late 1970s, the stiletto regularly soared to heights of four inches. Some women objected to the styles, calling them misogynistic implements of torture, but fashion is driven by what consumers buy and high-heeled shoes sold well. Shoes were being consciously designed to create sex appeal and the stiletto heel achieved that goal. For those who chose not to follow the fashion for high heels, there was a variety of styles available from low-heeled shoes to trainers, which were pulling in good sales by 1980.

Italian-made for Canadian export, red
patent-leather sandals, labelled 'Brown's,
Italy', c. 1977–80.

Italian black patent-leather D'Orsay pumps with high instep strap, labelled 'Casadei – Made in Italy – Tomaia Pelle', c. 1978–81.

French red and gold kid and snakeskin sandals, labelled 'Charles Jourdan Paris – Made in France', c. 1982.

French garnet-red leather pumps with decorative rosettes, labelled 'Charles Jourdan Paris – Made in France', c. 1979–82.

>> BOOT INSPIRATION

Boots were staples in women's wardrobes throughout the 1970s and 1980s. Historical and exotic sources were referenced, from riding, boxing and pirate boots to Cossack, granny and cowboy styles. Low-heeled boots hit the market in the 1980s providing yet more choice for fashionable women. There was an unending array of heel heights, styles, colours and designer brands offered every season. Before the 1980s only a few fashion clothing designers carried footwear, but by the mid 1980s it was common to find footwear in many collections. Consumerism was in: more was better and greed was good.

Women wore cowboy boots before the 1970s but they were usually only found on cowgirls at rodeos or wealthy wannabe cowgals on holiday at dude ranches. The original cowboy boots of the late nineteenth century were based on American Civil War cavalry boots. Fancy stitching and stamped leatherwork appeared on some styles by c. 1900, influenced by the Spanish colonial tradition of Mexican boot making. It was really the Tom Mix silent cowboy movies of the early twentieth century that made the American cowboy a cultural icon and developed the cowboy style.

The use of elaborate stitching increased and coloured leather inlays featured on cowboy boots in the 1920s and 1930s. By the 1950s ornately designed cowboy boots were made by a number of bootmakers specializing in custom-crafted styles for local ranch hands and tourists. Cowboy boots became part of mainstream fashion in the late 1970s and remained in vogue until the early 1990s, during which period the style was greatly modified to appeal to a broader audience, including Europeans who were unfamiliar with the tradition of cowboy boots as a fashion statement.

Opposite, left: Italian leather boots with riding-inspired spur straps, labelled 'Zemar – Made in Italy', c. 1979–81.

Opposite, right: Italian-made for export, olive suede boots with gold kid trim, labelled 'Brown's Italy', c. 1979–84.

Top: Italian brown leather ankle boots with back straps, labelled 'Varese Shoes – Made in Italy', c. 1978–81.

French garnet leather ankle boots with fur trim, labelled 'Charles Jourdan Paris – Made in France', c. 1979–81.

Italian deep-lavender-coloured kid boots
with woven kid inserts, labelled 'Valentina',
c. 1983–86.

Opposite, right: Italian black suede boots
with gold-and-silver-painted design,
labelled 'Arlene La Marca – Handmade
in Italy', c. 1984–87.

American white vinyl and leather cowboy-
style ankle boots, labelled 'Nine West',
c. 1988–91.

Brazilian-made for export, gold-flecked clear-plastic pumps, labelled 'Thierry Mugler – Grendene', c. 1985.

>> STYLE INJECTION

Injection moulding is the most recent construction method to change the shoemaking industry. Developed in the 1960s, the first entirely moulded plastic shoes became known as jellies and were marketed as inexpensive work shoes in the Third World, not as a fashion style. The leading manufacturer of the shoes, Grendene, is located in Farroupilha, Brazil, where they continue to make the shoe entirely by machine, keeping production costs low. The shoes caught on in Europe first in the mid 1980s and returned as summer favourites in 1995 and again in 2004.

>> STREET FASHION

Subcultures have been selecting their own clothing and footwear styles outside the realm of mainstream fashion for centuries. In the twentieth century Teddy boys and beatniks, zoot suiters and bikers adopted marginal, exaggerated or affected styles of dress and footwear to identify themselves as belonging to a group of like-minded individuals. The two largest subcultures, hippies, who came out of the United States in the late 1960s, and punks, who came out of Britain in the late 1970s, were so pervasive that their clothing influenced mainstream fashion. Fashionistas called it street style as fashion seemed to work in reverse now, taking inspiration from what was being worn and tweaking it for high fashion, rather than styles filtering down from haute couture.

Canadian black leather colonial pumps, labelled 'John Fluevog', c. 1984–86.

Canadian photograph of punks, Toronto, c. 1985. Most punks wore military surplus and Doc Marten boots, but some women punks also wore vintage stiletto-heeled shoes in the early 1980s.

Canadian black suede boots with skull buckles marked 'Canada' on reverse, unlabelled, c. 1990.

>> VARIATIONS ON THE STILETTO

The revival of stiletto-heeled shoes in the late 1970s continued successfully throughout the 1980s. The women's liberation movement had originally identified stiletto heels as debilitating and scorned their return, but by now there was a feeling of empowerment associated with the stiletto. Women at work were dressed like men from the waist up, in tailored shirts and broad-shouldered jackets, but as women from the waist down, in skirts, ranging from mid-thigh to mid-shin in length, and high-heeled shoes. The message was that the 1980s 'superwoman' had it all: she could run a corporation while retaining her femininity and she was empowered by her mixed-message outfits of masculine and feminine attire. A woman who dressed for success, however, had to be careful about the shoes she chose: a shoe too colourful with too high a heel might suggest she was not serious about her career. Power-dressers required the correct balance in their outfits, and retailers filled that need with fashionable but toned-down styles with almond toes and medium-height heels that were not too thin and sexy. The triangular-shaped stiletto heel originated in Europe in 1979 and was much copied in the mid 1980s, giving a new twist to the classic heel shape. Most American manufacturers were now involved only in the production of casual styles, with the bulk of high-fashion footwear being designed in France or Italy and made in Italy, Spain or Brazil. Cheaper styles coming from China tended to use all man-made materials in their production and were available at a much cheaper price. Chinese-made shoes improved in quality during the 1990s and began to displace the manufacture of high-fashion footwear in Europe.

French leather pump with metallic-finish heel, by Maud Frizon, c. 1982–86.

Right: French black kid and purple suede
pumps, labelled 'Charles Jourdan, Paris',
c. 1984–87.

Italian black textile sling-back pump with
beaded vamp, labelled 'Andrea Pfister,
Made in Italy', c. 1985–90.

Chinese printed-textile pumps with roses on
toes, labelled 'J. Renee Couture Collection,
Made in Hong Kong', c. 1982–87.

English midnight-blue leather pumps with patchwork inlaid pink and red leather vamps by Rayne, c. 1987–89.

Spanish-made suede patchwork pumps with V-shaped cut-out on heel, labelled 'Sacha London – Made in Spain', c. 1987–92. The Memphis postmodern movement of the mid-to-late 1980s, known for its angular modernism, influenced the design of these shoes.

Chinese-made for export, black vinyl stiletto pump with bow on back seam, labelled 'Agnew – Made in Taiwan', c. 1989–92.

Chinese-made for export, red vinyl and brass stiletto pump with cross-over instep straps, labelled 'Cabaret – Made in China', c. 1990–95.

>> LATE-CENTURY REVIVALISM

The Louis heel reappeared in the late 1980s and was a popular alternative to stiletto heels in the early 1990s. Some versions looked like near identical copies of post-World War I styles, while others exaggerated the curves for a more modern cartoonish look. For a brief moment in the mid 1990s fashion writers and stylists referred to stiletto heels as passé. Stores temporarily dropped them in favour of platform soles and low chunky-heeled styles that looked similar to those from the late 1960s. However, consumer demand would not let high-heeled shoes die and they came back a couple of seasons later, higher and thinner than ever.

American black kid and elastic pumps
by Stuart Weitzman, c. 1992–95.

Chinese black suede platform pumps with
exaggerated Louis heels, labelled 'Fantasy',
c. 1993–95.

Italian-made chunky-heeled 1960s-style pumps, labelled 'Calvin Klein – Made in Italy', c. 1996–98.

Italian-made embroidered-net Louis-heeled pump by Todd Oldham, c. 1992.

English black leather platform boots, labelled
'Magic Shoes – London', c. mid 1990s.

>> THE PLATFORM…AGAIN

Several designers showed platforms in the 1980s but over-exposure in the 1970s prevented the style from enjoying a popular comeback so soon. By the 1990s, however, enough time had passed and trainers and casual shoes were getting thicker rubber-tread soles, which prepared consumers for the return of platform soles. Platforms inundated stores in the mid 1990s, many of the styles heavily inspired by their 1970s ancestors. The most extreme versions appeared on the feet of 'club kids', fetishists and goths. As had been the case in the 1970s, older women tended not to wear platform shoes, letting their offspring take up the style while they continued to seek out Jimmy Choo and Manolo Blahník stiletto-heeled pumps and sandals.

Italian black carved-wood clog-sandal with aurora-borealis-finish printed-vinyl upper, unlabelled, c. mid-to-late 1990s.

Spanish-made for export, black leather platform shoes, labelled 'Made in Spain', mid 1990s.

?Chinese aurora-borealis-finish plexiglas
platform shoes with vinyl straps,
labelled 'Wild Pair', c. mid 1990s.

French platform pump with ankle strap, inspired by Manchurian Chinese shoe, by Jean Paul Gaultier, c. mid 1990s.

Chinese-made for export, rubber and cotton
open-toe sling-back platforms, labelled
'Made in Taiwan', c. 1973–75.

>> RUNNING OUT ON FASHION

From its 1870s origins, the rubber-soled sports-shoe market grew and by 1960 a pair could be found in every fashionable wardrobe. In the early 1970s branding was critical and Adidas and Nike led the pack. The 1980s saw many competing manufacturers use such gimmicks as gel pads, flashing lights and air pumps in an attempt to lead the field. Many women in the 1980s wore trainers most of the time, often with flashes of pink or purple to distinguish them from male versions. An unfortunate fad in the late 1980s was for women to wear their trainers to work, changing into shoes at the office. The practical nature of trainers did not make them high-fashion accessories but the high-fashion pumps (or court shoes) of the 1980s were not practical for commuters. The trainer had become indispensable and was now seen on the street more than any other kind of shoe. Expensive celebrity endorsements and costly advertising made them elitist objects of desire and increasingly pricey.

The popularity of trainers began to slow in the early 1990s. Less urban looking leather and suede rubber-soled shoes, known in the business as the 'brown shoe' market, gained favour, and when it was revealed that most trainers were made off-shore for pennies per pair in South East Asian sweatshops, some consumers resented the artificial profit margins and manufacturing practices. Sports-shoe manufacturers scrambled to diversify and readdress their waning market. However, the dominance of the sports-shoe market in the late twentieth century made the trainer an icon of the period.

Chinese-made for export, high-heeled rubber and cotton laced ankle boot, labelled 'Anne Michelle – China', c. 2004.

Chinese-made high-heeled rubber and cotton laced shoes, labelled 'Norma Kamali', c. 1984.

SHOEMAKERS, DESIGNERS AND MANUFACTURERS

American illustration of a woman trying on new shoes, from *Boot and Shoe Recorder*, 1922.

Shoemaking developed into a profession in ancient Rome when artisans congregated near city marketplaces. Apollo was the god of Roman shoemakers and images of him graced the entrance to streets reserved for members of the profession. Similarly, images of the patron saints of shoemakers, Crispin and Crispinian, adorned the churches and guildhalls of medieval Europe. Crispin and Crispinian have since lost their sainthood but their feast day, 25 October, remains a holiday for the shoe industry in France.

Like many craftsmen, shoemakers created guilds from the twelfth century, which acted as professional associations, unions and regulatory boards, protecting shoemakers, their suppliers and their clients from unfair business practices and pricing while ensuring quality products. Shoemakers learned their trade over a period of years through unpaid apprenticeship to master shoemakers. They were licensed by guilds only once they had mastered the skills of construction and finishing. This tradition remained unchanged for centuries and many of today's great Italian shoemakers began their careers as apprentices. Guilds were not open to cobblers, who were shoe repairers. Shoemakers were capable of doing repairs but it was considered beneath their abilities. From the twelfth century, English quality shoemakers were known as cordwainers, an anglicization of the French word *cordonnier*.

The European tradition of apprenticeship created masters of shoe manufacturing techniques, however, the shoemaker was not necessarily a designer. Prior to the nineteenth century, developments in fashionable style came from changes in construction techniques, invention through necessity, regional influence and clients' suggestions. Style was established by what was already being worn. Shoemakers with design talent, for example, might be able to finesse the gentle curve of a heel, but who these shoemakers were is mostly lost to history.

In the Middle Ages in Europe shoemakers began to make unordered pairs of shoes during slow work periods, creating off-the-rack products. Shoe sizing began in England in the late seventeenth century and was made possible by the adoption of standard measurements in 1324 under King Edward II. Consistent in size, three barleycorns laid end-to-end equalled one inch. The other standard measurement was the hand, used since Biblical times and still employed today for measuring the height of horses. A hand equals 4.33 inches or thirteen barleycorns. By 1700 standardized shoe sizes deemed children's shoes to be less than the measurement of a hand and adult sizes over a hand. It therefore became profitable for shoemakers to make footwear for speculative sale when not preparing clients' orders. Existing shoes dating from as early as the 1750s often have sizes written on linings, suggesting that they were pre-made. Paper labels giving shoemaker's names and addresses also began to appear inside shoes in the late eighteenth century to encourage repeat business. Footwear had become the first ready-to-wear fitted clothing article. By the end of the eighteenth century ready-to-wear shoe stores had appeared. One of the first, Edward Hogg, advertised his 'Ladies' Cheap Shoes Warehouse' on Jermyn Street in London. Similar shops popped up in American cities such as Boston. While a precedent had been set, there were not many products to fill this kind of retailing. According to a London advertisement in 1764 a pair of plain leather bespoke shoes cost 5 shillings, the approximate equivalent of £95 or US $170 today. An invoice for a pair of bespoke shoes for the Duke of Hamilton in 1673 (presumably of high quality) for 2 pounds 14 shillings is approximately £267 or US $481 today. These are comparable prices for leather shoes today, but there were no chain stores selling cheap imported shoes then and purchases could rarely be had on long-term credit.

The system changed in the nineteenth century with the advent of American mass-production. America had a great need for footwear but lacked trained shoemakers. To supply quantities of footwear at reasonable cost, an early form of a production line grew up in and around Lynn, Massachusetts. Individual labourers did piecework, meaning that several labourers, each specializing in one area, made one shoe. Parisian shoemakers also used this system in the early nineteenth century for the production of women's heel-less turn-shoe construction sandal-slippers. Exported all over the world, these shoes were profitable because production costs were low.

Numerous patented inventions in the middle of the nineteenth century, many of them American, resulted in the emergence of the successful American shoe industry. European shoemakers failed to adapt to mechanization as there was little worry about American imports usurping European trade. Early American shoes were generally not as well finished, consisted of cruder materials and were more expensive due to importation costs. By the 1880s, however, American factory-made Goodyear-welt-constructed shoes and machine-made and embellished fancy turn shoes were putting European shoemakers out of business. American manufacturers were exporting products at competitive prices, virtually eliminating the handmade tradition of European footwear. German, French and English manufacturers tried to adapt but the machine patents were mostly held in the United States and had to be purchased and shipped from there and royalties paid for their use.

Some European shoemakers realized that cost and quality were only two elements of what consumers wanted. Design quickly became the touchstone for elite elegance. Patrons still went to Joseph Box in London or François Pinet in Paris to have shoes made to complement their couture gowns. In these cases, uniqueness and design were of primary importance and not cost or durability. Shoemakers like Cedric, Alfred Argence and Greco made names for themselves as suppliers of exceptional footwear.

The American trade journal *Boot and Shoe Recorder* reported on 27 January 1923: 'Wannamaker's and Saks & Co. have been particularly strong in presenting models adapted from those of Perugia and Hellstern....It does indicate that style is becoming more pronounced in the footwear field than it has been heretofore.' With the rising hem lines of the early 1920s, the foot, ankle and lower leg became visible and the shoe was now an integral part of the ensemble. The *Boot and Shoe Recorder* noticed on the opening of a shoe store in New York in March 1921: 'Particular attention is called to the mirrors....These are placed on an angle so that the customer gets a view not only of the shoe but of her costume as well.'

Haute couturiers like Elsa Schiaparelli and Chanel offered accessories and footwear in their prêt-à-porter boutiques in the 1930s. Perugia started as a bespoke shoemaker for Paul Poiret's clients in 1920, but by the late 1930s was collaborating with many couturiers and manufacturers to create footwear collections. Most shoe designers worked anonymously. Even today a shoe designer must commission a manufacturer and negotiate a favourable contract or quietly accept that his or her designs will go under another label. In the 1940s David Evins was the first shoe designer to see his name appear in shoes alongside the American manufacturer I. Miller. In 1955 Roger Vivier was the first shoe designer to produce collections for a couturier, Christian Dior, in which his name sat next to the couturier's.

Until the end of the 1960s most clothing designers never worked with shoe designers. Couturiers required models to supply their own footwear for photo shoots and fashion shows. Since the 1970s the shoe has gained more prominence and many clothing designers now work with shoe designers to produce footwear under the clothing designer's own label. Whether or not the clothing designer actually designs the footwear is often unknown.

The divisions between shoemaker, designer and manufacturer are sometimes difficult to assess, especially today. There are designers who have little understanding of construction and must work with technical support. There are technical masters who create beautiful shoes but do not attempt to change classic design. There are manufacturers who rely on in-house and freelance designers while still receiving the design credit for products they simply cut and sew together. Many shoe retailers and suppliers are really distributors who import footwear from manufacturers in Brazil or Spain. Some manufacturers do not have a designer on staff and do not even hire outside designers. Instead, they build their own imitations of fashion footwear for general production by taking elements of established styles and having computer operators piece together designs that are made with almost no human contact.

Between 1920 and 1970 shoe fashions changed at such a rapid pace that stores sometimes could not sell their stock before the next style was introduced. Over this period almost every conceivable style was made fashionable and then discarded in favour of the next trend: from spiked stiletto heels to negative heels and from platform soles to ballerina flats. Shoe designers since the 1970s have revived past styles, reinventing them for a modern audience. Designers are always looking for innovative ideas, but there are only so many directions in which they can go before every conceivable type of heel, toe and embellishment has been explored.

The following list is far from a complete representation of all the designers, shoemakers, manufacturers and influential retailers who have shaped footwear history. It would take several lifetimes to research a complete history, culminating in encyclopedic results. Even the corporate histories of well-known American companies, such as A.E. Little, are not currently published. But out there in some archive lurks the raw research material of these companies and all the other companies and craftsmen who will someday become footnotes of shoe history.

Advertisement for Andrew Geller, autumn 1951.

Bandolino pink leather pumps with suede roses and net inserts on vamp, c. late 1980s.

Metallic brocaded silk tango shoe by Bally, 1923.

□ = **picture reference**

Adidas Manufacturer, active 1924–present
The German Dassler brothers Adi (Adolf, born 1900) and Rudi (Rudolf, born 1902), produced rubber-soled canvas shoes scavenged from tyres and rucksacks in the late 1910s. In 1924 they set up business together in Herzogenaurach as *Gebrüder Dassler Schuhfabrik* (Dassler Brothers Shoe Factory). The company distinguished itself by designing specific shoes for different sports, showcasing its early products on the German athletes at the 1928 Amsterdam Olympic Games. In 1936, American Jesse Owens wore a pair of double-striped 'Dassler's' when he sprinted his way to four gold medals in the Berlin Olympics. During World War II, the Dassler factory was commandeered by the Nazis to make boots for soldiers, and Adi remained running the factory while Rudi was called to service. A rift between the brothers occurred after the war, most likely sparked by Rudi's resentment toward Adi for not having negotiated his release from a prisoner of war camp. Adi had been on good terms with the American occupying army, even making shoes for an American soldier who competed in the 1948 Olympics in London. The brothers parted ways in 1948, and Rudi set up his own factory across the River Aurach where he made sports shoes under the brand name Puma, using a cat's paw in motion as his trademark. Meanwhile, Adi added a third stripe to the Dassler's trademark and renamed his shoes Adidas. Adi's son, Horst, joined the business and came up with the idea of promoting the shoes directly to athletes at the 1956 Melbourne Olympics. This marketing ploy worked. By 1972 Adidas was an official supplier to the Munich Olympics and the company dominated the world's athletic shoe market. Adidas was the first company to place logos on sports bags and clothing. Adi Dassler died in 1978 at a time when the market was flooded with competitors cutting into Adidas sales. Nike and Reebok captured the North American market in the 1980s. The company was sold in 1989 and production moved to South East Asia in 1993. It has been struggling to maintain a 20% share of the market ever since.

□ **Andrew Geller** Manufacturer, Retailer, active c. 1919–c. 1989
An American retailer before World War I, Andrew Geller added a wholesale line of women's shoes in around 1919. The family-operated business grew over the years picking up fashion footwear lines along the way, most notably **Julianelli** and Gamin. The company was liquidated in the late 1980s.

□ **Angiolini, Enzo** (1942–93), Designer, active 1978–93
Recruited in 1978 by Marx & Newman, a division of US Shoe Corp, Italian-born Angiolini was the exclusive designer for Bandolino. His designs increased sales tenfold and a later line, eponymously named Enzo, was added to his portfolio. He is credited with increasing the commercial value of both brands by facilitating a smooth transition from Italian to Brazilian manufacturing. He also shared techniques and workmanship between Italy and Brazil at a time when Brazil was known for inexpensive but second-rate production. Bandolino and Enzo brands were top sellers on most retailers' lists during the 1980s.

Argence, Alfred Designer, active 1900–c. 1983
Opening a shop in Paris at 89 rue du Faubourg Saint-Honoré in 1900, Alfred Argence was a member of the Syndicat des Bottiers de Paris, an early group of elite shoemakers. The Parisian actress Sarah Bernhardt was among his exclusive clientele. In later years, Alfred's son, Alfred Victor, took over the shop, which had moved to rue des Pyramides. The firm continued to garner awards and maintain an elegant clientele throughout the 1940s. Business gradually declined after World War II and Argence closed during the recession in the early 1980s.

Atwood, Brian (1967–), Designer, active 1996–present
Atwood was born in Chicago in 1967 and graduated from the Fashion Institute of Technology in New York in 1991 before becoming a male model. In 1996 he started working at Versace in the diffusion Versus line. He launched his own line of shoes in 2001.

Azagury, Joseph Designer, active 1990–present
Born in the early 1960s in Morocco, Azagury moved to London as a young man and trained at Cordwainers College. He learned the footwear trade while selling shoes in the Rayne department at Harrods. Financed by his brother, he produced a line of shoes that won 20,000 orders and facilitated the opening of his first store in London in 1990.

Bally Manufacturer, active c. 1851–present

Carl Franz Bally, the son of a silk-ribbon weaver, was born in Schönenwerd, Switzerland in 1821. He founded the Bally Company in 1851 and manufactured and supplied ribbons and sundries, including the elastic webbing used by shoemakers. The exact date the company began making shoes varies according to different corporate histories, but it is often reported that while on a visit to Paris in the 1890s Carl bought an entire stock of shoes with the intention of mass-producing high-quality copies. He died in 1898 after Bally had begun producing footwear. His son continued to develop the business as a quality manufacturer of fine shoes. Unlike many companies, Bally managed not only to survive the Great Depression and the material shortages caused by World War II but also to grow and prosper. Bally shoes were successfully exported around the world from the 1920s to the 1960s, with exports accelerating during the 1970s and reaching a pinnacle in the mid 1980s. Sales began to falter in the 1990s when competing brands took a larger share of the market, and Bally was sold to an American investment firm in 1999. The company has been reorganized with a view to taking its former position as lead manufacturer in the luxury footwear market.

Bass Manufacturer, active 1876–present

Founded in Maine, US in 1876 by the tanner George Henry Bass, the company made oiled-leather hunting boots and camp moccasins. In 1936 it produced a slip-on moccasin with a hard sole and instep strap from a Norwegian prototype, calling the brand 'Weejun', short for Norwegian. In 1960 *The Daily Tar Heel*, the student newspaper of the University of North Carolina at Chapel Hill, ran the headline: 'What are Bass Weejuns? – The Thing on the feet of those who are with it'. Sales rocketed.

Bata Manufacturer, Retailer, active 1894–present

Founded in Zlin in the present-day Czech Republic by Tomas Bata, the Bata Shoe Company used American-style factory-line manufacturing methods to quickly became the largest shoe manufacturer in Europe. After World War II, Bata's son, also named Tomas, rebuilt the company's headquarters in London and then in 1964 moved operations to Canada. Between 1950 and 1980, the company expanded into 68 countries as manufacturers and retailers of their own brand-name shoes as well as other popular brands. Never a leader in style, Bata aimed to meet the demand for everyday footwear at affordable prices. Competition from discount retailers and cheaper imports took its toll on the company during the 1980s and 1990s, and in 2005 the Canadian stores were closed. The headquarters relocated to Geneva, Switzerland where Thomas, the grandson of the founder, now operates the company.

Batacchi, Paolo (1945–), Designer, active 1980–present

After graduating from the prestigious Ars Sutoria in Milan, Batacchi designed shoes for a factory in Florence. He went on to become director of the Florence office of US **Genesco** Inc., supervising marketing, production and design from 1970 to 1979. It was there he learned the business side of the industry and met **Andrew Geller**. From 1980 to 1985 he worked for Andrew Geller, designing the Beene Bag collection. In 1985 Batacchi was hired by Intershoe to launch Via Spiga, which became the fashion footwear success story of the late 1980s and early 1990s. In 1988 he designed a cheaper line called Studio Paolo and in 1991 a more expensive couture line called V Spiga Couture.

Berluti Shoemaker, Designer, active 1928–present

Italian-born Torello Berluti was an apprentice in his father's workshop before going to Paris like his father, who had briefly worked there as a made-to-order shoemaker at the turn of the century. Opening a boutique in 1928 on the rue du Mont Thabor, Berluti created bespoke men's footwear. By the 1950s the firm had acquired a long list of jet-set clients. Torello's son Talbinio introduced a ready-to-wear line in 1959, expanding the client base. Talbinio took over operation of the company in the early 1960s with his daughter, Olga. They produced a more comfortable line of shoes and later designed and promoted the boutiques that opened around the world as the company expanded in the 1970s and 1980s.

Bikkembergs, Dirk (1959–), Designer, active 1985–present

Belgian national Bikkembergs was born in Bonn, Germany in 1959 and graduated from the Antwerp Academy in Belgium in 1982. He created his first shoe collection in 1985 and was well known as one of the young Belgian designers called the Antwerp Six.

Advertisement for Bass, 1925.

White leather pumps made by Bata for the American market, c. 1935. Bata became Europe's largest shoe manufacturer in the 1920s. They exhibited at the 1933 Chicago World's Fair and were exporting to the United States in the late 1930s. After World War II Bata concentrated on expanding into developing nations and did not seek to compete in the American market. This is why they are unknown in the United States but are the best-known shoe manufacturer in most of the rest of the world.

Brown suede pumps, labelled 'Via Spiga', c. 1985–88.

Flower-petal sandal by Manolo Blahník, 2003.

Multicoloured snake and kid leather shoe with wedge heel of wine corks by Gaza Bowen, c. 1983.

Pale-green silk shoes with white-beaded vamps and bows by Joseph Box, c. 1880.

Birkenstock Manufacturer, active 1964–present

The German Birkenstock family has a history of shoemaking dating back to 1774. In 1902 Konrad Birkenstock designed a flexible arch support with orthopedic structure, but it was his grandson, Carl Birkenstock, who in 1964 perfected the contoured-cork foot bed for which the sandals are famous. In 1967 Margot Fraser began importing Birkenstock sandals into the US, selling them through health stores and opening her own company, Footprint Sandals Inc., in 1972. Straddling the border between orthopedic and ugly in many people's eyes, the sandals enjoyed a cult status with a growing clientele. Sales increased slowly until the mid 1990s, when 1970s chic became fashionable and sales rocketed. In 1997 Birkenstock opened its flagship store in San Francisco; and in 2000 it formed a licensing agreement with the estate of Grateful Dead guitarist Jerry Garcia to produce sandals decorated with Jerry's paintings.

Blahník, Manolo (1942–), Designer, active c. 1970–present

Born of a Czech father and a Spanish mother in the Canary Islands, Blahník studied literature and law in Geneva, Switzerland and art in Paris. In 1971 Diana Vreeland, then editor-in-chief of American *Vogue*, saw his portfolio of theatrical designs but it was his shoe designs that impressed her. He began designing men's shoes for a tiny shop in Chelsea called Zapata and got his first break in 1972 when fashion designer Ossie Clark asked him to make the shoes for a runway show. Critics were encouraging and Blahník began to build a clientele. In 1973 he bought out Zapata's owner and set up his flagship shoe store with his sister Evangelina. He broke into the US market in 1978 when he launched a collection for Bloomingdales and the following year opened his first store on New York's Madison Avenue. He designed shoes for Perry Ellis in 1980, Calvin Klein in 1984 and Isaac Mizrahi in 1988. Blahník sales soared after George Malkemus, Blahník's American business partner since 1982, renegotiated the American distribution agreements. The first Manolo Blahník store opened in Hong Kong in 1991. Blahník continued to collaborate with designers throughout the 1990s, including John Galliano in 1992, Bill Blass, Caroline Herrera and Oscar de la Renta in 1994, and again with Galliano for Christian Dior in 1997. Blahník describes his style as good-quality shoes with just enough hooker chic for sex appeal. He admits that he is inspired by the work of **Roger Vivier**, modelling himself more as a shoe artisan rather than a 'star' designer. Blahník's best marketer was Carrie Bradshaw (played by Sarah Jessica Parker), the lead character in the *Sex & the City* series. Carrie's shoe fetish made Blahník a household name, and Sarah Jessica Parker ensured the shoes were hers to keep when Carrie was done with them!

Bowen, Gaza Shoemaker, active 1979–85

Bowen learned shoemaking from a master shoemaker at Colonial Williamsburg in 1976. From 1979 until 1985 she made shoes that blurred the boundary between art and fashion. Bowen also taught shoemaking before leaving the practical manufacture of footwear altogether in 1995. She died in 2005 and is considered more of an artist than a shoemaker by her followers.

Box, Joseph Shoemaker, active 1832–1956

In 1816 fifteen-year-old Robert Dixon Box was apprenticed to James Sly, the owner of a London ladies' shoemaking business founded in 1808. After Sly's death in 1832, Box bought the business at 187 Regent Street. In 1855, Robert's son, also at the age of 15, became apprentice to his father, taking over the business in 1862 and renaming it Joseph Box Ltd. The business gained a reputation for quality footwear, receiving royal warrants from Alexandra, Princess of Wales, and Victoria, Crown Princess of Germany. In 1882, Joseph sold the company to his cousins so that his daughters could enter society. By 1899 the premises were shared with Gundry and Sons, shoemakers to Queen Victoria since the 1830s. In the early twentieth century the business was relocated to various addresses, including 15a Hanover Square, 43 Conduit Street, 25 Hanover Square and 61 Grosvenor Street. In 1956 the business was taken over by **John Lobb**.

Brown Shoe Company Manufacturer, Retailer, active 1878–present

With the financial backing of Alvin Bryan, George Brown hired five shoemakers and opened Bryan, Brown and Company in St. Louis in 1878. Located far away from the then New England–based American shoe industry, the firm successfully made fashion footwear for the growing population of the American mid-west. The enterprise grew rapidly and in 1893 Brown, by then the sole remaining partner, renamed the operation Brown Shoe Company. The company introduced cartoonist Richard F. Outcault's Buster Brown comic-strip character in 1904 at the St. Louis World's Fair as a trademark for Brown's children's shoes. But, they failed to purchase exclusive rights and Buster Brown became the trademark for scores of products including cigars and whiskey. Buster's girlfriend Mary Jane was introduced to help market girls' shoes in about 1909, and the instep strap shoe became known generically as the 'Mary-Jane' style. Brown Shoes became a public company in 1913 and introduced the brand Naturalizer in 1927. The company entered the retail business during the 1950s, purchasing Wohl Shoe, Regal Shoe and G R Kinney, which they had to resell in 1963 to Woolworth because of antitrust litigation. Diversifying, Brown Shoes bought clothing, sporting goods and toy companies in the early 1970s and renamed themselves as the Brown Group in 1972 to reflect their larger holdings. Facing the changing American marketplace of the late twentieth century, the Brown Group restructured and closed all of its American shoemaking plants, moving all shoe manufacturing offshore by 1995.

Cammeyer, Alfred J Retailer, active 1875–c. 1960

Alfred J Cammeyer started selling ready-made shoes for men and women in New York in 1875. By 1885 his store had expanded to include 165, 167 and 169 Sixth Avenue. In 1893 Cammeyer went into partnership with Louis M Hart and opened a shoe store at the corner of Sixth Avenue and 20th Street in an area that was known as 'Ladies' Mile', New York's fashionable shopping district. Cammeyer was famous for high-quality footwear and cutting-edge retailing, and in 1902 became a leader in the field of shoe advertising. The store was known for promoting high-fashion styles, such as the spectator pump in 1914. When the fashionable shopping district relocated uptown, Cammeyer closed his store in 1917 and re-opened near 34th Street, at 381 Fifth Avenue. This store probably closed during the Depression but the Cammeyer name, synonymous with high-fashion quality ready-mades, continued to appear in shoes as late as c. 1960.

Caovilla, Renè (1938–), Designer, active 1955–present

In 1936 Renè's father founded the family's Italian business, taking his son into apprenticeship in 1952.

Renè took time to tour Europe and meet people like **Roger Vivier** and Valentino, for whom he would later work as a footwear consultant from 1973 until 1998. In 1955 he created his first collection and became successful during Italy's postwar restructuring. Emphasizing quality over quantity and renowned for his embroideries and inlays, Caovilla sold to an exclusive clientele all over Europe. In the 1980s he collaborated with Yves Saint Laurent, and by the end of the 1990s was producing shoes for Chanel and Dior. Caovilla opened his first signature boutique in Venice in 2000 and each passing year sees him expanding into foreign markets.

Capezio Manufacturer, active 1887–present

Italian-born Salvatore Capezio emigrated to the US and founded Capezio theatrical footwear in 1887. He was advantageously located at Broadway and 39th, diagonally across the street from the Metropolitan Opera House. By 1910 Capezio pointe shoes had become so well known among the dancing community that during a New York appearance Anna Pavlova purchased them for herself and her entire company. As the theatrical business exploded on Broadway in the 1920s and 1930s Capezio's business flourished and he created footwear for both stars and chorus-line dancers. In 1941 the young clothes designer Claire McCardell showed Capezio soft-soled ballet slippers with her collection. This prompted the store Lord & Taylor to carry a line of low-heeled street footwear built on dance footwear lasts, which catapulted Capezio into the fashion footwear world. Capezio was best known in the 1950s for popularizing toe cleavage in his low-cut low-heeled pumps.

Choo, Jimmy (1961–), Designer, active 1991–present

Born into a family of Malaysian shoemakers, Jimmy Choo made his first pair of shoes when he was 11 years old. He graduated from Cordwainers College in London and the London College of Fashion in 1989. Princess Diana was his best client for bespoke footwear in the early 1990s and she was frequently seen wearing his shoes after her divorce. In 1996 he went into partnership with Tamara Mellon, former British *Vogue* accessories editor, and launched a ready-to-wear line of shoes made in Italy. Choo sold his share in 2001 and the company was resold in 2004. Choo is no longer connected with the

Advertisement for the Jacqueline line of shoes by Wohl Shoe, a division of Brown Shoe, autumn 1950.

Advertisement for Cammeyer, 1930.

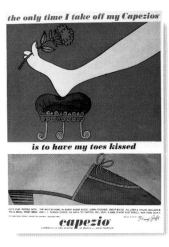

Advertisement for Capezio, autumn 1963.

Purchased at a closing-down sale, these tuxedo pumps date from the late 1980s, one of the last years in which Margaret Jerrold shoes were produced.

Advertisement for Clarks, spring 1963.

design of the ready-to-wear line. Jimmy Choo was awarded an OBE by the Queen in June 2003 for his services in making London a fashion design centre of the world.

Church's Manufacturer, active 1873–present
A family enterprise founded in 1873 in Northampton, Church's still remains in family hands. By 2000 Church's was operating three factories in Britain, one in Canada and one in Italy, producing primarily men's Goodyear-welted dress shoes but also men's casuals. The company is known for its quality ready-to-wear footwear.

☐ **Clark, Margaret** Designer, active 1954–late 1960s
Returning home to the US after World War II, Jerrold Miller started work in the family's shoe factory where the prestigious **I. Miller** line, founded by his grandfather Israel Miller, was produced. In 1954 he and his wife, designer Margaret Clark, who had started as an in-house designer for I. Miller in the 1940s, created their own line called Margaret Jerrold. Clark received a Neiman Marcus Award in 1963 for her sophisticated low-heeled designs. In 1964 Jerrold Miller launched the Shoe Biz department at Henri Bendel in New York, carrying fashion lines from Walter Steiger among others. That same year Miller founded a wholesale business called Super Shoe Biz, which sourced shoes in Italy and quickly branched out into Spain and later Southeast Asia. By the late 1960s the couple had divorced and Margaret was no longer designing. In 1978 Miller began phasing out the Margaret Jerrold brand in favour of imports and officially changed the firm's name to Shoe Biz. He retired in 1989, citing that the shoe industry had changed. He died in 2003; Margaret Clark died in 1994.

☐ **Clarks** Manufacturer, active 1828–present
The company was founded in Street, Somerset as a tannery in 1825. Quakers Cyrus Clark and his brother, James, began making sheepskin slippers in 1828, which they called 'Brown Peters'. The company grew slowly, with slipper sales eventually accounting for a third of the turnover. In the 1860s the company entered the industrial age, purchasing Singer sewing machines to increase production. Cyrus died in 1866, and James formed a new partnership focusing more on shoe production

with the launch of Torbrand shoes. In 1893 the company released Hygienic, a range of shoes designed on anatomical principles to enhance foot comfort. Clarks expanded into women's shoes in the early twentieth century and adapted American technologies. The Torbrand line was renamed Clarks in 1920 and another line of shoes, Wessex, was launched in 1927. Clarks became famous for its perforated and openwork children's and women's shoes in the 1920s. The company shod most British children for fifty years. In 1937 it began retailing under the name Peter Lord but in the 1950s retail outlets were renamed Clarks. In 1949 Nathan Clark, a descendant of the original founder, designed a crepe-soled suede boot he called the desert boot. The idea was taken from the North African English officers' regulation army boots he had seen during the war. The style was a huge success for the company throughout the 1950s and early 1960s and set a precedent for men's leisure shoes. Another winning style – the Wallabee – followed in the 1960s and used a moccasin construction. In the 1980s and 1990s the family firm began to encounter financial troubles. The traditional Quaker values of the Clark family had previously protected their workforce from lay-offs and had even paid sick benefits to workers as early as the mid nineteenth century, long before they were available in most companies. After 1996 however the situation became so dire that the company had to reorganize and production moved to Brazil and India. Clarks attempted to re-establish itself in Europe in 2001 with the acquisition of the German shoe manufacturer Elefanten, but by 2005 the last of the British production facilities had closed.

Clergerie, Robert Designer, active 1981–present
Starting a career as a shoe designer late in life, Clergerie studied at the Ecole Supérieure de Commerce in Paris and was an army officer, an accountant and an estate agent. In 1971 he answered an advertisement placed by Roland Jourdan to run the Xavier Danaud subsidiary of **Charles Jourdan** shoes. Clergerie got the job after a personality test awarded him high marks in persuasive authority. In 1977 Clergerie acquired the controlling interest of the **Unic** shoe company in Romans, France. He restructured the company and took on the design of the shoes himself in 1981, launching the line under his own name. His unornamented strong clean

designs won him *Footwear News* Designer of the Year awards in 1987 and 1990, and his architecturally designed heels won him a Fashion Footwear Association of New York award in 1992. About one third of his market is in the US, where his shoes are sold through high-end department stores and his own retail shops. Clergerie expanded in the 1990s to include a less expensive line of shoes called Espace, and a men's line called Joseph Fenestrier. In the late 1980s his son Xavier began to operate Première Classe Exhibition, a shoe exhibition that takes place in Paris twice a year, coinciding with the Prêt à Porter and Carrousel de la Mode shows.

Cole, Kenneth Manufacturer, active 1982–present

While working for his father Charles Cole, founder of El Greco Leather Products Corp, Kenneth recognized a fashion hit in a simple leather-strapped solid-bottom-unit mule called 'Candies' designed by Armando Pollini. The company imported more than 10 million pairs into the US in 1978 and 1979. Kenneth Cole decided to explore a higher end market and opened his own business in 1982. He called his company Kenneth Cole Productions to obtain permission to park a forty-foot trailer in midtown Manhattan during shoe market week, something that New York only allowed film-production companies to do. Kenneth Cole Productions began as a supplier and importer with a brand line called 'What's What' and in 1987 a junior line called 'Unlisted'. Cole opened his first store in New York in 1985, and in 1992 supplied a private label for the retailers Sears and J C Penney. In 1994 he launched the brand line 'Reaction'. Cole has failed to find a single shoe to equal the success of Candies, but he is known for providing affordable up-to-date fashion footwear marketed through socially conscious and humourous advertising campaigns. One of Kenneth Cole's early campaigns ran in 1986 shortly after the downfall of the Marcos family in the Philippines. It read: 'Imelda Marcos bought 2,700 pairs of shoes. She could've at least had the courtesy to buy a pair of ours.' The company went public in 1994 and has since branched out into clothing lines and accessories.

Converse Manufacturer, active 1908–present

In 1908 Marquis Converse established the Converse Rubber Shoe Company in Malden, Massachusetts. Basketball was growing in popularity and Converse seized the opportunity to create a shoe specifically designed for the game. The 'All Star' was launched in 1917 and had a thick rubber sole and high-cut canvas upper covering the ankle bone, over which a round rubber patch with a moulded star was placed. To increase sales, Charles H. Taylor, a basketball player for the Akron Firestones, was hired in 1921 to travel across the US promoting the game and endorsing the Converse All Star basketball shoe. In 1923 his name, 'Chuck Taylor', was added to the ankle patch. Converse fell into bankruptcy in 1929, but was bought out by a Boston family in 1933 who continued operations under the Converse name until 1972. Converse supplied the US military with footwear and equipment during World War II and grew quite profitable from the late 1940s to the late 1960s. Converse All Stars, or 'Chucks' as they were colloquially known, remained virtually unchanged from their original design and by the 1960s held the largest share of the American sports-shoe market. In 1968, Chuck Taylor was inducted into the Basketball Hall of Fame, a year before he died. However, sales slumped in the 1970s with the onset of new brands like Nike and Adidas. In 1972 Converse was sold to Eltra and expanded with the purchase of BF Goodrich's footwear division. All Stars enjoyed a brief revival in the mid 1980s when classic Chucks and new models sporting a variety of colours and patterns were popular with film stars and pop singers. Converse was bought by Interco in 1986 but has since been plagued by financial troubles and poor sales. All North American manufacturing plants were closed in 2001 and production shifted to the Far East. In 2003 **Nike** purchased Converse, operating it as a separate division.

Cox, George (1870–1960), Manufacturer, active 1906–present

George Cox founded his company in Northamptonshire in 1906 in a building that had been used previously as a swimming pool. The company has produced its own-brand shoes and footwear for other labels like **John Fluevog**, Katharine Hamnett, Lawler Duffy, John Moore and Vivienne Westwood. It became better known in 1949 when it launched Goodyear-welted shoes with crepe rubber soles, which became known as 'brothel creepers' and were the footwear of choice for the English Teddy boys. The company popularized the winkle-picker style for men in the early 1960s and revived pointed toes for the punk band The Sex Pistols in the late 1970s with the addition of **Dr Marten** soles.

Black satin pumps with Chinese frog closure trim by Patrick Cox, 1998.

Cerise satin boudoir mule by Daniel Green, c. 1940.

Pewter-finished kid evening sandals, labelled 'Diego Della Valle – Made in Italy', c. 1979.

Advertisement for Delman, winter 1952.

It became the licensed manufacturer of Dr Marten soles from 1973 until 1995. The firm also led in the field of rockabilly styles, which were popularly sold through the London store Robot during the late 1980s. In 1994 the company moved from their former swimming pool into a larger factory in Wellingborough.

□ **Cox, Patrick** (1963–), Designer 1984–present
Born in Edmonton, Alberta, Canada, Patrick Cox sourced accessories for Toronto fashion designer Loucas Kleanthous in the early 1980s. Kleanthous spotted Cox's raw talent when he customized a pair of shoes and advised Cox to study shoe design at Cordwainers College in London. In his first year of college Cox designed platform shoes for Vivienne Westwood's 1984 'Witches' collection and was soon creating footwear for John Galliano, Workers for Freedom and Anna Sui. Cox set up his own company in 1985, designing street-smart chic footwear, often incorporating unusual materials like chain mail. In 1987 he launched his own label collection. His earliest shoes were made in England with production later moving to Italy. Cox opened his first shop in London in 1991 and his style quickly moved toward classic looks and revisited favourites. His most successful design has been the 'Wannabe' loafer, a colourful revival of the hush-puppies classic, which hit the shops in 1993. In the same year he launched 'PCs', a cheaper diffusion line of shoes that once more popularized injection-moulded jellies. Since 1995 Cox has expanded and has stores in Paris and New York. Patrick Cox was recruited as the head designer for **Charles Jourdan** in 2003, leaving in 2005.

□ **Daniel Green Co.** Manufacturer, active 1882–2001
In 1881 Daniel Green, a travelling shoe salesman for the Wallace Elliott Company in New York City, visited a felt mill in Dolgeville, New York. He noticed that some of the workers had fashioned shoes from waste pieces of piano felt to keep their feet warm on the cold factory floors. Developing this idea, Green secured an agreement with the felt manufacturer to make felt slippers and sold 600 pairs in 1882 under the label 'Alfred Dolge Felt Shoes and Slippers'. By 1885 sales had jumped to 75,000 pairs a year and the company relocated, at first to Utica and by 1889 to New York. Green died in 1891 but the company continued, specializing in slippers made from a variety of materials. From the 1920s to the 1950s the

company was known for its high-heeled satin boudoir slippers. The Daniel Green trademark was sold in 2001 and the company, renamed Phoenix Footwear, now makes boots that are manufactured in Brazil, China and South America.

□ **Della Valle, Diego** (1954–), Designer, Manufacturer, Retailer, active 1970s–present
Third-generation Italian shoemaker Della Valle emerged in the 1970s as a quality manufacturer of ready-to-wear shoes for such designers as Versace, Gianfranco Ferre, Karl Lagerfeld, Fendi and Krizia. More recently Della Valle has made shoes for Christian Lacroix, Geoffrey Beene, Azzedine Alaia, Romeo Gigli and Calvin Klein. He is also known for his international 'Tod' boutiques.

□ **Delman, Herman** (1895–1955), Manufacturer, active 1919–88
The son of a shoe-store owner from Portland, Oregon, Herman Delman founded the Delman label in 1919 as a made-to-order shop on New York's Madison Avenue, producing high-class expensive footwear. Expanding into ready-to-wear, he understood the necessity for brand recognition and insisted that his name appeared on the label of his shoes. It was customary at that time for retailers to put their own labels in shoes, as it still is sometimes today. In 1936 he formed one of the world's first licencing agreements with **Rayne** in the UK, under which Rayne produced Delman shoes for the English market. Delman developed the business by hiring young shoe designers to create styles for his shops. He spied the young talent of **Roger Vivier** in 1938 and bought many of his designs under the Delman label. In 1940 Delman opened his salon in Bergdorf's, which led to further shop-within-a-store openings, including one in Saks on Fifth Avenue. In 1954 Delman retired from the shoe business and died the following year. His manufacturing and retail business was taken over by shoe-retailing conglomerate **Genesco**, which in 1961 sold half the Delman business to Rayne on the condition that they would operate it for at least ten years. In 1973, the British department store Debenhams purchased Rayne-Delman, selling the Delman interest in 1987 to Sam Wyly who closed the business in 1988. In 1989 Nina Footwear Inc. acquired the Delman name with plans to revive its tradition of elegant quality footwear.

Der Balian, Sarkis Designer,
active c. 1930–95

Little is known of Der Balian's early life. Born in Armenia, he arrived in Paris in 1929 to work as a shoe designer and by 1934 had secured a position with a shoemaker by the name of Enzel. At the same time, Der Balian worked as an independent model maker, selling his designs to various French firms. He also perfected models made from sketches for couturiers. Enzel closed in 1936 and Der Balian went to work for the French shoemaking-firm Cecile as a technical manager. He turned down an invitation to work for Delman in the US in 1939. Instead, he briefly ran his own shop in Paris during World War II before closing down and then re-opening in 1947. He received numerous awards and accolades for his work in the 1950s and remained in business until 1995. Much of his work was produced under other labels without credit to Der Balian.

Edelman, Sam & Libby Designers,
active 1985–96

Sam Edelman was the grandson of a founding partner in the Fleming-Joffe reptile tannery that supplied exotic leathers to the shoe trade. Sam's father, Arthur, joined his father-in-law's tannery in 1952 but closed the business in 1976 due to an increasingly environmentally aware marketplace. Instead, Arthur and his son opened a shoe business, which supplied the first shoes to appear in Ralph Lauren's collection. Later, Arthur left to go into partnership with his wife, Teddy, making leathers for interiors. Sam went on to develop a shoe division for Esprit in 1985 with his wife, Libby, and in 1988 they launched their own label Sam & Libby. Their first product, a ballet flat, was a huge success but additions to their line were never as popular. In 1996 they sold the worldwide rights to their trademarks and trade names to Maxwell Shoe.

Encore Shoe Corp Manufacturers,
active 1963–present

Founded in 1963 by Earl Katz, the family owned and operated company began making espadrilles under the label Pappagallos in Rochester, New Hampshire. The Zodiac label, headed by Encore's chief designer, Al Charette, was introduced in stores like Bloomingdale's as a fashion-forward brand, appealing to the twenty-something generation at a cost conscious price. Zodiac was a leading manufacturer of trendy footwear throughout the 1970s, but in the early 1980s sales and profits began to shrink and the company started to rely on imports over domestically produced footwear. The business was bought out by a group of investors in 1992 after a failed attempt to create an athletic line of Zodiac footwear. The original factory was closed soon thereafter.

☐ **Este** Manufacturer, active c. 1820–95

Este was a prolific Parisian shoe manufacturer who used a piecework method to manufacture silk shoes that were exported all over the fashionable world. The firm of Este was established in about 1820, located at 13 rue de la Paix, as advertised on the shield-shaped paper labels inside their shoes. In about 1838 they merged with Viault and the company was renamed Viault-Este, but the labels were not changed immediately to reflect the new name. In around 1849, rue de la Paix was renumbered and the address changed from 13 to 17. In 1853 Viault-Este formed an association with Thierry & Sons as their London distributors, with both names appearing on the labels of the shoes sold in England. At the same time they began to advertise as suppliers to the Empress Eugénie, who had married Napoleon III in 1853. Foreign exports began to fall during the 1860s and the company never recovered its huge export status when the American footwear industry began to boom in the 1870s. After 1876 Este moved to 20 rue de la Paix, and the association with Thierry & Sons in London ended at about the same time. In around 1890 the company moved again, this time to 18 rue Chauveau Lagarde, and went out of business a few years later.

☐ **Evins, David** (1909–91), Designer,
active 1934–90

English-born Evins moved to the US with his family when he was 13. He studied illustration at the Pratt Institute in New York. One of his first jobs was as an illustrator with *Vogue*, but Herman **Delman** did not like the artistic licence Evins took with Delman's shoes and had him fired, telling Evins, 'Get yourself a job as a designer if you want to be one'. So, Evins went to work as a pattern maker and opened his own studio, designing for various manufacturers. During World War II he served as a communications officer in the Army Signal Corps. After the war he opened Evins Inc. in New York with his brother, Lee, and started designing in conjunction with **I. Miller**,

Label typically found in Este shoes in the 1830s and early 1840s.

Custom-made shoes designed by David Evins with hand-painted sole waists, c. 1958–60.

Advertisement for Famolare, 1975.

Ferragamo is often remembered for his introduction of the platform and wedge heels in the 1930s and for his use of non-traditional materials. But the majority of his footwear was relatively subdued with perhaps one design flourish, as shown in these black suede low-heeled pumps from 1954.

where his name appeared on the label. In 1949 he received a Coty Award for his shell pump, which revealed toe cleavage, and he was unofficially crowned 'The King of Pumps'. He also promoted himself as a bespoke shoemaker and during his career made shoes for first ladies, royalty and film stars, including Claudette Colbert in 1934 and Elizabeth Taylor in 1963 for their roles as Cleopatra. In the late 1950s he entered into a partnership with the Mario Valentino factory in Italy, designing shoes for Mainbocher, Valentino, Charles James, James Galanos, Norman Norell, Balenciaga, Calvin Klein, Bill Blass, Ralph Lauren, Oscar de la Renta and Geoffrey Beene. In 1968 he sold his business to shoe retail giant **Genesco** but continued to design and oversee production of Evins footwear. In 1975, the US Shoe Corp acquired the Evins division from Genesco and he remained actively involved in the design and production of his shoes until he died.

☐ **Famolare, Joe** (1932–), Designer, Manufacturer, active 1969–87 and c. 1992–present
Famolare began working at his father's pattern and last company, Famolare Shoe Design & Engineering, at the age of 12. After studying musical theatre and experiencing a stint in the army, Famolare went to work for **Capezio** in the early 1960s and from 1965 to 1968 for the Bandolino brand under Marx and Newman, a division of US Shoes. In 1969 he founded his own company, Famolare Inc., and received a Coty Award for his moulded rubber clog in 1973. His next success was a shoe with a bicycle logo and the tag line 'Get There'. His wavy-bottomed thick rubber sole was designed for walking comfortably, and the shoe became a hit in 1975. However, his 3-inch-heel 'Hi There' shoe failed to capture the same interest in 1977. 'Get There' lost ground to knock-offs that even an expensive patent infringement suit in 1980 could not prevent. Trainers usurped the market for comfort shoes in the 1980s, and in 1987 Famolare licensed his name to US Shoes and took a break from the shoe business. He regained his name in the early 1990s when he produced a line of shoes for Pepsi, made in India.

☐ **Ferragamo, Salvatore** (1898–1960), Designer, Manufacturer, active 1923–present
Salvatore Ferragamo learned shoemaking as an apprentice. He followed his brother to the US in 1914

on his advice to learn American shoe-production methods. He studied chemistry and anatomy at various universities to learn more about the dyeing of leather and how the arch of the foot supports the body. Out of a small Santa Barbara shoemaking and repair shop he created footwear for the American Film Company, his largest order coming from Cecil B. DeMille for the 1923 epic *The Ten Commandments*. This contract bankrolled his purchase of The Hollywood Boot Shop, and Ferragamo began to build a clientele of film stars. By 1927, however, he was unable to fill his orders and he returned to the then fascist state of Italy. Ferragamo went bankrupt after the Wall Street Crash of 1929 and had to start all over again. In 1935, when Italy invaded Abyssinia (Ethiopia), the League of Nations imposed economic sanctions on Italy and Ferragamo found it impossible to import the leathers he needed. He began to use unconventional materials; inspired by Italy's illustrious past, he created platform shoes of wood or cork that resembled the chopines of Renaissance Venice. But he used non-traditional materials for the uppers, such as woven raffia and cellophane. His designs found international success and allowed him to purchase the historic Palazzo Feroni-Spini in Florence in 1938, which became the Ferragamo headquarters. When shortages occurred throughout Europe during World War II, shoe designers and manufacturers followed Ferragamo's lead, creating platform and wedge soles of wood or cork and developing innovative uses for unconventional materials. After the war, Ferragamo's 1947 shoe collection, which included an 'invisible' wedge-heeled sandal with nylon filament straps, was shown with Dior's 'New Look' collection at a fashion show in New York, where both designers had travelled to accept Neiman Marcus awards. Ferragamo regained his position as shoemaker to the stars during the 1950s, when his client list included royalty and screen stars who would travel to Florence to have bespoke shoes made by the master shoemaker. The Ferragamo business remained a family venture after his death in 1960. His wife and children continued to operate the company, particularly Fiamma, Salvatore's eldest daughter and the only child to work directly under her father before he died. She debuted her first official collection in London in 1961 and received her own Neiman Marcus Award in 1967. Each of Salvatore's remaining five children now heads a division of the company. Ferragamo is the largest exporter of high-end footwear in Italy, producing over

10,000 pairs per day, a far cry from the 350 pairs per day being made in 1960 under Salvatore.

Figueroa, Bernard (1961–), Designer, active 1980s–present

French-born Figueroa studied at the Studio Berçot, an avant-garde fashion school in Paris. For his student show he created a sculpted metal-heel shoe, decorated with abstract musical notes, fish and foliage. This brought him to the attention of Thierry Mugler who commissioned shoes for his own collections. Moving to Boston, Figueroa worked for two years at Rockport, a manufacturer of quality walking shoes. In 1992 he launched his own bespoke line in New York and is known for his hand-sculpted heels.

Fiorentina, Silvia Designer, active 1957–present

Silvia Sappia Baldi, who started the Fiorentina line in 1957, uses the name Silvia Fiorentina professionally. She was one of the first American designers to have her shoes manufactured in Italy. Known for elegant shoes, Fiorentina creates her 'look' with curved arches, high vamps and sweeping sidelines that dip to the back. Her line has been carried for a long time by the store Bergdorf Goodman in New York.

☐ **Florsheim** Manufacturer, Retailer, active 1856–1999, Importer, active 2000–present

German émigré Sigmund Florsheim worked as a shoe retailer in Chicago from 1856, branching out into manufacturing in 1892. He died two years later, leaving his son, Milton, in control. During Milton's tenure the wing-tipped brogue and oxford became wardrobe basics for businessmen and Florsheim stayed ahead of the competition by producing the best quality ready-to-wear versions on the American market. Florsheim became one of the first shoemakers to advertise nationally in magazines and also pioneered manufacturer-owned retail stores. Founded as a men's footwear company, Florsheim moved into women's shoes in 1929. Milton died in 1936 and his son, Irving, took over, passing the presidency to his brother, Harold, in 1947. Under Harold's direction the company recovered from the setbacks it had incurred during the Depression and World War II. Florsheim took on new looks, including one-eyelet tie shoes and tasselled slip-on loafers. Each season

new styles and colours were added to the Florsheim repertoire. Florsheim was a progressive retailer, securing prime locations for the company's stores and providing independent shoe stores who carried their products with free Florsheim signage, giving the label brand recognition. The bulk of the family stock was sold to Interco in 1953 but the company continued to operate as an autonomous division, quickly becoming Interco's most profitable unit. By 1963 Florsheim controlled the majority of the US high-priced shoe market, but inexpensive imports during the 1960s and 1970s made serious inroads into the company's profits. Florsheim discontinued its women's line in the late 1970s and began shifting production overseas. By 1989 less than half of the company's shoes were made in the US. Interco filed for bankruptcy in 1991 but managed to survive. Florsheim entered the 'brown shoe' market in 1993, carrying hiking and hunting boots, but the company failed to reverse its debt and in 1996 it was spun off from Interco. Renamed the Florsheim Group, they signed a deal to produce John Deere work boots in 1998 in an attempt to expand their market. Amid declining sales, mounting debt and rumours of scandal involving the CEO, Florsheim closed its last remaining US plant and moved production to India in 1999. In 2002 Florsheim filed for bankruptcy and began closing its stores but later in the year the shoemaker Weyco Group purchased Florsheim's assets.

☐ **Fluevog, John** (1948–), Designer, active 1970–present

John Fluevog met **Peter Fox** in Vancouver, Canada in the late 1960s, and they opened an avant-garde shoe store in Vancouver in 1970. An undisclosed reason took them in separate directions in the early 1980s. John Fluevog opened his own store in Seattle in 1986, followed by stores in Toronto and Boston and he began designing his own brand-name shoes manufactured by **George Cox** in England. Aiming for the street fashion crowd, his shoes have appealed to every subculture from the 1980s to the present day, including punks, goths and rockabillies. Fluevog also designs for the European manufacturer Dynamic, who produces Fluevog's brand for the European, Japanese and Australian markets. Designers Comrags, Anna Sui, and Betsey Johnson have used his shoes in their collections.

Advertisement for Florsheim, autumn 1953.

Black leather and gold kid boots by Fox & Fluevog, c. 1975. When John Fluevog and Peter Fox opened a shoe store in Vancouver in 1970, their boots and shoes were aimed at a stylish youthful market, appealing to disco divas and followers of glam-rock. After the duo went their separate creative ways, Fluevog continued to follow the street-fashion crowd from new wavers to rockabillies.

From 1981, Peter Fox began to open his own stores. His shoes are inspired by historical styles from Tudor velvet flats to Edwardian wedding pumps. These pink satin platforms from 2002 have Louis heels and are decorated with jewels.

Maud Frizon black suede comma-heeled pumps with net inserts, c. late 1990s.

Advertisement for Walk-Over shoes, spring 1940.

Fox, Peter Designer, active 1970–present

Peter Fox was born in London and attended Camberwell College of Arts in London and Maidstone Art School in Kent, where he studied sculpture. He entered the world of shoes in Harrods' shoe department in 1954. In 1956 he moved to Vancouver, Canada, where he became an apprentice to a traditional Italian shoemaker. He went into partnership with **John Fluevog** in 1970 and opened a shop that specialized in edgy youthful designs. He met his wife in the shop while fitting her for a pair of boots, and they opened Peter Fox Shoes in SoHo, New York in 1981. Together they create designs that are often solidly based on historical reference. They also manage to precede trends, as with their granny boots collection in 1982, their Louis-heeled pumps in 1985 and their platforms in 1986. Peter Fox produces footwear for Broadway Productions.

Fratelli Rossetti Manufacturer, active 1955–present

Brothers Renzo and Renato Rossetti set up Fratelli Rossetti near Milan in 1955. They made men's shoes and were leaders in promoting Italian-made men's shoes for export in the 1960s. (Italian-made women's shoes had been successfully internationalized in the previous decade.) Success really arrived when they translated the classic craftsmanship of men's footwear into a range of mannish women's shoes in the 1970s. They simultaneously launched a canvas-lined loafer that could be worn without socks. Renzo's three sons have been responsible for the expansion and internationalization of the brand, which boasts a stellar clientele, including Tom Cruise, Paloma Picasso and Lauren Bacall.

Frizon, Maud (1941–), Designer, active 1969–present

Maud (named Nadine at birth) Frizon began her fashion career as a model for such Parisian couturiers as Jean Patou, Christian Dior and André Courrèges. In the 1960s models were expected to use their own shoes on assignments. Unable to find the shoes she wanted, Frizon decided to make her own. She and her husband, Gigi de Marco, opened a shop on rue des Saints-Pères on Paris's Left Bank and presented Frizon's first collection in 1969, which included a pair of red leather boots. She was an overnight success, capturing interest from high-profile clients like Brigitte Bardot. Maud Frizon was a leading shoe designer in the 1980s when she created the cone heel and designed for Azzedine Alaïa, Claude Montana, Thierry Mugler and Sonia Rykiel. Financially overextended, Frizon sold her company in 1999 and no longer owns her name for the production of footwear. Frizon de Marco now operates Ombeline stores in Paris, St Tropez and New York for which Frizon creates new styles each season and is known for mixing colours and materials.

Genesco Manufacturer, Retailer, active 1924–present

James Jarman founded the Jarman Shoe Company in 1924. His son, Maxey, became president in 1933 and changed the company's name to General Shoe when the company went public in 1939. After World War II, General Shoe prospered, buying numerous shoe companies such as Johnston & Murphy in 1951 and **Delman** in 1955. They also brought **Charles Jourdan** to the US in 1953. General Shoe's success drew the scrutiny of the Justice Department, which, worried about monopolies at the time, filed antitrust charges directing General Shoe not to make any acquisitions in the shoe industry for five years. As a result, General Shoe diversified into apparel, renaming itself Genesco in 1959 to reflect the change. Genesco overextended itself in the 1970s and 1980s and in 1994 restructured, divesting itself of many divisions and focusing instead on men's footwear. In 1998 the company sold its slumping western boot business. Genesco ended its licence to sell Nautica-branded footwear in 2001, and in 2002 it closed the Nashville, Tennessee plant that manufactured Johnston & Murphy shoes.

George E. Keith Co. Manufacturer, active 1874–present

George Keith came from a family of shoemakers who had been operating in the Boston area since the 1750s. On 1 July 1874 he founded the company Green and Keith and incorporated the company as George E. Keith in 1896. A line of men's shoes was first produced in 1899 under the label 'Walk-Over'. The company was a prominent manufacturer and exporter of American-made Goodyear-welted shoes. By 1900 the company had offices in London, Melbourne, Cologne, Buenos Aires and Santiago. ` By 1912 an entire line of shoes was produced under the name Walk-Over Shoes. Dexter shoes purchased the company in 1997.

Golo Manufacturer, active 1915–86

In 1915 Adolf Heilbrun emigrated from Frankfurt, Germany to New York and relaunched his Golo Slipper Co., operating as a wholesaler until the end of World War II. Heilbrun's son-in-law, Arthur Samuels, then built a factory in Pennsylvania to manufacture women's casual Goodyear-welted shoes. His son, Arthur Samuels Jr, who trained under **David Evins**, was made fashion director of Golo Footwear when the company became a driving force in fashion footwear during the 1960s. Golo became a leader in boots and the Golo go-go boots were famous for their use of zips and stretch fabrics. The factory ceased operation in 1986 and the Golo name was later licensed to Caressa, which retired the brand.

Goodman, Georgina (1965–), Designer, active 2003–present

Born in 1965, Goodman worked as a stylist until deciding to study at London's Cordwainers College in 1996. She created her first line of shoes in 2003, which featured orange-peel-like upper patterns cut from one piece of leather that were folded, moulded and stitched into shoe and boot styles.

Gucci, Guccio (1881–1953), Designer, Manufacturer, active 1921–present

After working in a London hotel for several years, Guccio Gucci was inspired by the tailored English 'horsey' style. Returning to his birthplace, he founded a saddlery in 1921 in Florence and quickly branched out into luggage. The business expanded throughout the 1930s. In 1953 Gucci opened a store in New York and some accounts indicate that he first designed shoes in 1932. In 1957 he introduced a moccasin-constructed shoe with a gilded snaffle (instep chain strap). The style was available originally only for men in black or brown leather. In 1989 Gucci introduced a scaled-down version for women in a variety of colours.

Halpern, Joan & David Designers, Manufacturers, active 1968–present

Joan was studying psychology at Harvard when she met David, her future husband, who was the chairman of Suburban Shoe Stores. Learning the business at a small shoe firm in Boston, Joan designed snappy neutral-toned pumps and oxfords with sensible heels – the perfect attire for the modern liberated woman. The label 'Joan & David' was launched in 1977 and the following year Joan received a Coty Award for

design. A men's line, David and Joan, was launched in 1982 and a less expensive line, Joan & David Too, in 1987. The flagship store opened on Madison Avenue in 1985, and they have built an empire of shoe stores, franchises and boutiques in department stores. The company is now based in Italy.

Hardy, Pierre (1956–), Designer, active 1988–present

The son of a gym teacher and dance instructor, Hardy attended the Ecole Nationale Supérieure des Beaux-Arts in Paris. He began designing shoes for Dior in 1988 and Hermès in 1990. In 1998 Hardy launched his first eponymous line of shoes that featured the noteworthy blade heel, a thin rectangle that looks like a stiletto heel from the side and a block heel from the back.

Havilland, Terry de (1939–), Designer, active 1970–present

Born to English shoemaker parents, Terry Higgins was an apprentice to his father. In around 1960 Terry changed his surname to De Havilland when he was toying with the idea of pursuing an acting career. Terry worked in his father's business making winkle-picker boots for men and women during the 1960s. Upon his father's death in 1970 he took over the family business. While clearing out some of the shoes his father had made, he found a platform wedge shoe that his father had fashioned in the mid 1940s. Reinterpreting the style, Terry made up a few pairs in patchwork snakeskin and sold them through a Kensington market boutique. The rock'n'roll crowd loved them, and soon Terry was selling shoes as fast as he could make them for such clients as Bianca Jagger, Britt Ekland, Cher, Bette Midler, David Bowie and others. He opened a boutique called Cobblers to the World in 1972 on King's Road in London, a district that was popular with the glam-rock crowd at that time. In 1974 he was commissioned to make Tim Curry a pair of platform shoes for the film *The Rocky Horror Picture Show*. He was also instrumental in reintroducing the stiletto heel in the 1970s, first producing pairs for a Zandra Rhodes collection. In 1979 changing tastes forced his store to close, but De Havilland continued designing and launched a line called Kamikaze Shoes that featured winkle-picker stilettos for the New Wave scene. By 1990 however, the fashion for trainers, **Doc Martens** and almond-toed pumps forced Kamikaze out of business.

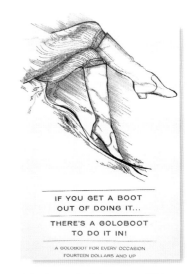

IF YOU GET A BOOT
OUT OF DOING IT...

THERE'S A GOLOBOOT
TO DO IT IN!

A GOLOBOOT FOR EVERY OCCASION
FOURTEEN DOLLARS AND UP

Advertisement for Golo, summer 1964.

Green suede and snakeskin platforms, labelled 'Terry de Havilland – London – Made in England', c. 1974–75.

Hellstern green silk satin and gold kid double-bar shoe with high gilded kid heels, c. 1925.

Advertisement for Charles Jourdan, summer 1959.

De Havilland worked on a freelance basis during most of the 1990s designing fetish and bondage boots as well as the occasional collections for Alexander McQueen and Anna Sui.

☐ **Hellstern, Louis** Designer, active c. 1872–c. 1970
Founded by Louis Hellstern in Paris following the Franco-Prussian War of 1870–71, the Hellstern company created some of the best quality men's footwear available at their first store on rue du 29 Juillet. Moving to Place Vendôme in around 1900, Hellstern became known for its women's shoes and was patronized by the same clients as Paris's top couturiers. Under Louis's son, Charles Hellstern, the company reached the height of its success in the 1920s, producing T-strap, instep strap and plain pumps. The company produced leather shoes throughout World War II but gradually lost business after the war. Their Brussels boutique closed in 1949, their London boutique in 1965 and their Cannes boutique in 1970.

Heyraud Manufacturer, active 1927–present
Heyraud was the first shoe manufacturer in France to mass-produce fashion footwear using American machines and production techniques. Their designs from the 1930s to the 1950s were in competition with **Bally** and other similar high-end ready-to-wear footwear companies. Heyraud is now operated as a division of ERAM, a French conglomerate of apparel manufacturers.

Hope, Emma Designer, active 1984–present
Trained at London's Cordwainers College, English-born Hope produced her first collection in 1984 and has designed shoes for Bill Gibb and Jean Muir. She opened her own shop in 1987 and received awards for her work in 1988 and 1989. Her shoes have always been heavily influenced by historical styles.

Jansen, Jan (1941–), Designer, active 1964–present
Dutch-born Jansen began his career in shoe design working under the Jeannot label in 1964. In 1969 he created the 'Woody' style, a new look for the Dutch *clompen*, consisting of a wooden clog sole and a leather upper. Copies by other manufacturers forced Jansen to abandon the design, but it set a fashion

for the return of the clog in the 1970s. By the 1980s Jansen was designing six collections per year, which were sold around the world. One of the most successful brands was the Bruno line. In the 1990s he started to produce shoes under his own name, which allowed him to explore unconventional materials and edgier designs.

Johnston & Murphy Manufacturer, active 1850–2002
In 1850 William Dudley set up a small factory in Newark, New Jersey that made high-quality hand-made men's shoes. He went into partnership with James Johnston in 1880 but died two years later and Johnston brought in William Murphy. The company was bought out by **Genesco** in 1951 and was moved to Nashville, Tennessee in 1957, retaining its reputation for quality and employing Italian master shoemakers. The company boasted that it had produced shoes for every president of the United States since Millard Fillmore (1850–53).

☐ **Jourdan, Charles** (1883–1976), Manufacturer, active c. 1921–present
Charles Jourdan worked his way up in the shoe industry in Romans, France, becoming a cutting-room foreman in 1917. Making his own shoes on the side, Jourdan built up a large enough clientele to start a small shoe workshop in 1921 (some sources say 1919). The company grew so rapidly that by 1928 it had moved into a larger building and a prêt-à-porter line under the label 'Séducta' was launched. The 1930s were difficult, so Jourdan produced a cheaper line under the label 'Feminaflor'. His sons joined the family business during World War II when, like most French companies, Jourdan was turning out shoes in substitute materials. It was in the postwar years that the company really took off, first expanding into the British market in 1950. His son Roland was responsible for establishing the company's reputation for chic elegance in the US. Roland met with American shoe retailer conglomerate **Genesco** and an agreement was reached in 1952 whereby a Jourdan sales office was set up in the Empire State Building in New York and Jourdan was the only French shoe factory to export shoes to the US. In 1957 Charles's three sons took over the business, which by then had a reputation for quality ready-to-wear footwear, and opened a boutique at 5 boulevard de la Madeleine in Paris. In 1959, the house of Dior granted the company

a licence to manufacture **Roger Vivier**'s shoe designs for Dior. Jourdan was now associated with haute couture and, through its connection with Genesco in the US, Jourdan was also making Dior's shoes for the American market. During the 1960s Jourdan opened shoe boutiques around the world and created lines for several prêt-à-porter collections, including Pierre Cardin. Jourdan shoes are synonymous with the 1970s, but this decade was also a difficult one for the company. In 1971 Genesco bought a controlling interest in Jourdan, which led to internal strife and resulted in Roland buying out his brothers' shares and becoming president of the company. The company expanded, perhaps too much, and in 1979 Genesco sold off their interest to a Swiss company. Roland stepped down from the helm in 1981 and non-family members have run the company since. In the early 1990s Jourdan was making shoes under its own labels (Charles Jourdan and Séducta), as well as shoes for Bis, Claude Montana (men's shoes), and Karl Lagerfeld (women's shoes). The company has cut back on its retail stores and has been focusing on restructuring since the early 1990s recession.

☐ Julianelli, Mabel and Charles Designers, active c. 1947–87

American husband-and-wife team Charles and Mabel Julianelli were a powerful duo, with Charles in charge of factory production and Mabel concentrating on design. Besides having her own line, Mabel designed for other companies like DeLiso Debs. Specializing in light and airy sandals, her footwear always had a feminine touch that made even low-heeled shoes seem delicate. Recognized in 1950 with a Coty Award for artistry and craftsmanship, Mabel designed for the couture end of the shoe industry. Paradoxically, she was one of the innovators of the masculine look in fashion footwear. Mabel Julianelli died in 1994.

Justin Boot Company Manufacturer, active 1879–present

H J Justin started a boot-repair business at a Spanish fort along the Chisholm Trail in 1879. He soon began making cowboy boots and moved his business to Nocona, Texas. He died in 1918 and his two sons took over the business, moving operations to Fort Worth in 1925, while his daughter remained in Nocona and opened the Nocona Boot Co. Third-generation John Justin Jr. was responsible for starting the

Justin Belt Co. in 1938, but rejoined the family boot business in 1949, becoming its president. In 1968, Justin Boot, the belt and leather goods companies merged to form Justin Industries Inc., which expanded into building products. In 1981 Justin bought back the Nocona Boot Co. and in 1990 also acquired Tony Lama Co. The southwest Tex-Mex fashion revival of the early 1990s saw boot sales peaking in 1993, but the falling interest in cowboy boots in the mid and late 1990s dragged down the profits. Justin split the footwear and building products businesses into separate companies in 1999 and moved boot-making operations to El Paso, Texas and Cassville, Missouri, closing the Nocona boot factories. John Justin stepped down as chairman in 1999 and died in 2001 at the age of 84. Berkshire Hathaway acquired Justin in 2000, ending the family-owned era of the business.

Kalso, Anne Designer, active 1968–present

Working as a yoga instructor, Danish-born Anne Kalso observed that when walking on the beach the heel sinks the most into the sand, as in the yoga mountain pose. Believing this stance to have health benefits, Kalso tested designs for shoes with lowered, or negative, heels. In 1968 Kalso opened a retail store in Copenhagen to sell her 'Kalso Minus Heel' shoe. The following year, vacationing Americans Raymond and Eleanor Jacobs discovered the store and entered into an agreement with Kalso to distribute the shoes in the US. Opening a store on 1 April 1970 on East Seventeenth Street in New York, they realized that they had accidentally coincided with the first internationally observed Earth Day, and Eleanor Jacobs put a sign in the window advertising the product as 'Earth Shoes'. To keep up with growing demand, the first Earth Shoe factory opened in the US in September 1972. By 1974 an advertising campaign was launched and extensive stories ran about the new product in news and fashion magazines, including *Time*, *Vogue* and *Cosmo*. Demand for the shoes rocketed. In 1977 franchise store owners filed a lawsuit against Earth for its inability to cater for the demand, resulting in the dissolution of the US Earth company. By 2000 the brand was being sold on a website in the US under a new partnership between Kalso and Meynard Designs Inc. The shoes were reintroduced to the retail marketplace in 2001.

Julianelli shoes of brown satin with black velvet brocade, c. 1960.

Red Cross Shoes catalogue, spring 1911.

Advertisement for Laird, Schober, autumn 1930.

White woven-leather pumps with brown leather toes, counters and heels, typical of Stephane Kélian's designs, c. 1985.

Herbert Levine Company introduced the aerodynamically designed 'Kabuki' pumps in 1964 to give the illusion of flight and walking on air. Levine later observed that they should have been named 'airplane' pumps.

□ **Kélian, Stephane** Designer, Manufacturer, active c. 1978–present

From Armenian roots, Stephane Keloglanian's family settled in Romans, France to work in the shoe industry in the 1920s. Stephane's older brothers, Georges and Gerard, opened their own shoe factory in 1960. In 1978 Stephane launched his first women's collection under the label Stephane Kélian and quickly became known for his high-quality, handmade woven uppers. The company produces **Maud Frizon** and holds the licence to make and distribute Claude Montana, Jean Paul Gaultier and Issey Miyake. In 1994 the Fashion Footwear Association of New York presented Kélian with the Fashion Medal of Honor Award. Kélian resigned as chairman of the company in 1995 but remains as a consultant working with the design team.

Knox, Nancy Designer, active c. 1960–present

Starting as an assistant shoe stylist at **I. Miller** in New York, Knox went on to create a small line of leisure footwear, called Renegade, for **Genesco** in the late 1960s. In the 1970s she created a line of men's shoes under her own label, which were manufactured in Italy. She was the recipient of the Coty Award in 1971 and 1975 for her men's shoe designs.

□ **Krohn, Fechheimer & Co.** Manufacturer, active c. 1905–c. 1965

This manufacturer based in Cincinnati, Ohio is best known for the brand 'Red Cross Shoes'. Produced from 1905 until the 1960s the brand was known for its comfort, bendable sole, attention to fashion and low price point. The brand's popularity with a vast number of urban and suburban Americans who wanted fashionable but not extreme footwear designs made the Krohn and Fechheimer families wealthy.

Kumagai, Tokio (1947–87), Designer, active 1980–87

After graduating in 1970 from the Bunka Fukuso Gakuin, the Tokyo college of fashion, Kumagai went to Paris where he worked for a number of companies, including Castelbajac, Rodier and Pierre d'Alby. In 1979 he began hand-painting shoes and in 1980 opened his first boutique. Inspired by modern artists such as Wassily Kandinsky, Jackson Pollock and Piet Mondrian, Kumagai often altered the structure of the shoe to accommodate his painting.

□ **Laird, Schober & Co.** Manufacturer, active 1869–c. 1965

Founded in 1869 in Philadelphia as Laird & Mitchell, the company became Laird, Schober & Mitchell in 1872. It exhibited at the 1876 Philadelphia Centennial Exposition, showing hand-stitched boots that had up to 64 stitches per inch (the most ever known). These boots are now in the collection of the Los Angeles County Museum of Art. The company became known as Laird, Schober & Co. in 1895 and won a Grand Prize at the Paris Exposition in 1900. It produced high-quality women's and children's shoes and was one of the American manufacturers who exported large quantities of shoes to Europe in the late nineteenth century. The company was prominent until the 1950s but became less so in the 1960s due to competition from Italian imports.

□ **Levine, Beth** (1914–2006) and Herbert Levine (1916–91) Designers, Manufacturers, active 1948–75

One of Beth's first jobs was as a size 4B shoe model for Palter De Liso in New York when open-toed shoes were first introduced – the scandalous fashion of the late 1930s. She met and married journalist Herbert Levine in 1944, and in 1948 they started their own shoe company. Herbert was the business manager and Beth headed the design. The Herbert Levine Company introduced the world to 'Spring-o-lator' mules and stocking boots (tights, or pantyhose, with heels attached) in the 1950s. They also popularized the return of the fashion boot in the mid 1960s, for which the company received a Coty Award in 1967. Anticipating trends, like the pointed toe of 1957, was the Levine strength. Fun heels, rhinestone-covered pumps, and the use of new, space-age materials such as vinyl and acrylic were trademarks of the Levine look. After testing a brand new material called 'Ultrasuede', Beth Levine decided it was not for shoemaking and showed it to her fellow designer Roy Halston. Some crazy styles, created more for publicity than to set a fashion, included paper shoes made of plaited candy wrappers, sandals sporting Astroturf insoles and upper-less sandals, where the shoe was glued onto one's nylons. Levine supplied boots for Nancy Sinatra and inaugural pumps for Patricia Nixon. The changing marketplace and foreign imports resulted in the company closing in 1975. Herbert and Beth Levine won a Neiman Marcus Award and two Coty Awards for their designs.

Lobb, John Shoemaker, active 1866–present

After a stint in Australia supplying boots to prospectors, John Lobb returned to London and in 1866 set up a bespoke shoemaker's business in St James Street, catering for London's male elite. He became boot maker to Edward VII, receiving his first royal warrant. Almost going out of business during the Depression in 1929 and damaged by bombs six times during World War II (the custom-sized lasts were stored in the country to avoid destruction), the company still managed to survive. In 1956 Lobb received its second royal warrant from the Duke of Edinburgh, followed by the Queen's warrant in 1963 and the Prince of Wales's warrant in 1980. A pair of Lobb bespoke shoes can take up to six months to make and costs over a thousand pounds sterling.

Louboutin, Christian (1963–), Designer, active 1991–present

Christian Louboutin describes himself as a bit of a shoe fetishist and explains that for him the most sensuous part of a woman's foot is the inside curve of the arch. Inspired by cabaret showgirls, Louboutin knew early on in his career that it was the flashy stage shoes he really wanted to design. He trained at **Charles Jourdan** and sold freelance designs before opening his own shop in 1991 at the Passage Vero-Dodat in Paris. He paints the soles of all his shoes bright red, regardless of their upper colour, and the top lifts of his heels are often shaped to leave rosette imprints. He refers to these as his 'Follow Me' shoes.

Maertens, Klaus Designer, active 1945–59

In 1945 Dr Klaus Maertens, a German orthopedic doctor, was recovering from a skiing accident when he decided to create a comfortable shoe to ease the pain of his injured foot. He designed an air-cushioned sole with the help of his colleague Dr Herbert Funck, who perfected, patented and marketed the soles in Germany. Looking for a larger manufacturer and distributor, Maertens came across the family-owned British manufacturer **R. Griggs Co.**, who was awarded the global licence in 1959.

☐ **Magli, Bruno** Designer, Manufacturer, active 1936–present

Although founded in 1936 it was not until the 1950s, when 'Made in Italy' became synonymous with quality and style, that the company became well known.

In the late 1960s Morris Magli, Bruno's nephew, became president and Morris's wife, Rita, took over the creative direction of the line. She has been credited with steering the collections on a more modern course and for instigating Magli's association with designer **Andrea Pfister**. Exports account for 80 per cent of sales.

☐ **Mancini, René** Shoemaker, Designer, active 1936–c.1985

A Parisian shoemaker who worked by hand, Mancini provided superbly made shoes to Balmain, Givenchy and Chanel. He also had an extensive list of private clients, including Jacqueline Kennedy, Greta Garbo, Princess Grace and Lauren Bacall.

Maraolo, Mario (1936–), Designer, Manufacturer, active 1956–present

At the age of fifteen Maraolo was apprenticed to his father's tannery. Five years later he opened his own shoe factory in Naples in 1956. By the mid 1960s he had opened stores in Europe and the US, which carried his brands 'Maraolo' and 'Coca'. He signed a deal with Giorgio Armani in 1979 to produce the leather goods for the lines Giorgio Armani and Emporio Armani. Maraolo also produces footwear for Donna Karan and **Joan Halpern**'s Joan & David line. About 40 per cent of the company's daily production of nearly 3,000 pairs of shoes for men and women is exported to the US.

☐ **Massaro** Shoemaker, designer, active c. 1894–present

Sebastien Massaro founded a shoe-making firm in 1894 at 2 rue de la Paix in Paris. Sebastien and his four sons, all trained in the business by their father, were bespoke shoemakers, little known outside their own exclusive circle of customers. Sebastien's grandson, Raymond, born in 1929, took the company in a different direction when he designed the beige pump with a black toecap and heel for Chanel in 1957. Produced as a closed pump and as a sling-back, the style has been in almost constant production ever since, even if not made by Chanel. Since this early liaison with Chanel, Raymond Massaro has produced shoe designs for a long list of couturiers and clothing designers. In 1994 the French government awarded him the title Master of Art for his consummate ability to produce finely crafted footwear.

Advertisement for Magli, autumn 1961.

Mancini black kid pumps made for Lauren Bacall, c. 1957.

Mid-1980s sling-back beige kid pumps with black patent toecaps by Chanel, showing little change from the original 1957 Massaro design.

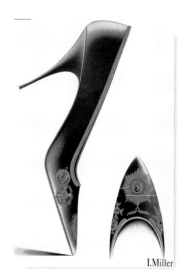

Advertisement for I. Miller, winter 1958.

Advertisement for Palizzio, summer 1964.

□ **Miller, Israel** Manufacturer, Retailer, active c. 1880–c. 1980

The House of Miller was a family dynasty of shoe manufacturers founded by Israel Miller, a Russian émigré who learned the business from an Italian shoemaker in New York. In 1880 Miller went into business for himself, opening a theatrical footwear suppliers store and factory on 23rd Street. He lived with his large extended family over the business. By the end of World War I the company had expanded into fashion footwear and Israel's son, George, led the business solely into fashion footwear when he took over the company on his father's death in 1929. Miller hired designers **André Perugia** and most notably **David Evins**, with whom he had a contract to make shoes with Evins's name appearing on the label. I. Miller was also known for its studio of talented in-house shoe designers. Jerrold Miller, great grandson of Israel, joined the firm after returning from service in World War II and went on to form his own business (see **Margaret Clark**). In the early 1960s Miller hired a young Andy Warhol to dress windows and produce charming shoe sketches for Christmas greeting cards. By the 1960s I. Miller had entered the lower-priced market with a line called 'Mademoiselle' and also the youth market with a line called 'Miller Eye'. In 1973 the company was sold to US shoe retailer conglomerate **Genesco**. It was part of the **Rayne** division until the early 1980s when it was sold to investors and, not long afterwards, went into bankruptcy.

Model, Philippe Designer, active 1983–present

In 1983 French designer Philippe Model was inspired by a piece of heavy elastic used in lingerie. He fashioned a simple flat shoe using the elastic as the upper, stitching it all over in arabesque designs. Model was an innovator of stretch shoes, and this simple design concept has been used on a large range of footwear, including boots, pumps and mules.

Nike Manufacturer, active 1972–present

Entrepreneurs Phil Knight and Bill Bowerman met through the University of Oregon's track and field department in 1957. The pair formed Blue Ribbon Sports in 1962, selling Japanese-made Tiger brand running shoes at track meets. In 1972 Knight and Bowerman renamed their company Nike, after the Greek goddess of victory, and paid Carolyn Davidson US $35 to design the 'swoosh' logo (she was later given an undisclosed amount of stock for her important contribution). At the 1972 Olympic trials in Oregon, Nike persuaded some of the marathon runners to wear their shoes and quickly advertised that four of the top seven finishers had worn the brand. In 1974 they added the waffle sole to their running shoes, literally created by placing a rubber sole in a waffle iron. Nike's running-shoe sales grew as the popularity of jogging increased throughout the 1970s, and they had captured a 50% share of the US running-shoe market by 1979. Nike went public in 1980 and expanded into other sports footwear, launching the Tailwind running shoe in 1980, the first shoe to feature the Air-Sole cushioning system. The technology was a hit and in 1985 Nike created a basketball shoe and, with the endorsement of Michael Jordan, the Air Jordan became the company's most successful product. In 1987 Nike introduced the cross trainer and, the following year, the familiar 'Just Do It' slogan was born. Throughout the 1990s, with a weakening market for athletic shoes, Nike diversified into athletic apparel and electronics. They acquired Canstar Sports, which included hockey-equipment-maker Bauer, in 1992, and opened stores called Niketown. Hoping for a repeat marketing success, Nike signed Tiger Woods for an endorsement contract that they renewed in 2000. Bill Bowerman died in 1999 and a line of shoes was named in his honour. In 2003 Nike acquired **Converse** but allow it to operate separately, keeping its name intact.

Nina Manufacturer, active 1962–present

The father of Stanley and Mike Silverstein emigrated to the US from Cuba in the 1930s and opened a small clog-making shop in 1944. In 1953, Stanley and Mike were put to work crafting basic leather uppers that were tacked to the wooden soles. In 1962 the brothers started a company, which they christened Nina, in a small SoHo loft. By the late 1960s, through a series of expansions and profitable purchases of Spanish boot exports, Nina had become one of the largest manufacturers in the US, producing more than 5,000 pairs a day. Stanley presided over design and manufacturing, while Mike headed the merchandising efforts. Today, the company manufactures four footwear lines: Nina, Touch of Nina, Nina Doll and Elements by Nina. It has also acquired the defunct **Delman** label from which they aim to build a luxury footwear line.

Nine West Manufacturer, active 1977–99
Nine West founder Jerome Fisher worked in his family's shoe factory before opening his own factory in 1958. His partner Vincent Camuto had worked for the Japanese shoe importer Sumitomo Corporation of America, where he developed marketing and distribution plans. The two founded the wholesale shoe business Fisher Camuto Corporation in 1977, importing shoes from Brazilian manufacturers. They started a sister company, called Jervin (the name comes from the first three letters of each of their first names), in 1988 to sell unbranded women's shoes made in Brazil to retailers and wholesalers. Fisher Camuto expanded between 1989 and 1992 due to their quick production of designer-style footwear at moderate prices. In 1993 they merged their two businesses into Nine West (after their first address, Nine W. 57th Street, in Manhattan) and went public. In 1995 they bought out American shoe manufacturing giant US Shoe and the following year began to dismantle US Shoe operations, closing their headquarters, discontinuing unprofitable brands and shutting down domestic factories to shift all production to Brazil. In 1999 clothing manufacturer and distributor Jones Apparel Group bought Nine West for US $1.4 billion and integrated it into their own company within a year.

☐ **Palizzio Shoes** Manufacturer, active c. 1950–88
Reuben and Leo Gordon were sons of a Russian émigré who went to the US in 1885. Reuben founded Thomas Cort Shoes in Philadelphia during World War II and Leo joined the company. Leo left to found Palizzio Shoes in New York in around 1950 with his son-in-law, Ralph Abrams. Ralph's son, Michael, and his son-in-law joined the company in 1967, buying it in 1980. Michael opened factories in Spain and Italy to manufacture the brands Palizzio, Proxy and Perry Ellis footwear. The Palizzio name was sold in 1988 to Arcadia International Shoe Corporation but Michael Abrams continued in the shoe business, opening Kasper Footwear in 1995.

☐ **Palter De Liso** Designer, Manufacturer, active 1919–75
The Palter Shoe Company was founded in New York in 1919 by Daniel Palter. In 1927 Palter went into partnership with James De Liso and renamed the company Palter De Liso. De Liso headed the design while Palter ran the business. The company promoted coloured leather shoes in the 1930s and received a Neiman Marcus Award in 1938 for introducing open-toed sling-back pumps. In the 1950s the 'De Liso Debs' line was added, aimed at a youthful audience. The company was taken over by Daniel Palter's son, Richard Palter, who ran the company until it closed in 1975.

☐ **Pancaldi** Manufacturer, active 1888–present
Pancaldi has operated in Bologna since Natale Pancaldi crafted his first shoe in 1888. His son, Romolo, took over in the 1930s. Third-generation Natalino expanded the family business by modernizing and exporting in the postwar period. Today, Stefano (Natalino's son) presides over the company. Most of its production is exported. Pancaldi has made shoes for **Manolo Blahník**, **Walter Steiger**, Isaac Mizrahi, Fausto Santini and **Philippe Model**. In 1986 the company was licensed to produce footwear for the German apparel company Escada.

Pasquali, Guido Designer, active 1967–present
The Pasquali company was founded in 1918 by Guido Pasquali's grandfather. Guido studied mechanics and engineering at Bocconi University in Milan before taking over the family business in 1967. During the 1970s, he supplied shoes to such Italian designers as Walter Albini, Giorgio Armani and Missoni. His own designs are available through his shop in Milan.

☐ **Perugia, André** (1893–1977), Designer, active c. 1920–77
Perugia was born in 1893 in Tuscany, but his family moved to Nice where André learned shoemaking as an apprentice to his father. One of his first commissions was for the wife of a hotel owner who agreed to put his shoes on display in the hotel foyer. This brought Perugia to the attention of Paris couturier Paul Poiret, who was holidaying there at the time. Poiret offered to set up Perugia in Paris, but World War I interrupted their plans. After working as an engineer at an aeroplane factory during the war, Perugia took up Poiret's offer. Poiret introduced Perugia to his clientele and in 1921 Perugia opened his shop at 11 rue du Faubourg Saint-Honoré. His client list quickly grew and included stars from film and the Folies Bergère, such as Josephine Baker. He expanded to Nice in the mid 1920s and in 1930 entered into a collaboration with

Advertisement for Palter De Liso, winter 1952.

Black suede pump by Pancaldi, c. mid 1980s.

Teal suede and gold kid D'Orsay pump, stamped on sole 'Perugia', c. 1930–33.

Peter Kaiser green leather and snakeskin platform pumps, made under the brand label 'Paradies', c. 1975.

Andrea Pfister pineapple-print cowboy boot with pineapple-shaped heel, c. 1999. Pfister was best known in the 1980s and early 1990s for the surface ornamentation of his shoes.

Advertisement for the opening of the Pinet store in New York, September 1930.

Elsa Schiaparelli that would last until 1950. In 1933 he moved to 4 rue de la Paix and introduced a ready-to-wear collection under the label 'Padova', which was distributed through Saks in the US. In 1937 he moved to 2 rue de la Paix, where he would remain for the rest of his career, designing under his own label as well as for **Rayne** in England and **I. Miller** in the US. Perugia registered numerous patents, including his 1942 French patent for an articulated wooden sole that was much used during wartime leather shortages, and a 1956 patent for interchangeable heels. Throughout his prolific career Perugia drew inspiration for his designs from the Orient, modern art, industrial design and history. Perugia worked for **Charles Jourdan** as a technical advisor from 1962 to 1966 and, upon his death in 1977, left his archives to Charles Jourdan.

Peter Kaiser Manufacturer, active 1838–present

One of the first industrial shoe manufacturers in the country, Peter Kaiser established a shoemaker's shop in 1838 in Pirmasens, Germany. By the beginning of the twentieth century Pirmasens had become the seat of the German shoe industry, as Northampton was to England and Romans was to France. The company specializes in women's high-fashion footwear.

Pfister, Andrea (1942–), Designer, active c. 1964–present

Andrea Pfister was born in Pesaro, Italy and was educated in Switzerland and Italy, attending the Ars Sutoria shoe design school in Milan. In 1963 Pfister, then a neophyte in the world of shoe design, won Best International Footwear Designer for his snakeskin pump called 'Comedie'. By 1964, he was designing footwear for Jean Patou and Lanvin. Pfister showed his first collection of shoes in 1965, and in 1967 established his own signature collection, which he and his partner, Pierre Dupré, used to open their first boutique in Paris at 4 rue Cambon. After expanding into handbags and belts, Pfister opened his second boutique in 1987 in Milan. The following year he was once again recognized as Best International Footwear Designer when he received the Grand Fashion Medal of Honour in New York, the first living designer ever to do so. From his studio in Positano, Italy, Pfister creates couture and prêt-à-porter collections twice a year. He is a master of colour and applied decoration, known for adorning his shoes with sumptuous displays of embroidery, sequins and exotic skins.

As well as running his own line, Pfister has held design posts at Anne Klein, Dell-Olio and **Bruno Magli**. His footwear is reproduced under licences in Japan, Turkey, Spain and South Africa, but the US accounts for the majority of his business.

Pinet, François (1817–97), Shoemaker, Designer, Manufacturer, active c. 1855–1940

François Pinet was the son of a French provincial shoemaker. As a made-to-order shoemaker of bespoke footwear he is thought of as the first great shoe designer to make a name for himself. Pinet catered for the fashionable elite of his day from his Paris shop at 44 rue Paradis Poissonière, which opened in 1855. Pinet's reputation rose as the foundations of haute couture became established, and a pair of Pinet boots was considered the perfect complement to a Charles Worth dress. By 1863 Pinet was employing 120 people in his studio and over 700 pieceworkers. Pinet is credited with popularizing the return of the high heel in the 1870s. His trademark high Louis heel became known in the late nineteenth century as the Pinet Heel. Pinet eventually handed his business over to his son, who continued to make footwear into the 1930s. The business had expanded just prior to the Depression, with outlets in Paris, London, Berlin, Vienna and New York. These proved difficult for the company to maintain in the changing political and economic times of the 1930s.

Pollini, Armando (1935–), Designer, active 1962–present

Italian-born Armando Pollini worked in his father's pattern-making company, leaving only briefly to train as a member of the Italian track and field team for the 1960 Olympics. Pollini then hit the pavements as a freelance designer, working for a variety of companies and travelling extensively throughout Europe, although he favoured London as a source of inspiration. He is counted among the designers who popularized the return of the platform in the early 1970s, and in 1975 created his first line of shoes. Pollini's clog consisting of a plastic bottom unit and a leather upper strap was a huge hit in the American market in 1978 and 1979, where it had been imported under the brand name 'Candies'. In the early 1980s Pollini became known for his version of ballet flats. In the late 1980s he introduced elastic textile uppers, which he called 'elast', and which, by the early 1990s, accounted for 50% of his sales.

Prada, Miuccia Designer, Manufacturer, active c. 1978–present

Mario Prada founded the Italian fashion house in 1913. The company did not become well known until the late 1970s when Miuccia revamped the business, promoting Prada's strength in shoes and accessories. In the late 1980s Prada launched a fashion collection of pared-down cutting-edge pieces and a younger, hipper secondary line called Miu Miu. They also released a collection of men's apparel and shoes. A third of Prada's business is derived from footwear, and Prada's influence on fashion footwear by the mid 1990s cannot be overlooked. Prada promoted the elongated vamp and squared toe and revitalized the fashion boot. Miuccia received a Neiman Marcus Award in 1995 for her contribution to style.

Puma Manufacturer, active 1948–present

Brothers Adi and Rudi Dassler founded the Dassler sports-shoe factory in 1924. But a rift between them resulted in Adi remaining with the Dassler factory and renaming his product **Adidas**, and Rudi opening Puma across the River Aurach in 1948. Puma got off to a good start when Germany's team won the first post-World War II international soccer match wearing Puma's Atom shoes. The company was renamed PUMA-Sportschuhfabriken Rudolf Dassler KG in 1959 when Rudi's wife and two sons, Armin and Gerd, joined the firm. In 1974 Rudi Dassler died and Armin took over the company. Puma introduced shoe technologies and products intended to capture the jogging market in the 1970s. By 1977 it was selling 40,000 shoes in 150 countries. In the mid-1980s both Martina Navratilova and Boris Becker won Wimbledon wearing Puma shoes, and in 1986 the company went public. Puma quickly fell from the forefront of the sports-shoe market, largely because it missed important trends in the fashion-conscious US sneaker market in which Reebok and Nike were leaders. After 1993 the company reorganized and ownership changed hands several times. Puma raised its visibility in 1998 by signing tennis phenomenon Serena Williams. It also regained some of the US market when its associate company LogoAthletic became an official supplier of the National Football League and the National Basketball Association until 2001.

R. Griggs Co. Manufacturer, active 1901–present

This family-owned British manufacturer was founded in 1901. The small firm, which specialized in work footwear, became very successful when it acquired the licence for a patented sole from Dr **Klaus Maertens** in 1959. Griggs anglicized the name to Dr Martens and changed the material from rubber to PVC to make them more resistant to oil, acids and petrol. The first model was dubbed '1460', after the date the first pair came off the assembly line on 1 April 1960. The boots were marketed as industrial and work wear, and the first steady customers were the British police, postal workers and labourers. In the mid 1970s the punk movement picked up on the brutal-looking but comfortable boots, and by the mid 1980s sales for this British street style had rocketed. Griggs's son, Max, took over the family firm in 1980 and bought out the various licensed manufacturers of Doc Martens, expanding control over the market. The product range grew to include thousands of styles and colours. By the early 1990s, the patented sole was found within every echelon of society. Skinheads adopted the boot as part of their uniform, using coloured laces to express their beliefs, the most negative of which was white laces worn by neo-Nazis. Meanwhile designers like **Manolo Blahník** fashioned high style couture shoes from the patented sole, and even the Vatican placed an order for Doc Marten footwear. Success was the footwear's downfall. Sales began to slump in the mid 1990s, so in 1996 Griggs purchased the distributor AirWair USA Ltd and tightened control of the brand. He fought to protect the look of the product, taking to court manufacturers who copied elements of the boot's style, including components that were not patented such as the contrast stitching of the uppers. Claiming Doc Martens were not just a brand but also a lifestyle, Griggs spent most of the late 1990s and early 2000s in litigation. The style had been overmarketed and consumers were moving on. Following massive losses, Dr Marten shifted production from Britain to China in 2003.

Rautureau, Guy Designer, Manufacturer, active 1975–present

Hailing from a 300-year-old line of shoemakers in La Gaubretière, France, Guy Rautureau and his brother aimed their company, Apple Shoes, at a hip young market. Their lines include Pom D'Api (1975), Free Lance (1980), Slugger (1983), Etnies (1986), Spring Court (1989) and No Name (1993). Known for their

Instep strap pump with red wedge heel by Prada, c. 1997.

Blue kid sling-back open-toed pumps with ceramic heels. Rayne produced a line of shoes with Wedgwood jasperware heels in 1959 and again in 1978.

chic platforms in the 1990s, they also produced creative packaging, replacing the standard cardboard shoeboxes with corrugated plastic containers and tin-plate boxes painted by Loulou Picasso. Their shoes are on sale in their Free Lance stores, located the world over, and their first US store opened in New York in 1994.

☐ **Rayne, H & R** Manufacturer, active 1920–94
This family-owned firm was founded in the late 1880s by Irishman Henry Ryan who opened a theatrical costume business in London. Ryan changed his last name to Rayne to avoid anti-Irish feelings. Rayne provided costumes, make-up and theatrical footwear to such notables as Anna Pavlova and all the members of the Ballet Russe. When Joseph, his son, took over the business in 1918, he focused on footwear, opening the first Rayne shoe store in 1920 on New Bond Street and a shoe factory in North London. Rayne was granted a royal warrant by Queen Mary in the mid 1930s. In 1936 Rayne signed one of the world's first licensing agreements with **Delman** in the US, under which Rayne produced Delman shoes for the UK market. By the 1950s Rayne's American design sources were drying up, due partly to a production shift to Italy and partly to US shoe-retailing giant **Genesco** taking over Delman in 1954. Rayne signed a licensing deal with Genesco in 1957 to produce **Roger Vivier**–designed Christian Dior shoes for the English market, and in 1961 acquired the rights to make Delman shoes for ten years. Under head designer Jean Matthew, Rayne created shoe collections for apparel designers, including Hardy Amies, Mary Quant, Bruce Oldfield and Jean Muir. In need of capital to expand in 1973, the business was sold to the British department store Debenhams. Edward Rayne, grandson of the founder, had joined the company in 1940 and was now at the helm. He made the fatal error of not shifting production to Italy. The company coasted for the next twenty years, losing ground to competitors and becoming more of a retailer of other brands. Debenhams was acquired by The Burton Group in 1985 but Rayne was resold in 1987 to entrepreneur David Graham. Edward Rayne retired in 1988, severing all family involvement, and due to the recession six years later, Rayne went into liquidation.

Reebok Manufacturer, active 1894–present
In 1894 English runner Joseph Foster started a company making spiked running shoes to supply the British Olympic team in 1924. In 1958 two of Foster's grandsons formed a companion company called Reebok, after the African gazelle, eventually absorbing their grandfather's business. In 1979 Paul Fireman, a distributor of sporting goods, noticed the shoes at a Chicago trade show. Acquiring the North American licence for Reebok, Fireman did not threaten the established markets cornered by **Nike** and **Adidas**. The wife of Fireman's California sales rep had taken up a new activity called aerobics that she performed either barefoot or in bulky running shoes. Fireman felt this was a niche market worth exploring. An error in communication resulted in shoes made of soft white garment leather rather than the intended stiffer shoe leather, but this proved to be an advantage. Marketed as 'Freestyle', the women's line of aerobic footwear was launched in 1982, followed by a men's line in 1983. Reeboks' sales rocketed, even temporarily surpassing Nike in total sales in 1986. In 1985 Reebok USA acquired the original British Reebok Company and went public. Reebok created the inflatable 'pump' basketball shoe in the early 1990s, and in 1993 signed Shaquille O'Neal to promote the 'Shaq Attaq' line, with the hopes of muscling in on Nike's Air Jordan market. By 1993 however the sneaker boom was fading in comparison to the growing recreational 'brown shoe' market. With its shrinking market share, Reebok released O'Neal in 1998. After a significant cut in the workforce, Reebok shifted production from Asian countries in 2000 to avoid human rights issues. Since then Reebok has sought to become the exclusive supplier and/or licencee to sports organizations, including the National Football League, the Canadian Football League and the National Basketball Association.

Rossimoda Manufacturer, active 1944–present
Founded in Vigonza as a family business shortly after Italy conceded in World War II, Rossimoda has grown to be one of the largest manufacturers of high-end footwear, supplying shoes under the label of Lacroix, Givenchy, Pucci, Marc Jacobs, Kenzo, Yves Saint Laurent, Dior and Vera Wang. Under the direction of the founder's son, Luigino Rossi, since 1956, the company also produces a line of footwear.

Rudofsky, Bernard (1905–88), Designer
active 1947–present
Austrian-born Rudofsky was a Renaissance man who worked as an architect, writer, teacher, designer and

social historian. New York was his home from 1941 until his death. Rudofsky frequently lectured on the topic of modern fashion and felt that contemporary dress was impractical and irrational. His wife, Berta, taught courses on sandal making. Both created designs inspired by Ancient Greek and Roman sandals. Encouraged by the *Harper's Bazaar* fashion editor Diana Vreeland, the couple made sandals that were often featured in fashion shoots using Clair McCardell's clothes as early as 1944. Their successful venture, Bernardo Sandals, became one of the first American companies to employ Italian shoemakers to create their products. The company still thrives and was influential in the adoption of the thong sandal for beachwear in the 1950s.

Salamander Manufacturer, Retailer, active 1885–present

Kornwestheim, near Stuttgart, is home to Germany's largest shoe manufacturer: Salamander. Although the company was founded in 1885 as J. Sigle & Cie., by 1904 Jakob Sigle had gone into partnership with Maxuel Levi and the company was renamed Salamander. In 1925 Levi died, followed by Sigle in 1935. In 1960 Salamander expanded into France and in 1969 into Austria. At the peak of production in 1967, Salamander was producing 13.5 million pairs of shoes per year. By 1981 that number had decreased to 8 million pairs. After German reunification in 1990 Salamander expanded into the former East Germany as well as the then Czechoslovakia, Poland, Hungary and Russia. Salamander also expanded its retailing into the US.

Sanderson, Rupert (1966–), Designer, active 2001–present

Sanderson worked for Sergio Rossi before attending Cordwainers College in London between 1998 and 2000. He continues to work out of London where he launched his own line of shoes in 2002.

☐ **Schwartz & Benjamin** Manufacturer, active c. 1924–present

People outside the shoe business probably will not recognize this manufacturer. They have operated under numerous licensing brands, translating the shoe designs of Anne Klein, Yves Saint Laurent, Michael Kors and other designers into actual shoes. Founded in the early 1920s, the company created a line of shoes in the 1950s called 'Customcraft'.

☐ **Selby Shoe Co.** Manufacturer, active 1869–2000

Operating out of Portsmouth, Ohio, Selby developed a trend for comfort footwear in the 1920s. Its most successful brand, 'Arch Preserver', was popular from the 1920s to the 1950s, especially with the older American lady with an interest in fashion footwear. Selby was acquired by the US Shoe Company in the 1950s, but continued trading under the same name until it was closed in 2000 after the division was resold.

Sperry, Paul (1895–1982), Designer, active 1935–82

Paul Sperry was an avid sailor who found the rope- or rubber-soled canvas shoes available for boating in the 1930s to be less than satisfactory on slippery decks. Observing the paws of his dog, who had no problem keeping its footing on deck, Sperry experimented with various sole designs for superior traction, eventually coming up with a herringbone-designed rubber sole called the Top-Sider. Sperry struck a deal with the Converse Rubber Company, and the shoes were first marketed in 1935 for US $4.50. Uniroyal bought out **Converse**, and Stride Rite bought out the Sperry Top-Sider account from Uniroyal in 1979 and continues to produce this boating shoe.

☐ **Steiger, Walter** (1942–), Designer, active c. 1966–present

Walter Steiger was born in 1942 in Geneva, Switzerland. Following in the family shoemaking tradition, he became a shoemaker's apprentice at the age of 16, after which he went to work at **Bally**. He moved to London where he designed shoes for Mary Quant and opened a studio in 1966. He showed his collection in Paris two years later and moved there in 1973, opening his first shop on the Left Bank. In 1981 he brought his collections of men's and women's shoes to the US. Steiger has designed shoes for Karl Lagerfeld, Chanel, Chloé, Oscar de la Renta and Nina Ricci.

Susan Bennis Warren Edwards Designer, Retailer, active 1973–present

Design and retail team Susan Bennis and Warren Edwards opened a store in New York in 1973. They aimed to appeal to the high-fashion market with Italian-made men's and women's shoes and accessories. The company came to prominence

Advertisement for Customcraft, summer 1955.

Advertisement for Selby, winter 1952.

Pewter metallic-finished kid with gold metallic kid lining and triangular stiletto heel by Walter Steiger, c. 1985–86.

Advertisement for Troylings, autumn 1951.

Advertisement for United States Rubber Company, autumn 1951.

in the 1980s when it was located at 440 Park Avenue. Later, in 1990, it moved to 22 West 57th Street. In 1991 the company expanded and sold through Neiman Marcus and opened a second store in Los Angeles.

Thatcher, Mark Designer, active 1982–present
Working as a river guide along the Colorado River, Mark Thatcher felt there was no appropriate footwear available for this kind of activity. In 1982 Thatcher designed a securely strapped nylon sandal with a rubber-tread sole. Calling it an amphibious utility sandal, he picked the brand name 'Teva' (pronounced teh-vah, not tee-vah), Hebrew for 'nature'. Working with a manufacturer, Thatcher sold only 200 pairs in the first year of production, but the style slowly caught on. In 1988 Thatcher received his US patent and entered into an agreement with Deckers Corp., who would produce and distribute the sandals. His design led to many similar styles from other manufacturers in the 1990s.

Timberland Manufacturer, active 1968–present
In 1968 Sidney and Herman Swartz took over their father's Abington Shoe Company. Working with Goodyear, they created a waterproof leather boot with a bonded synthetic rubber sole that was marketed under the brand name 'Timberland' in 1973. The boot was so successful that the firm changed its name to The Timberland Company in 1978 and opened its first store in 1986. In the early 1990s, due to the over-saturation of the brown-shoe (outdoor recreational footwear) market, the company closed its American plants and outsourced production by 1994. In 1997 Timberland introduced a sneaker-boot hybrid.

Tondowski, Alain (1968–), Designer, active 1989–present
Tondowski studied at Studio Berçot, Paris's fashion school, before becoming a design assistant at Stephane Kélian in 1989 and Christian Dior in 1990, where he remained until 1994. He launched his own line of shoes in 1997 and has worked exclusively on his own collections since 2003.

☐ **Troy, Seymour** Designer, active 1923–75
Born in Poland, Seymour Troy came to the US in 1910. In 1923 he opened a small factory under his name and later produced a line called 'Troylings'. He was responsible for originating half sizes, a shankless

shoe, asymmetric strap closures, rolled top lines and a high-cut shoe called 'Valkyrie', which was endlessly copied. He was given the first Mercury Award from the National Shoe Industry Association (NSIA) in 1960 in recognition of 35 years of pioneering design.

Truedsson, Gil Designer, active 1970–present
Recipient of the 1979 Coty Award for men's footwear design, Truedsson works more in the field of clothing and sportswear. He won his first design job in the late 1960s at Saks Fifth Avenue, at a time when Saks was developing its own sportswear line. In 1971 Truedsson moved to Ralph Lauren, who was in the process of expanding his collection. In 1974 Truedsson was hired by the Swedish Fashion Group but became so involved in production that he found it hard to concentrate on designing. In 1979, aided by his Coty Award and with an interest in sports, he pursued a number of freelance projects, including the design of the uniforms for the National Hockey League All-Star game and the design of the Yves Saint Laurent sportswear collection. In 1984 he entered into a contract to design the line of clothing for the Sears-owned Boston Athletic Club.

Unic Manufacturer, active 1895–present
In 1895 Joseph Fenestrier bought a small rubber-boot factory in Romans, France. Moving the factory to larger premises in 1901 and hiring the American-patented Goodyear welting machine, Fenestrier specialized in quality men's footwear. In 1904 the company launched brand names for their shoe lines, including one called 'Good Taste American Fashion'. In 1907 the company was incorporated as Unic. Receiving numerous awards for quality and production between 1910 and 1915, the company expanded its retail outlets throughout Continental Europe, Russia and the Middle East. Following Fenestrier's early death in 1916, his wife took over operation of the plant until his son Joseph Emile-Jean succeeded her in 1922. He added a line of women's sports shoes in 1930. Sarkis Der Balian was among the many shoe designers hired to create designs for the company. During World War II Unic was forced to adapt its output to shoes made from such materials as wood, raffia and felt. Joseph Emile-Jean died in 1961 and the company merged with Sirius in 1967, which in turn was taken over by Charles Jourdan in 1969. Robert Clergerie took over the company in 1977, restructuring it and continuing to produce a line of

men's Goodyear-welted shoes under the Fenestrier label. Clergerie also produced a line of women's high-fashion boots and shoes under his own label.

☐ **United States Rubber Company**
Manufacturer, active c. 1893–present
Rubber-soled tennis shoes were first produced by the United States Rubber Company in 1893 under the first-grade brand name of 'Defender' and the second-grade brand name of 'Champion'. The company referred to them as 'sneaks' in 1900 when they were producing over 7,000 pairs of rubber-soled tennis, gym, yachting, 'vacation' and bathing shoes daily. After US Rubber bought out Goodyear in 1916, they began a rubber-soled sports and casual shoe line called 'Keds', which became the name for the rubber-soled sport shoe division of the US Rubber Company in 1917. The division was later sold and is currently part of Stride Rite. The United States Rubber Company also produced a line of overshoes and galoshes under the brand name 'Gaytees'. From 1942 until 1987 the United States Rubber Company concentrated on tyre production made under the name Uniroyal.

Villon, François (1911–97), Designer, active 1960–97
François Villon was the professional name of the shoemaker Benveniste, who worked as a chief designer at **Perugia**. He left to start his own design house in 1960, setting up shop at 27 rue du Faubourg Saint-Honoré. He promoted thigh-high boots in the late 1960s and during his career designed for numerous couturiers including Louis Feraud, Hermès, Chanel, Ted Lapidus, Jean Patou, Nina Ricci, Jean-Louis Scherrer and Lanvin. Villon opened boutiques in Milan, New York, Singapore and Hong Kong and worked up until his death in 1997.

☐ **Vivier, Roger** (1907–98), Designer, active c. 1937–98
Born in France in 1907 (some sources say 1913), Roger Vivier studied sculpture at the Ecole des Beaux-Arts in 1926 and 1927. He considered becoming a couturier, but having previously worked in a shoe factory he decided to devote himself to shoe design. He was hired in 1936 as a shoe pattern maker and in 1937 opened his first store in rue Royale in Paris. He was soon providing freelance designs for such manufacturers as **Bally** in Switzerland and **Delman** in the US. Delman turned down one of Vivier's designs

for a platform shoe, which went on to be used by Elsa Schiaparelli in her 1939 collection. With the onset of war, Vivier went into service. He left for New York in 1941 just before Paris was occupied, intending to work for Delman. He met Suzanne Remy, the top milliner at Agnes in Paris, aboard the liner L'Exeter. With wartime restrictions on leather use he decided against shoe design, instead opening a millinery shop with Suzanne Remy in 1942. Vivier returned to France in 1947, and became busy with freelance work, which included making Queen Elizabeth II's coronation shoes in 1953. Later that same year he entered into an agreement with Christian Dior to create a line of prêt-à-porter shoes under the Delman-Christian Dior label. In 1955 the name would be changed to 'Christian Dior crée par Roger Vivier' (Dior created by Vivier), the first time a shoe designer appeared alongside a couturier on a label. Vivier perfected his variations on the stiletto heel while working with Dior and, after Dior's death in 1957, with Yves Saint Laurent. Vivier was an innovator with toes and heels during this period, popularizing the stiletto and introducing the 'comma' heel in 1962. This was the first of many heel shapes that he named after its shape; others included the ball, needle, pyramid, escargot and spool. In 1963 Vivier opened his own design studio on the rue François Premier in Paris and created his signature line. His association with Paris couture however continued until 1972 with designs for Yves Saint Laurent, Emanuel Ungaro, Chanel and Hermès. It was during this period that he became known for his interest in new and unusual materials like vinyl, metallic-finished leather, faux fur and stretch fabrics. Between 1972 and 1993 Vivier went into semi-retirement, carrying out some shoe design contracts, but not creating collections. In 1993, at the age of 86, he opened a new ready-to-wear boutique on the fashionable rue de Grenelle. He had a licensing agreement with Rautureau Apple Shoes to manufacture his designs, which included many styles from his past collections with their signature heel shapes. He worked at his atelier right up until his death in 1998.

☐ **Weitzman, Stuart** (1941–), Designer, Manufacturer, active c. 1965–present
Stuart Weitzman's father, Seymour, started work as a part-time cutter for **I. Miller** in New York, where he progressed to the role of designer. In 1959 he decided to open his own factory producing ladies' shoes under the 'Mr. Seymour' label. His son, Stuart, born in 1941,

Vivier gold kid and aluminium mesh sandal, c. mid 1990s.

Vivier black silk and silver kid sandal with rhinestone-ball heel, c. mid 1990s.

Advertisement for Stuart Weitzman depicting bridal shoes with sheer panels and floral ornamentation, a style for which he won a 1987 IRIS Award for Excellence for revolutionizing bridal footwear, c. 1987–88.

NEIMAN MARCUS AWARDS (1938–)

years when awarded for shoe design:

1938 – Dan Palter
1947 – Salvatore Ferragamo
1949 – David Evins
1954 – Herbert and Beth Levine
1961 – Roger Vivier
1963 – Margaret Clarke Miller (Margaret
      Jerrold Shoes)
1967 – Fiamma Ferragamo
1968 – Roland Jourdan

COTY AWARDS (1942–1985)

years when awarded for shoe design:

1949 – David Evins
1950 – Mabel and Charles Julianelli
1967 – Herbert and Beth Levine
1971 – Nancy Knox, men's footwear
1973 – Joe Famolare
1973 – Herbert and Beth Levine
1975 – Nancy Knox, men's footwear
1978 – Joan Halpern
1979 – Gil Truedsson, men's footwear

worked as a pattern cutter during his summer breaks from Wharton Business College. In the summer of 1965 he created an oxford with a bow on the vamp that sold so well his father had a pair bronzed for Stuart as a memento. Seymour died later that year, leaving Stuart in charge of design and sales and his brother, Warren, overseeing manufacturing. In 1971 the 'Mr. Seymour' label was sold to Caressa Inc. and his father's factory closed. Production moved to Spain with Stuart supervising the 'Mr. Seymour' division of Caressa until 1986 when Stuart reacquired the label and renamed the company Stuart Weitzman and Co. In 1982 his clear lucite Cinderella pump sold more than 70,000 pairs. *Bride's* magazine honoured the designer in 1987 with an IRIS Award for Excellence and for revolutionizing bridal footwear. Especially popular was his 'Sheer Delight' pump of embroidered lace. Weitzman has built a reputation for using unique materials in his shoe construction, including cork, 24-carat gold, vinyl and hand-painted python. He is also known for his sculpted heels that sometimes use unusual materials such as chrome, steel or bamboo. Stuart revived evening shoes paved with Swarovski crystals in the 1980s, a style popularized by **Delman** and **Levine** in the 1950s. Weitzman shoes were sold through other stores until August 1995 when he opened his first store on Madison Avenue. In the 1990s Weitzman became one of the leaders of retro style when he reintroduced the Louis-heeled pump and boot in 1993, and in 1995 he brought back the 1960s square-toed low-heeled pump.

Wolverine World Wide Inc. Manufacturer, active 1903–present

G.A. Krause and his uncle, Fred Hirth, founded the Hirth-Krause Co. in 1883, producing leather and shoemaking goods. The company started making shoes in 1903 and in 1922 became Wolverine Shoe and Tanning Corporation. The US government encouraged the development of pigskin as a new source of leather when Adolph Krause was president in 1957. Seeing a trend toward casual footwear after the introduction of **Clarks** desert boots, the company developed a pigskin shoe with crepe sole. The brand name Hush Puppies came from the company's sales manager who had seen some people eating corn fritters and tossing bits to their barking dogs (the slang term for sore feet being barking dogs) with the plea 'Hush, puppies'. The brand immediately caught on and sales rose from US $11.3 million in 1958, the first year

of production, to US $55.4 million in 1965, the year Wolverine World Wide went public. Sales for Hush Puppies fell in the late 1970s. The style enjoyed a revival in the 1990s but by then the company had shifted most of its concentration into work and motorcycle boot production. An industrial footwear line called 'Cat' after Caterpillar construction equipment was launched in 1994. Wolverine acquired the California shoemaking firm Sebago in 2003 after restructuring in the early 2000s.

Yantorny, Pietro (1874–1936), Shoemaker, Designer, active c. 1914–30

Little was known of Yantorny until his nephew released his uncle's archives. Before this, most of the information about the designer was inaccurate, likely fictionalized by Yantorny himself. Yantorny was born into a poor family in Calabria, Italy. As an illiterate young man he held several jobs, ranging from washing dishes to working in a macaroni factory. His father immigrated to Chicago when Pietro was twelve. So, Pietro sought an apprenticeship in the shoemaking trade and worked with various shoemakers in Naples, Nice and Paris. In the late 1890s he learned the art of making shoe trees in London. He was never a curator at the Cluny Museum in Paris as was previously reported, although the similarities between many of his lace-embellished shoes and eighteenth-century examples found in the Cluny Museum suggest he studied the collection carefully. When he finally set up his shoemaking business at the age of 40, he wished to attract only the wealthiest clients and placed a sign on his Paris store that reportedly read 'The World's Most Expensive Shoes'. Yantorny was apparently haughty with his customers, arrogant about his abilities, a perfectionist and slow to complete orders. He received his first order in 1914 and remained in business until 1930, when the onset of the Depression made it difficult for him to make a living from luxury bespoke footwear. Yantorny went on a two-year sabbatical to India, returning to Paris in 1932. Although not prolific, his shoes fitted superbly, were light as a feather and were made of sumptuous materials such as antique laces, velvets and brocades. His name is spelled in many ways, including Yantourni and Yantorni, but it is the spelling Yantorny that appeared on his business cards of the 1920s. Presumably his illiteracy never led him to correct any misspellings, and everyone from fashion reporters to business-card printers probably spelled his name phonetically.

FOOTWEAR GLOSSARY

Most American terminology relating to shoe styles and manufacturing is based on British terms in common use by the nineteenth century. As the American footwear industry grew in the mid nineteenth century, word usage began to differ. The same word was sometimes used to describe different things or different words were used to refer to the same thing. In addition, terminology changed over time. Cordovan leather, for example, had many definitions, ranging from alum-tanned goatskin from Spain to ass hide from Turkey. Shoe manufacturers also picked random words to describe their product that became common usage; for example, 'slide', 'kitten heel' and 'sneaker' all began life as marketing terms and are now used to refer to types or elements of footwear. Canadian terminology is a mixture of British and American terminologies and, of course, France, Italy, Germany and other countries have their own terminologies. Footwear terminology is not an exact science but rather jargon that changes over time and from region to region. The glossary is divided into four categories: footwear types, shoe terms, shoemaking terms and materials and attempts to cover international variation where necessary.

FOOTWEAR TYPES

Adelaide A nineteenth-century English term for a woman's side-laced boot, named after the queen consort of King William IV (1830–37). However, Adelaide boots were most fashionable in the 1840s and 1850s. The male version of the side-laced boot is called the Albert boot, after Queen Victoria's husband Prince Albert.

Albert slipper A slipper with the vamp extended into a short rounded tongue that rests on the instep, called the Albert cut.

Arctic An American term in common use by 1900 for a winter overshoe with rubber sole, cloth upper and fleece lining, covering the ankle and fastening with one or more clasp buckles. After 1930 the Alaska came into use, which was similar to the Arctic but was a slip-on style cut higher in the front and back than on the sides.

Ballerina A flat-heeled pump designed to resemble a ballet shoe, introduced in the 1940s.

Balmoral A front-lacing ankle boot with closed eyelet tabs. The term was in common use by 1860 and was named after Balmoral castle, the Scottish estate that Queen Victoria rebuilt.

Bar shoe An English term for a woman's shoe with any number of bars or straps fastened across the instep with buttons or buckles. They can be arranged in a variety of ways, for example, T-bars. The American equivalent is a strap, although the term strap shoe is rarely used. The term **Mary-Jane** is commonly used for single-bar shoes after 1910.

Beatle boot see elastic-sided boot

Blucher A term commonly used between 1820 and 1850 for men's half boots (ankle height), laced in front over a tongue with open tabs. It is named after the Prussian army general at Waterloo who, along with Wellington (who also had boots named after him), defeated Napoleon in 1815. The English use of this term refers strictly to boots. English shoes with this closure were referred to as **derbies** for men and gibsons for women. American usage extended to shoes, and derbies and gibsons were referred to as blucher oxfords. However, the term for a low-heeled woman's shoe using this construction was sometimes referred to in the US as newports in the late nineteenth century and usually consisted of a two-eyelet closure.

Boot Any kind of external covering for the foot extending above the ankle. In the nineteenth century different terms were used to describe boots extending only to the ankle, for example, bootees, half boots, high-lows, brogans, gaiter boots and demi-boots, as well as the French words *bottine* and *brodequin* (a term appearing only in early nineteenth century English and American fashion journals).

Bootee is sometimes used for short boots although this is used more today to describe women's or children's ankle-high boots.

Brodequin see boot

Brogan An American term for a heavy-soled work shoe, often with pegged or nailed soles. It has open tabs and lace closure. They were mass-produced in New England in the early and mid nineteenth century for domestic work wear and exported to the southern United States and Caribbean, where they were purchased for slave labourers.

Brogue A closed-front tie shoe, the upper comprising of several parts each decoratively punched and gimped. The style was historically developed from a punchwork shoe worn in Ireland in boggy or wet areas, the holes supposedly allowing water to drain easily from the shoe. Germans use the term *Budapester*, after the Hungarian city that was known for making elegant versions of the style in the early twentieth century.

Buskin The exact definition of this style varies, but in the nineteenth century it included tied shoes or short boots with no tongue and a thick sole suitable for country wear. They were usually cut with a gypsy (centre front) seam and sometimes decorated with a rosette at the throat. One version of a buskin was called a Jenny Lind, after the acclaimed Swedish opera singer of the mid nineteenth century. The lack of tongue meant that white stockings showed under the crossed-lace closure creating a peasant look. The term, however, was used loosely over the years, disappearing from the shoemaking lexicon by the 1920s.

Carriage boot A woman's overshoe worn for warmth in a carriage over shoes, usually of felt, quilted silk or velveteen and often with fur trim and front laces. This style was the precursor to the ankle-high **Arctic** galosh. The term was in use from the 1860s to the early 1900s.

Chameleons/Cameleons A style of shoe fashionable from the 1850s to the 1870s made of bronzed kid with machine chain-stitched embroidery on the vamp and cut-outs revealing a satin underlay. They were referred to as chameleons because the satin underlays were available in a variety of colours. In 1867 the *Englishwoman's Domestic Magazine* described this style as having a removable satin underlay so that different coloured satins could be placed to match the dress. But no surviving examples are known to exist and the term may have been misunderstood by the writer.

Chaussure French word for shoe used in English-speaking fashion journals of the nineteenth and early twentieth centuries to imply high-class footwear.

Chelsea boot see elastic-sided boot

Chukka A man's ankle-high boot with high-cut quarters and two-hole eyelet open tabs. Originally worn for playing polo in India (chukka is a period of play in the game), the style was produced in tan suede for British forces in North Africa during World War II. See **desert boot**

Clog All footwear made of wood, including styles with leather uppers. The term also refers to the wooden overshoes made from the fourteenth to early nineteenth centuries and worn to protect shoes from wet and mucky streets. Wooden overshoes with iron rings attached to the soles, fashionable from the seventeenth to the early nineteenth centuries, were known as both clogs and pattens in the eighteenth century but strictly as pattens by the nineteenth century. Plastic clogs were first made in the 1970s and are also referred to as clogs because of their rigid soles. *Sabot* is the French term for a wooden shoe or clog, and the word sabotage comes from the act of throwing wooden shoes into machinery during Luddite revolts.

Colonial A late-nineteenth-century to early-twentieth-century American term for a woman's shoe with a buckle (rarely functional) and a high-flaring tongue. Suggesting an eighteenth-century style, they were sometimes called a *Molière* in France or a Cromwell in the UK.

Court shoe A British term for a pump or woman's slip-on shoe. The name comes from the shoe's original purpose of being worn at court and other formal occasions.

Cromwell see Colonial

Derby A man's front-laced shoe with open eyelet tabs, not stitched into the throat but sitting on top of the vamp. A gibson is the female equivalent. Other names associated with this style include **blucher oxfords** and newports.

Desert boot Crepe-soled suede boots originally created by Clarks in England. Nathan Clark, a member of the Clark shoe-manufacturing family, took the idea from the English officers' regulation army boots in North Africa while he was in service. The army had borrowed the style from Indian **Chukka** boots worn for playing polo. Clark's prototype was first shown at the Chicago Shoe Fair in 1949. At first considered effete by many North American men, they eventually became the footwear of choice for American college students by 1960. They were the first of many leisure shoes popular in the 1960s and 1970s.

D'Orsay A dress **slipper** or **pump**, usually heeled, with the vamp and quarters curving downwards (sometimes overlapping) on both sides of the upper to the sole so that the shoe is held to the foot by the back quarters and the vamp only. Originally a man's style in the early to mid nineteenth century, it was adapted for women's shoes in the late nineteenth century and was known as a Grecian slipper in the UK.

Elastic-sided boot Elastic threads woven into webbing and inserted into gores at the sides of boots in the 1840s allowed boots to be slipped on and off easily. These boots have been referred to by various names throughout their history, including gored boots, Garibaldi boots, spring-

sided boots and congress boots or congress gaiters in the middle of the nineteenth century. By the late nineteenth century they were known as nullifiers, cambridges, Romeos for men and Juliets for women; in the twentieth century they were called Chelsea boots and more recently Beatle boots in 1964. The boots are now sometimes referred to as Blundstones, after the Australian boot manufacturer founded in 1870, which continues to make them.

Galosh/golosh In the nineteenth century the term galosh in the UK came to refer to vamp wings seamed at the back or the lower-half of a shoe or boot upper, known as whole-foxing in the US. It is also a rubber or patent leather overshoe worn in inclement weather. See **overshoe**

Ghillie A shoe of Scottish origin with laces criss-crossed through loops over the vamp.

Gypsy An American term for a style of shoe or boot with a seam running from the centre front, creating a split or two piece vamp. It was fashionable for a time, especially c. 1915–16, and was commonly found on skating boots up to the 1970s.

Health sandal A wood- or plastic-soled sandal with an adjustable strap across the forepart and a contoured foot bed intended to improve foot health, support the arch and force the foot muscles to work during the action of walking. Sometimes referred to as exercise sandals in the UK.

Hessian Calf-to-knee-high men's boots extended higher at the front than the back, with side seams and often decorated with a tassel at the centre top of the shaft.

High tops An American term for a high-cut sports shoe that does not extend beyond the ankle bone. Anything that extends beyond the ankle should be called a boot, although this term has been used erroneously for boots.

Jellies Inexpensive, mass-produced, flexible, waterproof and longwearing footwear made entirely of PVC by the injection-moulding process and fashionable in the 1980s. See **Shoemaking: moulded**

Loafer A lightweight slip-on shoe intended for outdoor wear. Essentially a low-heeled **pump**, a loafer always has an apron vamp and is usually of a moccasin construction with an additional sole. Loafers either use a fold-over tongue, often fringed (called a kiltie), or a wide instep strap across the throat. Commonly called penny loafers or penny mocs in the 1950s because a coin could be slipped under the strap, they are also known by their brand name of 'Weejuns' ('Norwegian') and have been made by Bass in the US since 1936.

Leggings

    Gaiters Leggings of textile or leather worn over a shoe and ending from just below the calf to mid thigh. They are fastened with buttons or buckles and were anchored with a strap under the instep. The term also

describes the leg or shaft of a woman's or child's boot in the mid nineteenth century, especially in footwear that had counters and caps, creating the illusion of an added gaiter or spat over a shoe.

    Puttees Leggings formed by wrapping a strip of leather or fabric around the leg up to the knee. The word is of Hindi origin.

    Spats Short for 'spatterdashes', spats are ankle-high protective coverings, usually of wool, canvas or leather, fastened over a shoe. They look as if they are a boot protecting the stockings and top of the shoe from spatters and dashes of mud.

Mary-Jane Mary Jane was Buster Brown's girlfriend from the comic strip by Richard F. Outcault. The Brown Shoe Company of St. Louis was granted the use of the two figures in its advertisements for children's shoes. Buster Brown was first used at the 1904 St. Louis World's Fair to promote children's boots, and Mary-Jane was introduced in around 1909 to advertise girl's single-strap shoes. The style became synonymous with the name, and by the late 1910s all girls' single-strap shoes were called Mary-Janes.

Mule A **slipper** made for outdoor wear, usually heeled, and having no quarters, thus exposing the heel of the foot. The term originated from the Latin word *muleus*, meaning reddish, and was used by the Egyptian Copts for their red kidskin backless shoes. Known as *pantouffles* in France, mules came to be known as pantables in England at the end of the seventeenth century. Other terms have since been used, including 'slips' in the mid nineteenth century and 'slides' since the 1980s.

Overshoe A shoe or boot worn over another for protection against wet, cold and mud. **Galoshes/goloshes** are the best known type of overshoe and are made of rubber or other water-resistant materials. A foothold is the English term for a rubber galosh with a closed forepart and a strap that hooks around the back but allows the heel to pass through. Pattens are overshoes with wooden soles sometimes raised on iron rings and date from the medieval period until the early nineteenth century. They were also sometimes called scatches (now archaic). Englishwomen used overshoes in the eighteenth century usually with leather soles and cork blocks fitted to the arches of the shoes and called **clogs**.

Oxford A laced shoe with closed tabs (eyelet tabs stitched under the vamp). A laced shoe with open tabs (eyelet tabs overlapping the vamp) is called a **derby** in the UK for a man and a gibson for a woman. In the US an open-tab shoe is called a **blucher oxford**.

Patten see clog

Plimsoll A canvas sports shoe with a rubber sole extended up around the upper. This style was previously called a croquet sandal. Plimsoll was the marketing idea of the Liverpool Rubber Company, registered in 1885. It was named after Samuel Plimsoll, a British reformer concerned with the welfare of seamen and who was instrumental in passing the Merchant Shipping Act of 1876. One provision of the act was to paint a line on the hulls of ships, which if not visible when in the water indicated that the ship was too heavily laden. This line became known as the Plimsoll line. The shoe was a forerunner of the **trainer**.

Polish A woman's front-lacing mid-shin boot with a contoured top line and usually decorated with a small tassel at the centre front (like a **Hessian** but without side seams on the upper). They were sometimes referred to as boots *à la Polonaise* during the 1870s when they were fashionable.

Pump A slip-on shoe made without any closures. Although the term appears in sixteenth-century England, it is the Americans who use it more now, while **court shoe** has become more commonly used by the British. Historically it is a unisex term, but is more vague when used for men's styles and included buckled, heel-less evening pumps in the early nineteenth century. The exact origin of the word is lost, although a French version suggests that it comes from *pompe*, meaning pump. Apparently early Parisian shoemakers were also volunteer firefighters because they made the leather buckets for fire brigades. However, this story sounds more like urban legend.

Russian boot A woman's pull-on boot popular in the 1920s. Also called leg boot and pull-on boot.

Sabot see **clog**

Saddle A laced **oxford** shoe with a 'saddle' across the instep, originally of contrasting colour but by the 1930s the shoes were also available in solid colours. It was first made as a sports shoe in the early 1920s.

Sandal An ancient and simple footwear construction in which a sole is fastened to the foot using a series of straps or laces. By extension, the term came to refer to any shoe on which straps or ties are conspicuous or where there is profuse slashing or cutting out on the vamp. In the early nineteenth century, as early as 1802, low-cut **slippers** with ribbon ties that crossed and tied around the ankles were known as sandals or sandal-slippers. In the late nineteenth century, sandal was sometimes used to refer to any strapped **pump**.

Shoe Any kind of external covering for the foot, not extending above the ankle and incorporating in its construction a separate sole and enclosed upper. Moccasins, **slippers** and **sandals** are not included in this strict definition but are often included in the broadest sense of the term.

Slipper The strictest definition for this term is an indoor slip-on shoe with no fastening or closure. The term today implies shoes intended for indoor home use only, such as bedroom slippers. In the nineteenth century slipper referred to any delicately turned shoe primarily intended for indoor use, such as ballroom slippers, but also included fine shoes with some form of closure, like ribbon ties. The term **shoe** implied sturdier footwear intended for outdoor wear.

Sneaker American term for a rubber-soled canvas sports shoe. The earliest reference to the term appeared in the publication *The Household* in 1893: 'tennis shoes with rubber soles…the kind known among boys as "sneakers"'. The term features again in the publication *The Shoe Retailer* in 1900, referring to the rubber-soled tennis shoes sold by the United States Rubber Company under the brand name

'Champion': 'These are the popular "sneaks" that have been widely advertised by this euphonious name by hundreds of dealers from Maine to California.' The term was certainly in common usage by 1916 when Keds marketed tennis shoes as sneakers. Even so, there were outcries from some shoe manufacturers in the United States in the early 1920s who felt the term inappropriate, preferring to use instead 'tennis shoes'.

Spectator A woman's heeled shoe usually with a light-coloured upper and contrasting toecap and counter. A correspondent is a man's spectator.

Trainer A category of shoe originally designed specifically for sports training and consisting of a textile and leather shoe with a moulded or cemented rubber sole. Trainers are also known as tennis shoes, runners (this term is particularly popular in Canada), **sneakers**, joggers and other colloquial terms, including manufacturers' names such as Reeboks and Adidas, or brand names such as 'Air Jordans' or 'Chucks'.

Wellington A man's calf-length pull-on boot with side seams and plain straight cut along the top. A shorter version, extending a few inches above the ankle, is called a half-Wellington. Named after the Duke of the same name, they were made of leather although most versions today are made of rubber or plastic and worn in wet and mucky conditions.

Winkle-picker An English term for sharp-pointed toes. Winkles are edible molluscs, and shoes with toes so pointed that they look as if they could extract the winkles from their shells were given this name in the late 1950s.

SHOE TERMS

Adjustment A fastening of any kind: button, buckle, lace, and so on.

Aglet A tag is a metal or plastic tip reinforcing the end of the lace to allow the lace to pass easily through holes and to prevent fraying. Ornamental tags that have no other purpose than to be decorative are more correctly identified as aglets.

Arch The side and bottom of the foot below the instep on the inner side, and by extension the corresponding part of the shoe or last.

Back strap A British term for a strip of leather or other material strengthening the back seam of a boot or shoe (back stay in American). If it is made of textile it serves a purely decorative purpose and the strip of material can be referred to as a galloon.

Ball The widest fleshy part on the bottom of the foot directly across the joints behind the toes. The corresponding part of a shoe's sole is more correctly referred to as the tread.

Binding see Galloon

Bottom part All elements comprising the bottom part of a shoe, including the insole, sole, welt and heel. Also called a bottom unit, the bottom part is one piece of moulded synthetic material.

Chiropody Remedial care of the foot, especially dealing with corns and toenail disorders.

Closed front When the eyelet tabs are stitched under the vamp it is referred to as a closed front.

Clump A half sole added to a shoe, usually as a repair.

Counter A British term for an exterior reinforcement at the back of the shoe used to stiffen the quarters. If the counter is placed between the upper and lining and is thus invisible to the eye, the British refer to it as a stiffener. American usage calls a stiffener a counter, and an exterior counter is called heel foxing.

Domed sole A modern term used to define a sole rounded up at the sides, as seen in early-eighteenth-century footwear.

Domed toe A modern term for a square toe blocked into a curved or domed shape on the upper, as seen in early-eighteenth-century footwear.

Eyelet In its broadest sense, eyelet can describe any purposefully created hole through cloth or leather, such as those made and bound with thread, for the purpose of making eyelet lace. In shoe terms, an eyelet referred to a hole through which a lace was threaded, until Englishman Thomas Rogers patented a metal eyelet machine in 1823. The term then came to describe the metal rings used to

reinforce the eye holes. Holes reinforced in any manner other than by a metal or plastic ring for the purpose of threading a lace were then more clearly defined. Eye holes bound with thread are more properly referred to as worked eyelets or stitched lace holes. Blind eyelets refer to holes reinforced with rings from the reverse so that the eyelets are unseen. Holes that are not reinforced are called lace holes or eye holes.

Eyelet tab This is the extension of the quarters over the instep bearing the eyelets for a lace.

Facing A strip of leather or other material applied externally to strengthen and reinforce the eyelet tab. A 'facing stay' is the British term used to describe this same strip but used on the inside of the eyelet tab, the American term for which is 'lace stay'. An 'eyelet stay' is a reinforcing strip inserted between the outer material and lining.

Feather line The line around the bottom edge of the last (see shoemaking terms) and the corresponding edge or boundary around the upper of a shoe where it joins the welt or the sole.

Foot bed An insert shaped or moulded to match the approximate contours of the bottom surface of the foot. Commonly used in sports shoes and health sandals.

Foxing An American term that refers to decoration or reinforcement, usually of leather or rubber, that runs around the perimeter of the shoe just above or over the sole seam or on the lower half of the upper. It is similar to the British term 'galosh' and is sometimes known as a 'curtain' when crepe rubber is used. Toecaps were referred to as 'toe foxing' in the US in the nineteenth century.

Galloon A thin strip of metallic, silk or other textile tape, lace or braid used to cover seams. It was also found as a centre strip down the front of late-seventeenth- and early-eighteenth-century shoes. When used to bind top lines it is called 'galloon binding' and sometimes 'French binding'.

Gimping A saw-toothed edge to leather, resembling pinking.

Goring Fabric woven with elastic thread and used for gussets in elastic-sided boots and shoes.

Gypsy seam The centre-front seam on the vamp, extending from toe to throat.

Heel A solid raised base or support attached to the sole of the shoe or boot under the back part of the foot. Heels are measured in eighths of an inch, so a 12/8 is a one-and-a-half-inch heel. The heel consists of the seat, breast, neck and top lift. The seat is immediately below the heel of the foot; the breast is the front surface under the sole; the neck is the back face visible when viewing a shoe from the back; and the top lift is the bottom of the heel resting on the ground, and also called a top piece. There are two basic types of heels: those made from blocks of wood or plastic; and stacked heels (sometimes called 'built heels') made

from layers or lifts of leather, rubber or leatherboard that are fastened together with glue, nails or wooden pegs. A heel can be attached in one of two ways: either knocked on (known as 'inside-nailed' in the US) after the rest of the shoe is completed; or constructed with the sole, which is made evident by the continuous sole down the breast of the heel. Originally, a knock-on heel was rarely high because it was not very strong. However improvements in the twentieth century enabled most heels to be attached in this manner. Many heels have a quarter tip, a piece of rubber or iron added to a leather top lift off centre toward the outer edge where greatest wear occurs when walking.

Cuban A straight-sided low heel with a slight taper to the neck. A similar higher version of this heel was sometimes called a military heel around the turn of the twentieth century, although this term is now largely unknown and its original definition was used differently by different makers. The term 'Cuban' came into use in about 1905 and originally referred to stacked heels but was extended to include covered heels through common usage.

French (pompadour, hourglass, Louis, Pinet, spool) The heel's name reflects its eighteenth-century origin as a breasted heel whose neck is in a graceful reverse curve to harmonize with the curve formed by the sole as it continues down the breast. The heel is usually waisted with a flaring bottom section.

Opera An archaic term used in the late-nineteenth and early-twentieth centuries to describe a knock-on heel with a straight breast and curved neck commonly used on evening shoes and high-heeled boudoir slippers. By the 1910s this heel was often referred to as a 'kidney heel'.

Italian A high thin heel made of wood and usually covered, it has tapering sides and neck and often employs a wedge extension that partially fills the hollow beneath the waist to add strength to the heel. Fashionable in the 1780s and early 1790s and known as an Italian heel to reflect its origin, the heel style disappeared with the term in the mid 1790s.

Spanish When the high wooden heel covered with leather and shaped with straight, tapering sides and neck was revived in the early twentieth century it was called either a 'Spanish' heel or sometimes a 'Spanish-Louis'. The term was commonly used in the 1920s and early 1930s.

Spring One or more lifts inserted between the sole and the heel seat, commonly used from the late 1790s to the 1810s.

Stiletto A thin tapered high heel with a small top lift and a metal reinforcing rod running the height of the heel. The term is derived from the bladed weapon of the same name.

Wedge A heel made from a series of lifts or layers of leather or from a block of wood or some other material that extends forward to fill the space under the **waist** of the shoe and gives a flat surface in contact with the ground.

Heel grip A small suede-covered pad used to prevent the foot from slipping out of the shoe.

Insole The sole to which the upper and the outer sole are attached to make the shoe. Not to be confused with a **sock**.

Instep The area on the top of the foot, and the corresponding part of the shoe, between the rear of the toes and the front of the leg.

Lace Any cord, string or ribbon that closes a shoe around a foot and is led through holes, hooks, loops or **eyelets**. Lace hooks are often used on the upper part of a laced-boot's closure and are typically found on ice-skating boots. They were introduced on women's bicycling boots in the late 1890s.

Latchet The extension of the **quarters** into straps resting on the **instep** that have eyeholes for closing with a ribbon or lace. Technically, latchets do not quite touch each other and are closed only with a ribbon or lace, while straps overlap and fasten with a buckle.

Leg The part of the boot above the ankle. Also known as the 'shaft' or 'top'.

Lining An added layer of material attached to the inner side of the upper. In the back part only it is referred to as the quarter lining, but if it reaches the toe it is called a full lining.

Monkstrap A broad **instep** strap fastened with a buckle on the outer side.

Quarters The sides of a shoe **upper** that join the **vamp** at the front and meet at the back of the heel, where they are usually joined by a seam and reinforced by a **stiffener**. Whole-cut quarters are made from one piece of leather without a back seam.

Rand A **welt** inserted between the **sole** and **upper**, the rand was usually in a contrasting colour to the rest of the footwear and was folded over and sewn through from the side. From the mid seventeenth century to the mid eighteenth century, the rand was made a visible feature of footwear. All rands are welts but not all welts are rands. Welts are not usually visible and are blended in with the outer sole of the shoe.

Seat see **heel**

Seg A metal stud attached to the **sole** to protect it from wear.

Shank A strip of wood or leather (and after 1855 a metal piece) used to reinforce the **waist** of a shoe between the **sole** and **insole**. It keeps the shape of the **arch** when the shoe has a heel.

Side seam The seam connecting the **vamp** to the **quarters**. It can be of any design: straight, dog-legged or curved.

Sling-back A woman's shoe with a strap around the back of the ankle in place of **quarters**.

Slit-vamp A shoe style in which the **vamp** is slit from the centre of the **throat**. It was commonly seen in the early nineteenth century. The slit is bordered by lace holes and there is no **tongue**. Shoes were sometimes altered in this manner if the wearer found them too tight.

Sock The thin lining of leather or cloth glued onto the **insole** inside a shoe. A heel sock covers only the heel area of the insole; a half sock covers the insole from the **waist** to the heel; and a three-quarter sock covers the insole from the ball to the heel. It is decorative and functional as it hides any nail heads or stitches used in construction and is usually where the brand or maker's name is printed.

Sole The bottom or under surface of a shoe or boot, excluding the heel.

Split vamp see **gypsy**

Stiffener see **counter**

Straights Symmetrical shoes that were not made for the left or right foot.

Swing The degree of crookedness or curvature on the outer side of the **sole**.

Tab A small rounded **tongue** protruding from the **vamp** over the **instep**. It can also refer to a **latchet** or strap that fastens with a lace or buckle over the vamp.

Tag see **aglet**

Throat The front edge of a shoe's opening or the central portion of the **vamp** resting on the **instep** of the foot. It is usually a place for decoration, such as bows and ornamental buckles. The throat line may be rounded (Albert cut), squared, peaked, tabbed or serrated (Van-dyked).

Toe The extreme forward part of the **vamp** and **sole** that can range in shape to include pointed, elongated, rounded, oval- or almond-shaped, square and splayed.

Toe box The American term for a **stiffener** used inside the toe area of a shoe to protect the wearer's toe and keep the shape of the shoe's toe. The British term is toe puff, but this can also refer to a wad of cotton wool that keeps the shape of the toe.

Toecap An extra reinforcement or decoration over the toe area of the **vamp**. Toecaps may be straight, peaked or winged. The American term is 'tip', as in 'wing tip'.

Toe spring The elevation or upward curve of the toe of the **sole** above a horizontal surface upon which a shoe is

standing. Most commonly found on stiff-soled shoes where the spring enables the wearer to proceed in a rolling action without stressing the foot.

Tongue An extension from the **vamp** throat resting on the **instep** of the foot, the tongue either protects the wearer's instep from the laced or buckled closure or it is purely decorative. A bellows tongue is cut very wide and attached at the sides of the opening under the **eyelet tabs**. The tongue folds flat when the shoe or boot is closed and is designed to keep out water or snow.

Top band A strip of material stitched or folded over the top of the **leg** of a boot.

Top facing A binding or lining sewn inside the **top line** to reinforce it and often bearing the maker's stamp or label.

Top lift see **heel**

Top line Literally the top line of a shoe or boot, also called the top edge.

Tread The widest part of a sole that comes in contact with the ground, corresponding with the ball of the foot.

Upper The entire shoe or boot that covers the top of the foot normally consisting of a **vamp**, **quarters** and **lining**. It does not include the sole or heel.

Vamp The upper forepart of the shoe that covers the toes and part of the instep, most commonly found on shoes where two symmetrical side seams exist about midway between toe and heel. When the **upper** is contoured to the **sole** line in a rounded shape it is called a winged vamp. If the upper extends directly to the back seam it is called a whole vamp or a whole-cut shoe. An apron vamp is a U-shaped insert on the top of the vamp, sometimes extended to include a tongue, and derived from the moccasin.

Velcro A fastening system developed in 1948 by Swiss inventor Georges de Mestral in which a strip of material composed of very small plastic hooks engages with a looped material. As it provides variable closure sizes it is used for securing straps on shoes, particularly sports and children's shoes.

Waist The narrowest part of the **sole** under the **arch** of the foot and also the narrowest part of the heel.

Walled toe A toe that rises vertically from the **sole** then turns sharply across the **vamp**.

Welt A strip of leather or material inserted between seams.

Wings The side of the **vamp** extending backwards on either side of the **throat**. Often seen in two-tone oxford styles and called 'wing-tips'.

SHOEMAKING TERMS

To ensure quality craftsmanship, shoemakers were apprenticed and controlled by guilds from the Middle Ages to the nineteenth century. A fine shoemaker was often referred to as a cordwainer, taken from the French word cordonnier, and first appearing in English in 1100. By the late thirteenth century there was a distinction made between cordwainers alutari, who used only the best leathers, and cordwainers basanarii, who used inferior tanned leathers. Cordwainers worked only with new leather, whereas cobblers were repairers and were even sometimes prohibited by law from making shoes.

The process for making a pair of welt shoes (in its most basic form) begins with accurately measuring the client's foot and translating those measurements onto a wooden last. Either a custom last is crafted, or a pre-existing last has layers of leather added to its surface until the measurements exactly match the girth required. A pattern is then traced onto the upper material, cutting out or 'clicking' the leather. Traditionally a rounded moon knife (used for cutting leather since Ancient Egypt) was used but straight knives and scissors are also used. Lasting pincers or 'dogs' are used to pull the sewn upper tightly around the last, securing it with tacks to the underside using the opposite side of the pincers, which has a peen or hammer. A separate hammer is not used for setting the tacks because it would require changing tools in the process of pulling the upper onto the last, complicating the process. The welt and sole are sewn using awls to create holes through which waxed linen thread is inserted; traditionally a boar's bristle was used to guide the thread. When the stitching is complete, the welt and sole edge are trimmed, and a wooden shoulder stick is used to burnish the welt and edge of the sole. A final buffing and perhaps waxing completes the process.

Beading A British term for the edges of the top line when they are skived until very thin, folded over and secured by adhesive. The American term is folding. The term 'bead' is also sometimes used to refer to a welt on the upper of a shoe.

Bespoke Made-to-measure footwear.

Blacking Originating in the sixteenth century, blacking is a mixture of soot and wax and sometimes ink, which is applied to the surface of footwear as a dressing or polish.

Bottom finish A term for the finish on the bottom of a sole and includes dyeing, waxing and wheeling (a fancy patterned iron that is sometimes used over the sole to produce a decorative sealed seam and is referred to in Britain as a Fiddle finish).

Butted seam When the edges of adjoining sections are butted together and sewn without any overlap. Commonly used from the seventeenth to the nineteenth centuries on heavy leather boots and shoes.

CAD CAM Computer Aided Design and Computer Aided Manufacture. Since the early 1990s most shoe manufacturers design their shoes using CAD CAM. After a design is approved in a three-dimensional format the computer can create sectional patterns with all grading calculations. The data is then used to control cutting tools, presses, lasers, sewing machines and even the machines for moulds and lasts.

Channel A shallow slit made around the edge of a sole to recess stitching. After the stitching is in place this channel is closed, protecting the stitches from wear.

Clicking Cutting the components of a shoe's upper by hand. The term cutting is now more commonly used.

Closing A British term for sewing together the upper; the American term in the nineteenth century was binding.

Construction types

Blake sewn/McKay sewn Lyman R. Blake invented a machine to sew on soles in 1858. Blake sold the principal interest to Gordon McKay who financed the construction of the first machines, working with Blake to perfect them. The machines sewed the sole to the upper by a single chain-stitched seam directly through the insole inside the shoe to the outsole, using no welt. Blake and McKay persuaded the Union Army to commission boots made using the new process. The process was in common use by the mid 1860s.

California A construction method, developed in California in the early 1940s during World War II, in which the upper, sock and a strip of material used to cover a mid sole or platform are sewn together. The last is then forced in the upper, the platform is attached (glued) to the bottom of the sock and the strip is pulled around the edge of the platform and lasted (glued and nailed) under the bottom of the platform before an additional sole is attached. This process used less leather and less skilled labour, both of which were in short supply during the war, and was suitable for women's and children's casual-wear platform sandals.

Cement A construction method that bonds the sole to the upper by means of an adhesive and is usually heat- and pressure-activated. It produces an inexpensive, flexible and lightweight shoe and has been much used for making ladies' dress shoes since the 1930s.

Moccasin An Algonquin native word for foot covering, with variations depending on the dialect ranging from makisin in Ojibwa to m'cusun in Micmac. It is traditionally constructed from one piece of semi-tanned hide, sometimes with a U-shaped apron vamp insert. The style was copied especially for slippers and baby bootees. Most loafers, which imitate this apron

insert style, are constructed as moccasins although an additional outer sole is added over the integral sole. Sometimes even an inner sole is added obscuring the moccasin construction.

Moulded There are three basic methods of moulding. Slush moulding uses a dry-blend plastic compound poured into a heated mould until it becomes more solid. Injection moulding injects a melted thermoplastic under great pressure into a mould cavity. Or, polyvinyl chloride, PVC or another material is moulded directly onto an upper; this method is most commonly used to produce rubber-soled canvas shoes. In any moulding operation some excess may exude at the moulding lines. The excess is called 'sprue' or 'flash' and is trimmed off by hand or machine.

Pegged construction Wooden pegs were first used for securing top lifts of stacked leather heels in the seventeenth and eighteenth centuries. The earliest American patent for making shoes with wooden-pegged soles was granted to Samuel Hitchcock and John Bement of New York on 30 July 1811. The process used small diamond-shaped wooden pegs to secure the soles of heavy-soled shoes and boots. The pegs swelled when wet, creating a waterproof sole. This construction style remained common in rurally produced footwear until 1859, when a successful pegging machine was developed. Pegged shoes remained popular in the US into the 1870s. McKay and later Goodyear welting machines made pegged-sole construction less popular although it continued into the 1940s, especially in Europe, but more as an art form applied in decorative patterns.

Screwed soles A similar construction technique to pegging but using threaded wire instead of wooden pegs. Popular in the 1870s for sturdy-soled shoes but displaced by McKay and later Goodyear welt shoemaking processes.

Stitchdown Eighteenth-century term now referred to as Veldtschoen.

Turn shoe A shoe that is made inside out by sewing the upper to the sole, sometimes including a welt in the seam, and then turning the upper the right way round so that the sole seam is on the inside. This method of construction dates back to Roman times but is rarely used today except in the construction of some slippers and babies' shoes.

Veldtschoen A construction technique in which the upper is turned outwards and sewn to the sole, forming a durable and waterproof seam. The term Veldtschoen (field shoe) comes from the Afrikaner Boer farmers in South Africa during the nineteenth century.

Welt construction A narrow strip of leather sewn between the upper and sole, this method was used from the fifteenth century onward. The sole is then attached to the welt by a second seam, creating a waterproof attachment of the sole to the upper. Welted shoes are more complex to manufacture and are now only used for high-quality men's footwear. They are however easily resoled by removing the old sole and reattaching a new one through the welt. Goodyear welt is a shoe made by Goodyear welting machines and patented in 1877.

Drunkship A collective term for professional shoemakers.

Folding see beading

Grindery A trade name for tacks, staples, rivets, stapling wire, and so on, used in shoemaking. Also known as findings in the US.

Last A shoe-shaped form traditionally made of wood upon which a shoe's upper is shaped before being attached to the sole. A shover is a piece of leather added to a last by a shoemaker to increase the girth and to customize the last

shape for a pair of bespoke shoes. Lasting stretches the upper over the last using tacks to secure the upper in place. A lasting margin is the lower edge of the shoe upper that is turned under and fixed during lasting. Tack holes used to secure the sole in place before sewing it to the upper are visible on the sole of a completed shoe and are sealed and hidden with a sole stamp, resulting in circular or floral-like stamps called lasting marks. A last should not to be confused with a tree, which is a form inserted in a shoe when not being worn to help retain its shape.

Lingel A shoemaker's waxed thread.

Mulling The process of dampening the uppers to make them more pliable before attaching them to the last.

Setting The process of dampening and heat drying the lasted upper into shape before attaching the sole.

Sizing

Brannock device A foot-measuring device that has adjustable slides to measure length and width to give the required shoe size. It originated in the US.

Mondopoint An intended international method to designate shoe size. The marking would consist of two numbers, the first corresponding to the length and the second to the width, both in millimetres.

Paris points The system of measurement used in Continental Europe since the eighteenth century and also now used by some Southeast Asian countries. One Paris point equals ⅔ of a centimetre.

Skiving A method that trims the thickness along the edges of leather so that they are thinner than the rest of the leather, reducing the thickness of seams. Also known as feathering, although this term is specifically used to refer to the skiving of the leather on the instep of the sole to create a thin graceful join with the upper.

Tunnel stitch A modern term for a seam used to attach one piece of leather to another. The awl enters the surface of each piece of leather, passes a short distance between the grain and flesh and reappears on the same side, never piercing the leather's surface.

MATERIALS

Crepe Natural rubber made by drying latex from the rubber tree. Hardwearing and flexible but slippery on wet surfaces, it is cut using a wet knife. Small pieces are used in the finishing room to 'rub out' marks on suede.

Gutta percha A flexible although not elastic material made from tree resin. Gutta percha does not stick to other materials and can be softened with heat, becoming hard when cold. It is not affected by water but blackens in the presence of oxygen and light. Commonly used for buttons and experimented with as a sole material in the mid nineteenth century.

Latex The milky emulsion exuded from the rubber tree. It is coagulated to separate the water from the natural rubber.

Leather The cured or tanned hide (large animal: horse, cattle, moose) or skin (small animal: calf, pig, snake, goat) of an animal. The tanning process maintains the fibrous structure of the hide but prevents rot through the application of tanning agents, either vegetable (oak, willow bark) or mineral (chrome, alum). Leather has two sides: the grain or outer surface originally bearing the hair or fur; and the flesh where loose fibres are usually prominent. Each animal has a characteristic grain pattern. If a thick hide is cut into layers, each layer is called a split. Splitting of hides was not possible until the 1830s. The grain split and the flesh split are the most common but sometimes a third split between those two layers is made and is called a middle split. The unit of measurement for leather thickness is an iron: one iron equals ¹⁄₄₈ of an inch.

Boarded leather Leather finished with an embossed, indented or stamped surface. Usually used to give the impression of a different finish grain from the natural one. Most commonly used to create a faux reptile finish to leather. Box calf is chrome-tanned calf leather finished by boarding the grain side with irregular rectangular crossed lines.

Bronzed kid Kid treated with cochineal, a dye made from the dried and crushed bodies of a female scale insect. Although it dyes cloth red it gives a semi-iridescent bronze-like glow to leather and was popular from the late 1840s to the 1920s.

Buckskin Technically this is male deerskin; more loosely, this term is often used to refer to any fine suede-finished leather in a light tan colour.

Buff The word buff is from the French word *buffle* and is also the origin of the word buffalo. Originally made from bison, buff was made from cowhide from the sixteenth century onward. Buff is oil dressed and as such requires the surface of the grain to be sanded to create a velvety surface (like suede) so that the oil can penetrate the hide evenly. It is not tanned and

is therefore light in colour, similar in appearance to chamois but much thicker. Occasionally used for shoe soles, its most common use is for military coats and belts and it was particularly popular in the seventeenth century.

Calf Leather made from the hide of an immature bovine. To be classified as calf, the hide is defined by the green (preprocessed) weight of the hide. In the UK, this is 16kg, although the weight classification varies from country to country.

Chamois An oil-dressed antelope hide that is soft, supple and washable. Used for breeches, vests and linings, including shoe linings, it is not used for the exterior of footwear as it is too fragile.

Chrome tanned see Vici

Cordovan This term has several definitions depending on when it was used. Originally it referred to alum-tanned goatskin, but it has been used to mean any high-grade leather, such as ass hides from Turkey in the eighteenth century. In the twentieth century it described the leather from the butt area of horsehide. It is named after Cordoba, the city in southern Spain where it was first made.

Curried leather A nearly obsolete term for finishing vegetable-tanned leather by impregnating it with oil to render it waterproof. It was used for work footwear worn in wet conditions. It is similar to oil grain leather, but has a boarded pebble surface on the grain side for the oil to distribute evenly into the hide. Today these kinds of leather are more often referred to as water-resistant leather and use water-repellent agents other than oil.

Dongola A vegetable-tanned goatskin leather made to look like French kid. It is named after the region in the Sudan where it originated.

Glacé kid A kidskin leather with a smooth glossy surface. Also called glazed kid.

Kid Leather made from the skins of goats. Sheepskin was sometimes called kid when used for gloves.

Kip Heavy calfskin.

Leatherboard A sheet material made from agglutinated shreds of leather and a binding agent, typically used for lifts and insoles.

Morocco A sumac-tanned goatskin originally made in Morocco and usually finished in red (although black, green and blue are also common after 1780). It is soft and firm with a fine grain. Eventually the term was expanded to include any goatskin used for shoes or any thin leather made to imitate the grain and finish of Moroccan kid.

Nubuck Leather sanded on the grain side to give a velvety surface (suede). Also later known as a brand name for white- or cream-coloured buck leather.

Oak sole The best quality vegetable-tanned leather used for soles.

Ooze The old name for **suede**, a vegetable-tanned leather sanded on the grain side to create a velvety surface. This term was applied to suede until the nineteenth century but survived in usage well into the twentieth century.

Patent leather Leather given a glossy finish using various methods. Originally called japanned leather in the late eighteenth century in imitation of Japanese laquerwork, it was achieved by painting the flesh side of leather with layers of black varnish and oil, pumicing the leather between each layer of varnish. Peal of London patented the process in the 1790s. By the 1840s the process had been modified and used layers of linseed-oil-based dressings for the glossiest of finishes. The modern process usually involves a plasticized coating and is less susceptible to damage and changes in weather than the older method.

Reptile All kinds of reptile leathers are used in the shoe industry. Crocodile and alligator are similar in appearance except for a dot in the middle of each scale where a hair follicle grew on the crocodile. Both are thick leathers and often used for shoe uppers. Lizard and snake skins are thinner and unsuitable for use as uppers but are often used for trims, or are completely lined in leather before use. Python is the largest snake used and its leather bears distinctive markings that show through after dyeing.

Russet Tan-coloured, undyed leather.

Shearling Sheepskin with the wool on, used for slipper and boot linings. Sheepskin is too fragile for making shoe uppers.

Suede The word is derived from the French word *Suède*, meaning Swede, because the velvety surfaced leather was commonly used for gloves in Sweden. Previously known as **ooze**, it is made from the grain side of leather that has been sanded to raise the nap. The terms ooze and suede were used concurrently until the 1920s when ooze generally fell from use.

Vici A trade name used by Robert H. Foerderer (who perfected the development of chrome-tanned leather) for his chrome-tanned glazed kid. The name, in common usage by 1900, was extended to include all chrome-tanned leather, not just that produced by Foerderer.

Rubber An elastic, waterproof material produced from the sap of the rubber or caoutchouc tree, originally found in the

Amazon. Vulcanization mills rubber with sulphur and heat, allowing it to be moulded, increasing durability and inhibiting deterioration. The process was patented in 1844.

Synthetics Manmade materials have now been used commercially for over a century. Some have been more useful to the shoe industry than others. Rayon had a huge effect on ladies' wear after World War I but little effect on footwear, other than for making shoelaces. Celluloid, a plastic made by combining nitrate cellulose and camphor and invented in 1883, and Bakelite, an urea-formaldehyde resin patented in 1907 by Leo Baekeland, both found limited use for sheathing heels and making buckles and buttons, primarily in the 1920s and 1930s. However, some synthetics revolutionized the footwear industry.

Corfam A trade name used by DuPont for a synthetic upper material that reproduced most of the properties of leather. Seventy-five million pairs of Corfam shoes were sold by 1969 after DuPont's aggressive marketing in the mid 1960s. However, it failed to meet expectations and DuPont sold the rights. Japan developed a refined version of the substance giving it the name 'ultrasuede'.

Neolite Styrene-butadiene rubber (SBR) is a synthetic resin rubber introduced in around 1950 by the Goodyear Tire and Rubber Company. Sold in sheets and die-cut to sole shapes for adhesive attachment, it has excellent flexibility and durability, feeling and behaving like leather underfoot.

Neoprene A trade name used by DuPont for the synthetic rubber polychloroprene, and developed in their laboratories in 1931. Used as an adhesive in shoemaking and in soling compositions. Many saddle shoes were made with neoprene rubber soles in the 1950s.

Polyurethane (PU)/Polyvinyl chloride (PVC) PU can be expanded into moulded flexible soles that are soft and light as well as being durable and slip resistant. Laminated onto textile backings, both PU and PVC can imitate a variety of finishes from wet-look patent leather to a quality split cowhide suitable for women's dress shoes. Not necessarily cheaper than leather they are however more adaptable to mass-production methods. Their biggest drawback is that neither are permeable and thus can cause odorous feet.

Textiles

Brocade A weaving technique with a pattern, usually worked in different coloured or metallic threads. The threads float on the reverse so it is not reversible.

Damask A reversible fabric, usually of linen, silk or cotton, characterized by a flat jacquard woven pattern.

Commonly used in the eighteenth century, the technique has been around since at least the fourth century.

Jet Real jet is fossilized pinewood. French jet is imitation jet made of black glass. Jet is quite fragile, expensive and was mostly used for mourning jewelry. Seed bead embroidery on the toes of shoes in the nineteenth and twentieth centuries always used black glass. References to jet beading on shoes should be understood to mean that French jet is used.

Nankeen/Nankin A cotton originally from Nanking, China, which had a natural tan-yellow colour. Imitations were being made in the West by the mid eighteenth century by dyeing cotton yellow. It was used in the early nineteenth century for women's boot uppers and for gaiters.

Prunella A strong worsted-wool warp-faced fabric in a satin weave, usually a dark plum or black colour, that was used for shoe uppers in the nineteenth century.

Ticking A heavy cotton or linen twill woven cloth with a lengthwise woven stripe, sometimes in a contrasting colour. It was used in eighteenth century shoes, particularly as linings.

Vesting A patterned fabric of silk and wool with a figured pattern, used for the legs of boots and occasionally high-cut shoes.

BIBLIOGRAPHY

Bossan, Marie-Josephe. *The Art of the Shoe*. Parkstone Press, 2004.

Durian-Ress, Saskia. *Schuhe*. Bayerischen Nationalmuseum Munchen, 1992.

Heard, Neal. *Sneakers*. Carlton Books, 2003.

McDowell, Colin. *Shoes: Fashion and Fantasy*. Rizzoli, 1989.

Mitchell, Louise. *Stepping Out: Three Centuries of Shoes*. Powerhouse Publishing, 1997.

Rexford, Nancy E. *Women's Shoes in America, 1795–1930*. The Kent State University Press, 2000.

Sedler, Irmgard. *Auf Schritt und Tritt…Schuhe*. Galerie der Stadt Kornwestheim, 1999.

Swann, June. *Shoes* (Costume Accessories Series). B T Batsford, 1982.

Trasko, Mary. *Heavenly Soles: Extraordinary Twentieth-Century Shoes*. Abbeville Press, 1989.

For further research, there are excellent archives of footwear- and shoemaking-related books, periodicals, trade journals and more at the Essex Institute in Massachusetts, The Bata Shoe Museum in Toronto, Canada, and the Northampton Museum in Northampton, UK.

Websites

Shoe Icons www.shoe-icons.com

The Honourable Cordwainers' Company www.thehcc.org